Jerry Pinto is a poet, novelist, translator and journalist based in Mumbai. His books include the novels *Em and the Big Hoom* (winner of the Hindu Literary Prize and the Crossword Book Award), *Murder in Mahim* (winner of the Valley of Words Award for Fiction and shortlisted for the Crossword Book Award) and *The Education of Yuri*. Among his other works are widely acclaimed translations from Marathi and Hindi: Daya Pawar's autobiography (*Baluta*); Baburao Bagul's first and classic collection of stories (*When I Hid My Caste*); novels by Sachin Kundalkar (*Cobalt Blue*) and Ganesh Matkari (*Half-open Windows*); and the memoirs of Malika Amar Shaikh (*I Want to Destroy Myself*), Vandana Mishra (*I, the Salt Doll*), Eknath Awad (*Strike a Blow to Change the World*) and Swadesh Deepak (*I Have Not Seen Mandu*).

Jerry Pinto was awarded Yale University's Windham-Campbell Prize and the Sahitya Akademi Award in 2016.

HELEN

The Making of a Bollywood H-Bomb

Jerry Pinto

SPEAKING TIGER

SPEAKING TIGER BOOKS LLP

125A, Ground floor, Shahpur Jat, near Asiad Village
New Delhi – 110049

First published by Penguin Books India 2006
This edition published by Speaking Tiger Books 2023

ISBN: 978-93-5447-477-4
eISBN: 978-93-5447-479-8

10 9 8 7 6 5 4 3 2 1

Typeset in Goudy Old Style by SÜRYA, New Delhi
Printed at Chaman Enterprises, New Delhi

Contents

Introduction

A Book on Helen, the Dancer?

Congratulations on 5th-century score! Hazel-Eyed-Chic-Sleek-Gorgeously glamorous twinkle-toed Charmer of the Silver Screen has finished the 500th film of her career in 'Dil Daulat Duniya'... a record all over the world for any film artiste.

—Publicity material for *Dil Daulat Duniya* (1972), quoted in James Ivory's film *Helen, Queen of the Nautch Girls*

The first indication of trouble is a pair of stocking-clad legs, rubbing languorously against each other.

The camera travels up a svelte body dressed in red and black for a rousing flamenco. It stops to linger on a pretty, dark head slumped against a bar, a half-filled wine glass next to it. The woman raises her head, in slow motion, and looks into the camera, her eyes filled with frank longing, her mouth a moue of challenge. It is a beautiful face, even if the eyes have been picked out with huge quantities of blue eyeshadow, and the orange crescents in her ears rest almost on her shoulders.

The camera draws back to show us a cityscape. Couples dance in a dimly-lit outdoor café, men in suits, women in dresses—an evocation of a public square somewhere in Europe—if there is a square in Europe equipped with plastic flamingos in military formation and a life-sized golden birdcage, from which, tongue-like, a slide emerges.

The clock strikes twelve, and the couples leave, middle-class Cinderellas all. Alone now, a creature of the night at its darkest, the woman drains her glass and begins to sing, softly:

Piya tu...ab to aa ja...
(At least come to me now, my love...)

A voice answers her offstage in a musical shout: *Monica*!

She snaps out of her languor, speaks: *Woh aa gaya. Dekho, woh aa gaya*! (He's here; look, he's here!) She begins to pant, her torso heaving in our faces. The drunkenness, the apathy of the betrayed, falls away.

The call comes again: *Monica, Monica*!

Now she is electrified. She whirls and runs, arms outstretched, pushing at imaginary obstacles, towards the golden cage. She races up the steps to the cage, slides down the other side, and resumes her song, faster this time:

Piya tu, ab to aa ja/ Shola-sa man deheke/ Aake bhuja-ja/ Tan ki jwala thandi ho jaaye/ Aise gale laga ja/ Aa-aa-aa-aha...
(Come to me now, my love. Come, put out these fires. Come hold me, cool this volcano within me.)

However, she must still wait for her lover, for another verse and a refrain, during which she has offered her body to the camera in a frenzy of longing, squirming and thrashing about on the floor and the tables. The absence of any audience in the sequence, of the lover even, implicates us as the real audience. This is a soliloquy, a declaration of the character's innermost thoughts. And since it is about love, we know that this is a woman who lives in her senses.

Dressed as a matador, the lover comes running up over the edge of the square and into the golden cage. As she runs to him, her skirt gets caught in a metal strip on the bar and in her impatience she rips it off. Halfway to him, she divests herself of the rest of the flamenco costume, using her hands and teeth, so that she is left in a gold half-skirt and halter blouse. When they finally make it into each other's arms, the bartender puts off the lights and the lovers slump to the floor in a series of syncopated jerks.

Ladies and Gentlemen: the 'queen of the nautch girls', the Bollywood sensation, the H-bomb—Helen Richardson, now Helen Khan, but always, Helen.

~

When Ravi Singh, then a commissioning editor with Penguin, asked me who could write a book about Helen, I said, 'Me.' I said it instinctively, without thought. But the more I considered it later, the more the idea worked for me. First, I was pretty sure that Helen would not cooperate. Others before me had come up against a wall of perfectly civil non-cooperation. But that was not important. In fact, it would be liberating: I had read interviews and suspected that Helen had no idea what she meant to Hindi cinema, and that with age, she might be keen to put the past behind her. 'My greatest high is spirituality now,' she had said to a journalist some years ago.

Second, I was convinced that Helen is important. Although she is technically of Franco-Burmese descent, she was perceived as a white woman. She entered a world dominated by North Indian men who had very definite notions about how women should look and behave on-screen and she managed to redefine those requirements.

Third, she was no ordinary phenomenon, no flash in the pan of male lust. As a dancer, she should have had a short shelf life. Younger women with firmer flesh and deeper cleavages should have usurped her position. It isn't as if they didn't try. Without thinking too much, I can name Padma Khanna, Aruna Irani, Komilla Wirk, Jayshree T., Meena T. and Bindu. They came, they were seen in hot pants and bikinis and without body stockings, and time conquered them all. But from *Shabistan* (1951) to *Bulundi* (1981), Helen was dancing. She was there while the studio mastodons were shivering in the Ice Age; she was there when the triumvirate of Raj Kapoor–Dev Anand–Dilip Kumar dominated the box office; she sashayed through much of the Bachchan era.

This means that she defied the rules of gender. It is a truism that Hindi commercial cinema has no place for the mature woman. Women must either excite the front-benchers with their youth or bring tears to their eyes portraying suffering maternity. Men play by other rules. Jeetendra, for instance, danced his way through four generations of heroines. Amitabh Bachchan played Raakhee's younger brother-in-law (*Reshma aur Shera*), then her lover (*Bemisaal*, *Jurmaana*, *Kabhi Kabhi*, *Muqaddar ka Sikandar*, *Barsaat Ki Ek Raat*), before turning into her cinematic son (*Shakti*). And Helen? She vamped three generations of men—Prithviraj Kapoor (*Harishchandra Taramati*), Raj Kapoor (*Anari*) and Rishi Kapoor (*Phool Khile Hain Gulshan Gulshan*). That's a sublime feat of gender reversal, even if by the end of it her admirers wanted to avert their eyes from the ageing coquette.

And then, when it should have been curtains, a final bedraggled last bouquet: another Helen was born. She resurfaced as a star mother and grandmother, performing only when her stepson Salman Khan or the son of an old friend (Amitabh Bachchan's son Abhishek) needed her presence to lend a special something to the cast.

And it *was* a special something. Suddenly, the notion of Helen as a mother, the notion of Helen as granny, was laced with charm. No one grudged her the *Filmfare* Lifetime Achievement Award in 1998. Every reviewer had something nice to say about her cameo in *Khamoshi—The Musical* (1996). When she launched into a quick recap of one of her item numbers in *Mohabbatein* (2000), we were enchanted by the sudden po-mo break from the realist narrative into a history of one of the actors. Helen was back and we loved her more than ever. She had achieved what few manage: she had become an icon.

If we take her word for it, she managed these awesome feats through her discipline. 'Friends often ask me how I manage to stay slim,' she told *Filmfare* in 1958. 'The magic formula is strict dieting and I advocate it for every woman, more so if she happens to be a dancer. The grace and appeal of a dance can be ruined by a heavy figure.' To 'stay trim', she would skip for half an hour every morning and avoid breakfast, unless she required energy for a particularly vigorous dance, in which case she would swallow a raw egg and drink half a cup of milk. Once in two months she allowed herself the luxury of eating Chinese food, 'which I love'.

She added that her passion for dancing came out of the French and Spanish blood in her. 'I have quite a mixed pedigree! Father was French and mother half Burmese and half Spanish. My great grandfather was a Spanish pirate!'

I think there's more to it than diet, discipline and a great genetic cocktail.

I also said I would write the book because I like Helen. Does that mean Helen the person? I don't know that Helen at all. I'm not sure I want to. In the course of my career as a journalist, I have met enough stars to know that even the most perfunctory interview can mean the death of a dearly held image. I like Helen, the projection. She did not haunt my dreams in the way Waheeda Rehman and Nutan did. She was not the object of a pubescent infatuation as Zeenat Aman and Parveen Babi were. Helen was different. She created a feeling that you might like to get to know her better. Her mouth and eyes were warm and friendly.

It wasn't quite lust that Helen aroused, although her dance numbers were chiefly about the pleasure men derive from the female form in motion. Helen was the desire that you need not be embarrassed about feeling. You could forgive yourself that feeling because there was something about her that transcended the tawdry clothes, the bizarre make-up, the invasive camera angles, the inane lyrics and the repetitive choreography and suggestive movements. These days she is often spoken of as 'the original item girl'. Like all journalistic short-forms, this one has its elements of truth, but Helen was not just an 'item girl'. As we'll see in later chapters, she had a much more important role to play in defining the moral universe of the Hindi film. And if she managed to break out of the slot of the item—as she did in many of her films—it was because she had charisma. She had the mix of innocence and sensuality that separates the girls from the women.

The imitators were exciting too—Padma Khanna's *Husn ke laakh rang* (The myriad aspects of beauty) in *Johnny Mera Naam* (1970) as she is stripped by a lecherous, bloated Premnath is still spoken of in hushed whispers among middle-aged film buffs. But there was something of the bazaar about them. Perhaps this was because Helen was always an unseen presence that they were all, without exception, desperate to exorcise. Perhaps it was because they were not very good dancers, or that they did not seem to be enjoying themselves in the way Helen appeared to enjoy herself. Whatever the reason, the imitators did not seem present as people. It is not as if they acquiesced to being objectified; just that the male gaze succeeded with them. It did turn them into dancing dolls, into faceless women with generic bodies. Helen escaped that fate by leaving a very personal imprint on the dances by which we best remember her.

Part of this is the inimitable ease with which she executed whatever steps she was asked to do, moving from flamenco to belly dancing to Kathak as to the manner born. But the most important element was her joyousness, the exhilaration of her dancing. She could create the ultimate male fantasy: the dancer who *wanted* to dance; the woman for whom dancing was as much about her enjoyment of her own body as it was about *your* enjoyment of it.

Looking back, it seems odd that Helen had such a hold on my generation. I grew up in the seventies—the decade when Helen's career was already in decline—and like most middle-class boys, I was allowed one film a month at the theatres by parents suspicious of its moral and aesthetic values (in that order). Helen could not invade my space through television, either. Hindi films had exactly four hours a week on the air. There was the three-hour pre-censored film on Sundays, the half-hour of uninterrupted film songs that was *Chhayageet* and another half-hour of a film interview, *Phool Khile Hain Gulshan Gulshan*, conducted by the bubbly, harmless child-star-turned-character-artiste Tabassum. This was all the government would allow on Doordarshan by way of bread and circuses. The rest of the time, we were 'educated' on such improving topics as the use of copper sulphate on the farms of the hinterland or we watched kabaddi tournaments played in deserted stadia.

So I shouldn't have remembered Helen at all, or barely. Or, at best, remembered her as a woman past her prime, showing up only in a song sequence or two and then vanishing, for that was her major contribution to cinema in that era. Instead, I think of her as The Vamp, the first name that comes to mind, the only name sometimes, the rest only as also-danceds. I watched the final moments of the Helen era, knowing that they were the final moments without saying it out loud. Or maybe I did, just once. Coming out of *Don* (1978), I remember turning to a friend and saying, 'Gosh, what a body Helen still has!'

Implicit in that remark was, 'For a woman her age.' I did not know her age then but I did know that she had been around for a while. I did not even know how long a while.

Helen had already transcended my slice of time.

~

This is not a biography of Helen, except where the story of her screen transformation, that transcending of the limitations of age, gender and public memory, implicates her life. It will not answer the question: what is Helen really like? I know this is an important question for all fans. How close or far is the truth from the image on screen? We want information either way (though in the end this information is of little use; we will make of it whatever suits our fantasy, our conviction of the moment). I cannot answer the question about what Helen is really like because I have never met her. I sought to meet her but never got past the household help. I apologize but I gave up after about a hundred telephone calls.

Which, as I've said before, is just as well.

In India, the whole viewer–star attitude is complicated by the way in which we perceive reality. Even when the film magazines were awesomely polite, the Nargis–Raj Kapoor affair was public knowledge; but this did not prevent Nargis from being seen as the woman in white. Hema Malini was never considered a home-breaker although she married a married man, Dharmendra; her conversion to Islam (and his) was not even a political issue to the Bharatiya Janata Party which elected her to the Rajya Sabha in 2003 and fielded Dharmendra from Bikaner in the 2004 Lok Sabha elections. (Nor did it seem to matter to voters who elected the latter with a respectable majority of 57,000-plus votes.) The star is no fixed entity; the star is everything about him or her—the true and imagined life, the performances, the promo material, the public appearances, the gossip, the interludes, the biographies and press coverage. This book, of course, by being about Helen, extends Helen further. The most common reaction that I received when I told people I was writing a book about Helen was, 'Yes, she was popular and she was a good dancer, but does she merit a book?' I do not know whether Helen the person merits one. I believe that Helen the persona created by Hindi cinema, crafted out of its need for Others, does.

This, therefore, is a book about the construction of Helen, the dancer who when she retired from the screen left several myths lying around, myths that slowly began to become the stuff of legend.

And so it will not assess the other question: can Helen act?

Definitions of acting have changed radically in the decades between 1950 and the present and, no doubt, will continue to do so. Sohrab Modi was considered a good actor in his time. If you watch *Yahudi* (1958) today, you might find him mannered and bombastic, his lines delivered in a melodramatic style. However, Modi might have defended his performance by asking how anyone could judge the correct way a Jew in the Roman empire should actually speak. The same argument could, of course, be used for almost anyone else. Since no one has ever met a child scarred by a tattoo that says '*Mera baap chor hai*' ('My father is a thief'), a child who grows up to take on organized crime at the docks with only the power of his body, we have no parameters against which to judge Amitabh Bachchan's performance in *Deewar*. We have never met such cold, concentrated rage before, but we agree that Bachchan's performance is a good one because he convinces us that that is the way such a young man would behave. And if Helen managed to turn into The Vamp for me, for someone who grew up when her career was in a downslide, I take it for granted that she was a good performer, one who satisfied some need in me, in all of us. We needed Helen and were willing to accept the silliness of songs in which she sneezed on people or sang *Nainon ki gaadi chali, gaadi chali chhuk-chhuk-chhuk-chhuk* (The train of the eyes has begun to run, chhuk-chhuk-chhuk-chhuk).

We needed an Other around which to build fantasies and Helen was available, a white woman in a brown world, a woman who could produce sensuality out of golden cages, flamingos, an excess of blue eyeshadow and oversized orange earrings. When we needed an icon on which to build the notion of the wise grandmother, there was Helen again, now a potent mix of nostalgia and charm. She has turned her entire career on its head, defied the notion that you can't come in out of the cold, turned respectable in a way that no one would have imagined possible.

She was good enough and valuable enough to survive and to be allowed the ultimate accolade: screen time in which to reinvent herself.

Perhaps, this is also a good time to deal with the methodology on which this book is based. I began by looking in the archives of film magazines and found precious little. Helen was not enough of a star to merit too many column-inches. It was time to go back to the films.

But which films? Thanks to the Internet, every star seems to have a site devoted to her or him. But there wasn't a single one exclusively on Helen. No filmography, either. When Helen won her Lifetime Achievement Award from *Filmfare*, she told the magazine that she had worked in more than a thousand films. This was an awe-inspiring number. It meant that if I watched them all I would be spending 1000 times 180 minutes which works out roughly to 3000 hours of Hindi films. While I am an addict, I am not into mainlining the stuff. Some choices had to be made.

The first step, then: to create the filmography. With Rajendra Ojha's indispensable filmography, *80 Glorious Years of Indian Cinema*, in one hand and a highlighter in the other, I trawled through five decades of Hindi cinema and found approximately 350 films. Careful investigation of video parlours and other websites yielded another 100 or so. Harish Raghuwanshi sent me his filmography and filled in the blanks on a few of the Bhojpuri, Magadhi and Rajasthani films, as well as the period between *Shabistan* (the film that all the articles on Helen say was her first) and *Malika Salomi* (the first mention in Ojha).

I have no idea of how to account for the other 500 films in which Helen has appeared. In 1964, she told *Filmfare*: 'I cannot quite recollect... [but] I have danced in films in almost every Indian language: Tamil, Telugu, Assamese, Bengali, Punjabi, Marathi, Urdu and now Bhojpuri.' But the missing 500 cannot all be her non-Hindi-language films. I have seen three Bhojpuri films with her in them: *Hamaar Sansaar*, a rural melodrama in which she performs a celebratory dance, *Aag laago saiyyaan tohaar piritiya re* (A curse on your love, my love) at the birth of a child; *Laagi Nahin Chhute Rama*, ditto, in which she dances the six-minute long *Patna ke babu, Jabaniya sambhaal* (Watch your mouth, you clerk from Patna) with the Hindi film comedian Mehmood; and *Bidesiya*, ditto again, where she dances to the song *Hame duniya karela badnaam balamwa tore bade* (My reputation has been ruined, my love, and you're to blame). She shines in all three, and I don't doubt that she was much sought after. But I do not think that she could have acted in almost as many Bhojpuri and Rajasthani films as Hindi films, simply because there aren't so many.

Of course, a thousand may just be a number. When she signed up for the Hindi television serial *Do Lafzon ki Kahani*, the number most commonly mentioned in publicity interviews was 700. As we know from the now-deleted Lata Mangeshkar entry in the *Guinness Book of World Records* for the most number of songs by a single artiste, in the world of Hindi cinema numbers may mean different things to different people. A thousand may be Helen's way of saying, 'I did a lot of work.' Or it may be a number someone told her, and if that person has a record I would be delighted to see it and include it in a future edition.

The second step was to see some of these films. I had to see, I decided, films from each decade of her career. I had to revisit those films by which she is still remembered, the ones in which she 'sizzled', such as *Howrah Bridge* and *Don* and *Inkaar*, the ones imprinted in popular memory. I had to see some of the films in which she was heroine. I had to see the films made on her and films that in some way implicated the construction of the Helen figure, such as V. Shantaram's Marathi film *Chaani* (1977) which dealt with a white woman in a brown village and the way in which she is seen as fair game, literally and metaphorically, for the men in the village. I watched them and made my notes.

Then I wrote this book. A book on Helen, not just a dancer.

Dancing through Helen's heart...
Happy and relaxed after an exciting dance number for her current film, Helen was asked who it was that captivated her heart.
She laughed. 'Oh dear me— just my pets. I love my poodle and all the rest of my dogs.'
'I love travelling. Especially abroad.'
'And I love dressing up. I feel I'm a thousand different people, so want to dress and dance like them.'
Asked what kept her so youthful and lovely, she thought for a moment. Then 'Why I think it's Lux.'
LUX
LUX
'The pure mildness of Lux helps my complexion stay lovely.'
Helen

One

The Making of an H-Bomb—I

...a slit-eyed teenage girl of Spanish–Burmese ancestry arrived in Bombay, having escaped from Burma. The legs that carried her through the jungles of the North-East were later to take Helen to fame.

—Dinesh Raheja and Jitendra Kothari in *The Hundred Luminaries of Hindi Cinema*

Mera naam Chin-Chin-Choo...
(My name is Chin-Chin-Choo...)

—Lyrics from the Helen song in *Howrah Bridge*

Helen Richardson was born on 14 July 1938 or 1939. (All these dates are uncertain since they vary from telling to telling.) Her mother was Marlene, a half-Spanish, half-Burmese woman, and her father a Frenchman. After his death, Marlene married again, a British officer this time whose name Helen took, becoming Helen Richardson. The family was stationed in Burma when the Second World War broke out. Japan joined the Axis powers in September 1940 and by December 1941, Japanese troops had invaded Burma. By May 1942, the conquest of Burma was complete, which means that the retreat of the British troops and non-indigenous British subjects must have begun earlier that year. The women and children were sent by boat to what was then Calcutta. The men walked.

Marlene and her family had left it too late to get on to any of the boats. They were forced to walk from Burma to Assam. Helen told *Filmfare* (3 April 1964) the story of their flight to India. It reads like a first-person account but, going by the journalistic practices of the 1960s, would probably have been an 'as-told-to' piece (a journalist talks to the actor and then writes it up as a first-person account):

> It was a cold December night in Rangoon. The year was 1941. Burma was being mercilessly bombed by the Japanese. Everywhere people were fleeing the country. My mother packed a few things and we went to the airport with my baby brother in Mother's arms. That night, the aerodrome was bombed. Frightened and nervous, we returned home.
>
> Life in Rangoon became unbearable for us. Father had been killed on the battlefront early in the war and there was no one to take care of us. Besides, life was insecure in the war-stricken city. When friends decided to come over to India with their families, Mother agreed to join them. Then from Upper Burma began our long, gruelling trek to Assam.
>
> I was only about three years old at that time. But I was to hear about that torturous journey often from Mother.

For weeks, she goes on to say, they trekked alternately through wilderness and 'hundreds of villages', surviving on the generosity of people, for they were penniless, with no food and few clothes. Occasionally, they met British soldiers who provided them with transport, found them refuge, 'treated our blistered feet and bruised bodies and fed us'. By the time they reached Dibrugarh in Assam, their group had been reduced to half. Some had fallen ill and been left behind, some had died of starvation and exposure. The survivors were admitted to the Dibrugarh hospital for treatment. 'Mother and I had been virtually reduced to skeletons and my brother's condition was critical. We spent two months in hospital. When we recovered, we moved to Calcutta.'

Helen spoke of the trauma again to Khalid Mohamed, then editor of *Filmfare*, of walking and running for months, of ducking bombs, of her mother miscarrying a baby girl on the way, of seeing dozens of people killed. So traumatized was she that her hands would shake for the rest of her life, especially when she heard sirens or saw anything that reminded her of those times.

In Nasreen Munni Kabir's television special, *Helen: Always In Step*, she said: 'It's surprising, I was so young but I can still remember a moment when in the middle of the night we were running out of the house and we passed a place where a bomb must have fallen. It was a shop and there was hair and blood and [bits of] skull on the wall. I still have that dream sometimes. It's very vivid in my mind.'

Returning once more to the *Filmfare* story:

> Life in Calcutta was no bed of roses. Mother, a trained nurse, slogged at odd jobs to feed us. Despite her best efforts to save my ailing brother, he died [of smallpox]. Mother felt the blow deeply. Calcutta now stifled her...After living for some years in Hyderabad and Deolali [in northern Maharashtra], we moved to Bombay in 1947. Here life really began for me. So far, I had known only a rolling-stone existence.

In later interviews, Helen would speak of the small place in Bandra, then a suburb of the city of Bombay, where they lived. The house did not boast too many creature comforts; its outhouse was so infested with cockroaches that the young Helen carried an umbrella to prevent roaches from falling into her hair. In *The Britannica (India) Encyclopaedia of Hindi Cinema* (2003), she talked of how the family was so poor that she would make toys out of broomsticks and wear hand-me-down uniforms to school (St Joseph's Convent in Bandra). 'My own unhappy childhood draws me to children,' she 'wrote' in the April '64 *Filmfare* article. 'I do my best to please them.'

Helen has mentioned her unhappy childhood often, in scattered details over different interviews. In the June 1978 issue of *Cine Blitz*, she said, 'I left school at the age of twelve, in the third standard, to learn dancing. I never really liked it...I used to detest those long hours of practice which I had to put in, because my mind was always on my friends playing outside. Only the cane in my mummy's hand kept my mind on dancing.' Years later, she repeated this familiar story of the child star to Khalid Mohamed: 'Whenever I wanted to play with the other kids, mum would beat me up with a cane. She wanted me to make something of myself. If she hadn't been tough with me, maybe I would have just floated through life without doing a thing.'

Marlene, apparently, had contacts in Hindi cinema. One of the most important contacts—in terms of her daughter's career—was Cuckoo, a dancer who was then in great demand. Cuckoo first appeared in Nitin Bose's *Mujrim* (1944) and then in Mazhar Khan's *Pahli Nazar* (1945). In the next five years, she had appeared in forty-nine films, including Mehboob Khan's *Anokhi Ada* (1948), H.S. Rawail's *Patanga* (1949) and Devendra Goel's *Aankhen* (1950). Cuckoo and Marlene played bridge together (or Cuckoo's parents and Marlene did, depending on the version you prefer) and it was at Cuckoo's urging that Helen was sent to a certain Ratti Bapu to learn Manipuri dance, although she has claimed in other places that she learnt it in school. (Later she said that she had learnt Kathak and Bharatanatyam too, from P.L. Raj, the choreographer of many of her most famous dance sequences.) In a couple of years, probably with Cuckoo's help, Helen began to get intermittent work as a chorus girl in Hindi films. As she wrote in the *Filmfare* story:

> My own love for dancing, the family's poverty and mother's determination made me enter films as a

chorus girl in October 1952 when I was thirteen. I worked as a chorus girl for nine months, envying the lead dancer and dreaming of the day when I too would be decked in gorgeous costumes and leading the dancers.

If you look very carefully, you might spot Helen in the background of her first films, such as *Khazaana* and *Shabistan* (1951), or *Ambar*, *Badnaam*, *Nazariya* and *Rangeela* (all in 1952), dancing in a group of twenty or thirty other girls. In Munni Kabir's television feature, she says that her first film was *Shabistan* in which Cuckoo had a big role. 'I think she was a side heroine. And after that I went on doing chorus dancing for about, maybe, a year... *Uske baad*, in a chorus song itself there was a close-up to be done, like one of the girls had to play the dholak. And they tried all the other girls, there were about fifteen to twenty of us. Since I was the youngest, they never bothered thinking I could do it...After trying all the girls, they said, Helen, now *you* try. And by chance, I got it all right! It was a good close-up.'

In her photographs from the mid-1950s, Helen has the kind of unblemished, untroubled freshness that can bring a smile to your lips. It isn't surprising, then, that the close-up led to better things. Helen was selected for a duet dance in the same film, D.D. Kashyap's *Badnaam*, though it wasn't easy: 'When I got ready for that dance and went on the sets...the director just refused to have me as the dancer because I [looked] too young for the part. And that made me feel very bad and I started crying. Anyway, the cameraman, the hairdresser and the make-up man...sort of took me back to the make-up room and dressed me up and padded me all over and gave me a little more make-up. After that I went back and [the director] was quite pleased with it. I did the dance in the end. From then onwards I started doing duets...I stopped chorus dancing after that.'

~

But as late as *Mayurpankh* (1954) Helen was still not a featured dancer, though she appears in the credits. This is a depressing film, a cross between a Ministry of Tourism handout and an intercontinental love story. A British couple—engaged to be married—come to India and bump about the countryside, seeing the sights. After a tour of South Bombay, on their way to Banaras, the car breaks down. A tiger hunter (Kishore Sahu) rescues them. The British woman (Odette Fergusson) and the hunter start to fall in love. After we have been shown the ghats at Banaras, a child dancer, a snake charmer and a village fair, the couple fight and hare off to Agra. The hunter follows them and confesses his love. It is here that Helen, playing a busker, sings *Mohabbat ki daastaan aaj suno* (Listen to a tale of love). Even before she has got to the antara, she has faded out of the scene and two other extras turn up as Jehangir and Mumtaz Mahal wandering lovelorn around Fatehpur Sikri. There are three more dances put on for the guests as part of the local exotica but Helen does not feature in any of them. (Cuckoo does.)

Helen's first solo dance came in K. Amarnath's *Alif Laila*, a year before the dud *Mayurpankh*. I have not had the pleasure of seeing that dance, although I have spent three fruitless years trying to find the film (despite the VCD and DVD revolution, some of Helen's films remain steadfastly out of reach, and the archives aren't much help). However, Helen told *Filmfare* (ibid) that it was the making of her career. Talking about the opportunities that opened up for her after *Alif Laila* was released, she said: 'One fateful day in November 1954, I was resting in our small Bandra tenement, when a limo drove up. A man walked in. He said producer P.N. Arora would like to see me at his office. I was too thrilled for words, for I sensed a great opportunity coming my way. My intuition proved to be true. I was signed up by All India Pictures who wanted a girl for a small role in *Hoor-e-Arab*.'

Perhaps P.N. Arora had seen her in *Alif Laila*; but it is more likely that he spotted her in the Madhubala-Shammi Kapoor starrer *Rail ka Dibba* (1953), made under his own banner, All India Pictures. According to the canonical Urdu short story writer Saadat Hasan Manto, who also dabbled in film journalism of the more gossipy kind, Arora started his career as a sound recordist, but rose fast in the movie business to become a producer. Other bits and pieces of information suggest that he was a man of some influence, and well aware of his power. In his profile of Sitara, titled 'Dancing Tigress of Nepal', to be found in *Stars from Another Sky* (translated and edited by Khalid Hasan), Manto also writes that Arora was having an affair with the formidable dancer and 'man-eater' Sitara Devi. Arora produced and directed a series of B-grade films, including the aforementioned *Hoor-e-Arab* (1955), *Neelofar* (1957), *Khazanchi* (1958), *Sindbad, Alibaba & Alladin* (1965) and *Dil Daulat Duniya* (1972), all of which starred Helen, none of which left any particular mark on film history.

It is difficult at this remove to tell exactly what impact *Hoor-e-Arab* had on Helen's career. She would have to dance her way through several films until she got to her first hit song-and-dance number in *Baarish* (1957). It is a confident dancer that we see featured in the song that takes place just before the climax. By this time in the film, Ramu (Dev Anand) is already married to Chanda (Nutan). He is a small-time hood who has just discovered that the gang he works for engineered the death of his revered elder brother. He infiltrates the gang—disguised as a madman, although it is unclear why the gang would accept a madman into their ranks—and begins to leak information to the police. A huge deal involving smuggled gold is to go through at the Moonlight Club and Ramu betakes himself there.

We see a woman at the club, back to us, perched on the balustrade of a staircase, swinging her trouser-clad legs, slowly, sensuously. This back-to-camera pose would become something of a signature with Helen. Even if the mystery is dispelled soon enough, it is a hint of suspense, a visual quickfix for hold-your-breath-boys-there-she-blows. This was borrowed from various earlier dance forms, including the mujra, which generally began with the dancer under a veil, or the Maharashtrian folk dance laavni, where the dancers have their backs to the audience. The camera moves up to a face swathed in a veil. Three men, waiting under streetlights, snap to attention. She steps off the balustrade and begins to sashay through a series of fountains until she is in the square with the three of them. They fight over her as she poses for them. One of them, Mr John, survives to have his cigarette lit by the dancer, now lying on the floor.

She begins: *Mr John, Baba Khan ya Lala Roshandaan/ Jo bhi dekhe mera jalwa ho jaaye qurbaan* (Be it Mr John, Baba Khan or Lala Roshandaan/ One glimpse of me is all it takes to fell any man).

The three men in chorus: *Ya qurbaan!* (We'd die for you!)

This is one of Helen's first songs of self-adulation and the men are completely at her mercy. They fall on their backs, their limbs waving feebly in the air, like so many cockroaches. She revives them, zapping each back to his feet by pointing a finger at him. A career in female power had been launched.

In comparison, Nutan, the other female presence in the film, is a tomboy, a village belle, and later a married woman. She trips lightly through her songs, never actually dancing.

But while *Mr John, Baba Khan* is a spirited little number, Helen's real breakthrough came in *Howrah Bridge* (1958), a crime thriller in which an impecunious young man tries to sell a family heirloom to pay his debts. He is murdered and the money taken from him. His brother (Ashok Kumar) comes to Calcutta to find the murderer and the heirloom with the help of a family retainer (Om Prakash) and Edna (Madhubala), a lovely young lady who is mixed up, thanks to her wicked uncle, with the villains. In search of his brother's murderers, Ashok Kumar enters a bar in which he encounters a young woman introducing herself: *Mera naam Chin-Chin-Choo/ Chin-Chin-Choo baba Chin-Chin-Choo/ Raat chandni main mein aur tu/ Hullo Mister, how do you do?* (My name is Chin-Chin-Choo/ Chin-Chin-Choo, sir, Chin-Chin-Choo/ On a moonlit night, just me and you—/ Hullo Mister, how do you do?)

This is as much as Helen does in the film. She isn't even a vamp in the way we understand vamps. She does not offer any sexual challenge, direct or indirect. The dancing is not titillating so much as it is enthusiastic. Miss Chin-Chin-Choo is an ingénue here more than anything else, offering only a certain physical energy and a bodily charm. She is surrounded by what will later become a standard trope of the Helen figure, a group of male dancers, but even they are not as lascivious or as submissive as later dancers would be. However, the words are instructive. Her name establishes her alienness—and it would be a name that would turn up for a long while after that. Her use of English establishes her westernization, underlined by the dress she is wearing, the honky-tonk music, and the way she dances with the sailors, those international symbols of the serially monogamous male, reputed to have a 'girl in every port'.

The basic outline of the Helen figurine was born.

In one sense, at least, the intuition that Helen had when P.N. Arora's limo drew up outside her door was justified. Arora and she would enter into a relationship that would last a good many years, since she was still acting in his *Dil Daulat Duniya* as late as 1972. However, it was not a happy time for her. It was only much later, when she had found happiness as the second wife of the legendary scriptwriter Salim Khan, that she spoke of those days to Shashi Baliga, then a journalist with *Savvy*, a monthly features magazine. Before he became a scriptwriter, Salim Khan was an actor, and in 1963 he played villain opposite Helen in *Kabli Khan*. They met each other off and on over the years, Helen told Baliga, and enjoyed each other's company, but that was all, for she was still involved with Arora. In Baliga's words: 'It was a relationship that, years later, she was struggling to get out of. "It gives me nightmares to even think about it today," she shudders. When P.N. Arora finally released his clutch on her, it was to leave her penniless, without work, and desperately in need of money. The industry folk, while sympathetic, preferred to "play safe" and keep out of it. Salim came to her rescue then, getting her work, and guiding her out of the mess she was in. Helen began to increasingly depend on him, and that was when she realized that her feelings for him were deepening. "The fact that Salim was a married man disturbed me, and I did feel guilty in the beginning," she admits, "but however hard we tried, we couldn't break off."'

Perhaps the long relationship with Arora explains why there was so little written about Helen during the high period of her career. The film magazines need more than just a successful dance number or two. They need a young woman and a young man and the suggestion of a romance. Arora affected well-cut suits but he was an older man, trailing wisps of white hair rather than the reek of testosterone. So there were no rumours, nothing else to link Helen to any other man. Helen herself worked hard at this, telling *Filmfare* (ibid): 'Believe it or not, I am the home-loving type. I suppose you could even call me reserved. But I love children. The neighbourhood children treat my flat as a veritable playpen. They [read] comic books and play with the toys I buy them and make their Aunt Helen dance.'

Arora, it is said, managed Helen's career and controlled her finances through the 1960s and up to the early '70s. During this period, you could not see a film without bumping into Helen. She seemed to lead two independent and simultaneous lives: there was the Helen of the films we all remember, the Helen of *Jewel Thief* and *Ganga Jamuna* and *Kaalicharan* and *Caravan*. And there was also the Helen who was heroine in a huge amount of B-Grade trash. But I'm not sure Arora, alone, was to blame for the latter.

No one comes to Bombay to become an extra or a character artiste. Every 'struggler' (as the tribe of wannabe film stars is now known) wants to be a hero or a heroine. While fortunes have certainly been made by directors, scriptwriters, musicians and other technicians, no one wants a backroom job, however well-paid. Not initially, at any rate. Salim Khan, for instance, who became a star in his own right as a scriptwriter in the seventies, co-authoring with Javed Akhtar such milestones in commercial cinema as *Deewar*, *Sholay*, *Zanjeer* and *Don*, came to the city with the proverbial stars in his eyes. He did act in a few films, including two with Helen—*Kabli Khan* and *Sarhadi Lootera* (1966). However, one

can guess at the lack of success from the billing he accepted in *Ramu Dada* (1961), playing second fiddle to Sheikh Mukhtar. He is the romantic hero but not the pivot on which the plot turns; and that, in a patriarchal industry, is what the real hero of the film must be. It is Ramu Dada's conversion from heartless villain to caring member of society that is central to the plot. Prince Salim gets the songs and the girl but it is the plug-ugly Mukhtar who dominates the show.

Helen, it is true, was never a struggler. At thirteen, she could scarcely be said to have chosen a career—from what she has said about her childhood, it is clear that her mother chose Helen's career for her. However, as part of an industry that pays stars astronomical figures and every other actor a pittance, being a star must have become Helen's dream soon enough.

There are at least fifteen films in which she was the female lead, including *Elephant Queen* (1961), *Miss Chaalbaaz* (1961), *Hawa Mahal* (1962), *Jadoo Mahal* (1962), *Been ka Jadoo*

(1963), *Captain Sheroo* (1963), *Kabli Khan* (1963), *Maya Mahal* (1963), *Sunehri Naagin* (1963), *His Highness* (1964), *Chor Darwaaza* (1965) and *Flying Man* (1965). None of these were hits. Her only success as a heroine was the sleeper hit *Cha Cha Cha* (1964). She plays a dancer who is in love with the hero Chandrashekhar but abandons him to marry a rich businessman. When she goes lame, the businessman abandons her. The unsigned review in *Filmfare* that year was all praise: 'And of course there's Helen, who slides across the film with the grace of a leopardess, whose femininity and quiet behaviour are in pleasing contrast to Bela Bose's enthusiastic flaunting of over-emphasized charms.'

The only other film we can add to Helen's list of successes as a heroine is *Hum Hindustani* (1960), a film that brought her very close to playing the female lead, and not in B-Grade trash. The two heros, Sukhen (Sunil Dutt) and Satyen (Joy Mukherjee) are *nouveau pauvre* brothers; their father's fortune is locked up in litigation. Satyen is already engaged to Kalpana (Helen). We meet her on her birthday and the anniversary of their engagement. The song they sing together—*Neeli neeli ghata/ Bheegi bheegi hawaa/ Hai nashaa hi nashaa/ Kahin kho jaayen na* (These blue clouds, these wet breezes, we might lose our senses to their intoxication)—is a romantic duet that takes them across South Bombay, almost as much a Mumbai darshan as it is a love song, and ends on a darkening skyscape with both of them silhouetted against the fading blue light. Helen seems out of her element, washing her feet in the Arabian sea, tripping along the beach. These are Romantic tropes and she was, it seems, at this remove, already a product of dim interiors.

Otherwise, the figure of Helen has all the requisites of a heroine. When Satyen tries to break off his engagement, Kalpana insists that a woman loves only once and his poverty does not matter. When they get wet and need to change their clothes, director S. Mukherji does not turn the male gaze on his heroine; we watch Satyen's bare back instead of hers. In the standard romantic song that follows—sung by the ready-to-stray hero, for it is night and they are alone—Kalpana behaves with perfect propriety. In other words, there is very little physical contact. She does draw an arabesque on his naked back, but when he reaches for her, she eludes him. He tries to rest his back against hers, one of the most innocent of gratifying contact positions, but she lets him fall over.

By the time I saw *Hum Hindustani*, in the 1970s, I had already internalized a certain viewing of Helen: she was a dancer and there was no one like her. That she was rarely, if ever, given the status even of a second heroine after that film may be an accident of cinema, or it may be that the film industry, too, could not look beyond the undeniable excellence of her dancing.

Here is the conundrum: a competent actress with a pretty face and a pin-up body never manages to get into the A-list of heroines. Various explanations have been offered for this: she looked foreign; her accent was funny; she had already appeared as a dancer and could not make the transition since she was seen as a fallen woman and heroines had to be presumptive virgins. None of these explanations work perfectly.

Helen looked far less foreign than Nadia 'Mary Evans' Wadia or Saira Banu in a blonde wig. A simple change of name should have done the trick. Dressed in ghagra-cholis or saris, as she was in several of her films, Helen was never awkward and looked every bit as Indian as Sandhya, Rekha or Reena Roy.

Her accent shouldn't have been any great impediment, either. She could have been dubbed, as I suspect she was in Babubhai Mistry's *Sampoorna Ramayana* (1961), where her trademark gurgle does not show up in Shurpnakha's voice at all. This might have added to the budget, but several heroines made do with dreadful Hindi accents, including Hema Malini, Zeenat Aman and Jayaprada.

Categories, too, are easily transcended. Mumtaz went from clumsy B-grade films with Dara Singh to huge hits with Rajesh Khanna. Vinod Khanna and Shatrughan Sinha started out as villains and ended up as heroes. Aruna Irani succeeded as a Gujarati film star, the heroine of several social films in which she tamed successive mothers-in-law. That she had been a dancer in Hindi films did not work against her, on the contrary, this helped establish her credentials in regional cinema.

And as for virginity, we have a complex notion of reality in relation to the stars. In the hugely successful *Karz*, Rishi Kapoor and Tina Munim sing a song in which he claims to be seventeen and she, sixteen. It is clear from the inflections in the *mukhda* that they don't believe this, and don't expect us to believe it, either. Through the song they are followed by the girl's chaperones who wave a huge pair of scissors, thus representing the Indian Censor Board. Instances can be multiplied endlessly.

A more cogent argument could be made that the problem lay in the trajectory of Helen's career, in the films that she did accept, either out of economic necessity, or because of poor judgment or the hold that P.N. Arora had on her.

Take, for example, *Hawa Mahal* (1962). It starred Helen as Champakali, a fairy, who is in the power of her sister Neelampari (Bela Bose). Neelampari sends Champakali to lure some hapless princes to their death so that her lover (Tiwari) can rule all three worlds. Champakali is expelled from the underworld because she saves one of the princes (Ranjan) instead of killing him. However, she is almost immediately abducted by a magician, Jaadugar Vetaal, who is in search of the perfect spirit to achieve immortality. Ranjan gets to rescue her with the help of a wish-granting statue that gives him a flower to protect him from evil.

As the synopsis alone should tell you, *Hawa Mahal* is a dreadful film. It has nothing to redeem it. It even wastes its principal asset, Helen, giving her only a single dance—*Nayi nayi manzil hai/ Naya naya geet hai* (Our destinations are new, our songs are new)—in which she trips about like any common or garden heroine of the sixties.

It pretty much set the tone for the rest of Helen's career as a heroine.

Sunehri Naagin (1963) was one of the earliest of a genre now called snake-dance films. Helen plays a princess in it, with the predictable name of Rajkumari, who falls in love with a poor musician, Mangloo (Mahipal)—ostensibly because he rescues her when her horse bolts (we know Mangloo is poor because she is taken to his house which is built at a geometrically perfect 45 degrees to the horizontal). All indications till now are that this will be a film about love, the kind that respects no barriers. But then we see Helen dance at the Naag Panchami festival, where a snake—the eponymous sunehri naagin—appears, drinks all the milk from a steel cup and vanishes. This might lead us to believe that we are in the realm of the mythological. Only, there's also a magician here who has to free the father of his fairy lover (Pritibala) by acquiring a bunch of magical bangles, for which purpose the fairy gives him the Stone of Invisibility and a Flying Carpet...All of which belongs to the realm of fantasy. Thus the film is a confused mix of poor special effects (zombies, snakes that turn into swords, trees of homicidal bent), Errol-Flynn-style swordplay, *Ivanhoe*-style jousts, dream sequences, smoke clouds and a sprinkling of bhakti.

Helen dances in several songs. There are a couple of snake dances—*Main baawariya, naachoon tere aage saari umariya* (Love-mad, I will dance for you all my life) and *Been na bajaana/ Yeh jaadu na jagaana* (Do not play that flute, do not evoke that magic); a romantic song with Mahipal—*Tujhe chaand kahoon ya phool kahoon* (Should I call you the moon, should I call you a flower?); a song of parting—*Mil ke bhi hum mil na sake* (Although we fell in love, it was not meant to be); and a song danced to divert the magician—*Dono haathon se dil kyoon sambhaala hai* (Why do you shield your heart so carefully?).

While she dances well, you know you're watching a last-ditch attempt to get some life into a dead film.

Likewise, *Aaya Toofan* (1964) is full of hams, the largest and worst being the male lead, Deepu (Dara Singh). Helen plays another princess, Rajkumari Chand, of another Cloud Cuckoo Land. Another magician, this time one with evil intent, descends from an extraterrestrial globe that falls out of a cardboard sky, but not before you see the string holding it up for the camera. He presents Chand with a little cupboard, which has a littler doll that mimics her movements. In the night, the doll metamorphoses into a golem and abducts Chand. Deepu rescues her—princesses exist only to be rescued—and they fall in love.

Once again Helen dances in practically every other reel. There's a tribal song. There's a romantic song with Deepu (through which she behaves like a good Indian heroine of the time: a few languorous movements and a few flowers chucked in the direction of the hero). There's a song of misdirection in which, trying to rescue Deepu, she distracts a band of guards with lots of spinning skirts and gypsy jewellery. There's a song to lull the magician into thinking she is responding to his overtures, with a supporting chorus in pastel gowns out of a Goan Catholic wedding. Through it all, you can see Helen working at it. Compared to Dara Singh, she acts up a storm. As always, she dances well. But it is difficult to care when Deepu is blinded at the king's orders and Chand sets off to find the *netraprabha moti* (the pearl of eyesight).

It becomes obvious quite early in the film that casting Helen was not the point. Dara Singh was enough of a name to draw in crowds in the north-Indian mofussil. His films relied on the reputation he had gained as a freestyle wrestler. In *Aaya Toofan* he fights and defeats four featured wrestlers: Baron-von-Heczev, Trilok Singh, King Kong and Ray Appolen. Helen could have been Pritibala or Jaymala or Chitralekha. It did not matter.

In 1972, she was still playing heroine to Dara Singh in *Sultana Daku*. By this time, she was an established dancer, a name for the marquee. But in this film she has only a single dance, *Tere haath jodoon/ Tere paiyaan padoon* (I plead with you, I fall at your feet), which is a standard Hindi film heroine performance. She is a gypsy who falls in love with and marries the dacoit Sultana Daku. She also dies in the film, felled by a stray bullet, which might have been the director's way of acknowledging her status as just a dancer after all, since an on-screen death with glycerine and speeches is usually reserved for a star.

In *Hulchul* (1971), Helen is the female lead, but only in a manner of speaking, for it is O.P. Ralhan, the producer and director of the film who also acts in it, who is the centre of the action. Peter (Ralhan) overhears a conversation in which a certain Mahesh Jetley is telling his mistress that he will marry her as soon as he manages to kill his wife. Ralhan finds three Mahesh Jetleys listed in the telephone directory and warns all Mrs Jetleys. They begin to suspect their husbands who, it must be admitted, behave pretty suspiciously.

There are no songs in the film at all, which makes it something of a rarity. We are never sure what Peter's girlfriend Kitty (Helen) does for a living although she does a dance in a hotel in which she represents, in order, the British, the Russians, the Spanish, the Scottish, the Egyptians, the Japanese, Africans (for which she wears dark makeup and a frizzy wig and is lifted out of a cooking pot) and finally Malayalis. Her role is largely comic since Ralhan fancied himself a kind of philosophical comedian, a Fool in the Shakespearean sense. She jumps, grimaces, giggles, turns away and coquettes efficiently but she was not meant to be a comic actress. Her mother is played by Tun Tun, who was believed to be funnier, simply by virtue of being fat. This means that Tun Tun gets more screen time with Ralhan than Helen does.

Things had not improved for Helen as leading lady even as late as 1976. The hero in mainstream cinema, as we have noted, is the pivot on whom the plot turns. He is the one who does and to whom is done. And the heroine is usually only his love interest. By that definition, the real heroine in the 1976 film *Ginny Aur Johnny* is not Helen but a child artiste, Ginny. The titles describe her as the 'most lovable, adorable, sensational discovery of the decade'.

Johnny (Mehmood) is a small-time con who makes his money by getting free Bibles, Gitas and Korans and then selling them at high costs to the widows of recently deceased men. Ginny is the daughter of a prostitute—Rosie (Hema Malini), who dies when one of her clients tries some one-hand driving. Johnny pretends to adopt Ginny and uses her to blackmail the john out of some money. When he has succeeded, he tries to ditch Ginny. But the little girl has taken the adoption seriously, and since she also makes sure

she has the purse strings firmly in her clutches, Johnny falls in with her plan. She wants new clothes, so they go shopping and meet Ruby (Helen), also shopping, for 'better-quality bras in size 42'. Johnny falls in love with Ruby. Ginny feels abandoned. The rest of the film is devoted to the way in which this love triangle plays out.

Once again, it need not really have been Helen in the lead, although she does play a cabaret artiste and does a couple of dances including the remarkable *Mutthu kullika vari kalla* (which I have been told means 'Come dive with me for pearls' in Tamil). And it is evident that Mehmood isn't expected to find love in this relationship, since Ginny and a good-hearted maid Sweety (Preeti Ganguly) concoct a Wodehousian charade to reveal Ruby's mercenary instincts. Helen is not the heroine; she just about passes muster as Mehmood's lust-interest.

Helen herself does not even try to explain her lack of success as a heroine. 'I was never ambitious,' she says in *The Britannica Encyclopaedia of Hindi Cinema*. 'I took life as it came.'

The oldest explanation—she was ahead of her time—has some validity here. At the point of time where she burst on to the screen with her combination of vivacity, expressive body language and sensuous enjoyment of movement, we had no use for these things. They did not fit in with the stereotype fixed for the heroine. A series of angels in white stalked the national imagination, their flowing clothes usually concealing all evidence of the body. They did not dance; they glided. When they smiled, it was from the Olympian heights of Virtue. They were happy in the confines of the home. They might throw it all up for love but the audience was always reassured of the purity of their passions. Duty came first, devotion next, love thereafter and nothing much mattered after that. The world of passion was *tamasik*; these women were *satvik*.

The sixties brought us the first gamine heroines, but look at the men who accompanied most of them: Joy Mukherjee, Jeetendra and Biswajeet. We could believe in them as heroes when someone equally juvenile was their leading lady. Even Shammi Kapoor would need pretty puppets for his overgrown-boy routines. It would have taken too much effort to believe in Helen as a complacent foil to these chocolate-box heroes with their epicene faces and pretty-boy looks. This would be a problem that would dog her throughout her career: she was far too threatening, far too female, far too sexual to ever play complacent foil to the leading man. By the time the seventies brought us the westernized heroines and the potent, sexualized threat of Amitabh Bachchan, Helen was fixed, a victim of her success, in the role of the dancer, the additional enticement to the theatre.

Another possible explanation could be her name. During the course of a televised tribute to Helen, Amitabh Bachchan remarked that he had heard of her, heard her name, since the time he was young. '*Pehle to aakarshan unke naam se hua. Aam Hindustaani kalaakaron se yeh naam alag tha.*' (First, I was attracted to her name. It was different from the names of other Hindi cinema artistes.) This remark, which you can still hear on Volume 2 of *Helen, The Golden Girl: The Concert of a Lifetime* (HMV), was meant to be a tribute but it did point up a fundamental problem. The leading ladies of the fifties and sixties had names that were identifiably Hindu or, sometimes, attractively Muslim, in origin. As a name, Helen was too reminiscent of a religion and lifestyle that was associated with the British, even if Christianity has a much more ancient lineage in India than colonialism. Being an alien was useful, as we shall see in the next chapter, for a vamp; perhaps it was only those who were deemed Indian who could play cinema's virgins.

Helen's failure to make the grade to heroine also has to do with the natural tendencies of a streetwise cinema. The first is a tendency to superstition. No film fails because an actor fails, but since by virtue of being the audience magnets the lead actors get the most publicity, they also get the lion's share of the blame for a flop. Take the year 1963. Helen was heroine in five films, while Meena Kumari was the lead in three, Nutan in three, and Asha Parekh in four. In addition, Helen appeared in *seventeen* other films, including three Bhojpuri and one Gujarati (they're in the filmography; count them). Although *Laagi Naahi Chhoote Rama* in Bhojpuri is still something of a standard and her song in it is hummed in the villages of Uttar Pradesh and Bihar to this day, the rest were substandard films with casts that included names which no one but the most committed of film buffs would remember—Indira, Mahipal, Vijaya Chowdhury, Pritibala and the like. There are only four films out of the total of twenty-two with saleable stars in them: Pradeep Kumar in *Mulzim*, Raj Kumar in *Pyaar ka Bandhan*, Shammi Kapoor in *Pyar Kiya To Darna Kya* and Pradeep Kumar-Bina Rai in *Taj Mahal*. Of course, a dancer can't afford to be choosy. A day or two of work would not amount to much money, so Helen the dancer probably had to take what came her way. But Helen the heroine? That's a different matter altogether. By appearing in twenty-two films in a single year, she was not doing her career any favours. She was overwhelming the demand with the supply.

The second tendency in cinema is to put to economic use what is available. Heroines? There were plenty of them. Dancers? There weren't so many, even in the sixties. It wasn't even required that actresses should dance well. While Waheeda Rehman and Vyjayanthimala were trained classical dancers, most others walked, tripped or glided through their songs. Helen herself says something of the sort in the television special *Helen: Always in Step*: 'They couldn't get anyone else to be Helen. But they could always get actors.'

And anyway, she has had her revenge. Few would remember Chitra from *Patal Nagri* (1963) or Gitanjali from *Parasmani* (1963), both heroines then, both nonentities now. Helen achieved a kind of immortality from the sidelines, which is a much greater achievement than the achievements of those acknowledged as stars.

Two

The Making of an H-Bomb—II

The dancer had to be a vamp in those days. The public would take to the vamp because she related to the real world. You know, a woman is not only sugar, she has to be spice too. The heroine was too goody-goody, wishy-washy for my liking. The vamp had to be seductive, a brazen hussy, have a cigarette in one hand, a glass of whisky in the other. I could never walk on the streets. I had to wear a burqa *(veil). They used to go berserk if they saw me. I'd get a lot of fan mail, even from women. I became a sex symbol in the sixties. I was known as the H-Bomb—H for Helen; that made me laugh a lot!*

—Helen, quoted in *Bollywood: The Indian Cinema Story* by Nasreen Munni Kabir

It is true that there were other dancers before Helen; Azoori is often mentioned, as, of course, is Cuckoo. But in the Roman costume drama *Yahudi* (1958) where Helen and Cuckoo share the song *Bechain dil, khoyi-si nazar/ Tanhaaiyon mein shaam-seher/ Tum yaad aate ho* (My heart is restless, my gaze distracted; through the lonely nights and days, memories of you come back to haunt me), there is a fragility about Cuckoo. Helen was twenty or thereabouts while Cuckoo had been dancing for fourteen years. Against Helen's puppy fat, Cuckoo's face has a certain battered, gamine knowingness.

There is history behind her smile, a past. Her body is thin, her movements feline. In the contrast between rounded contours and high cheekbones, expectant eyes and eyes that

have, perhaps, seen too much, it is clear that Helen is the future. Although at this stage only the coquettish eyebrow and arched hands foretell the diva of the sixties.

Women were, by then, commonplace in cinema. No longer would men have to play women as in Dadasaheb Phalke's early mythologicals. Nor would actresses have to be drawn from the lower strata of society. Durga Khote, a Brahmin, had managed to break the taboo associated with cinema. There were genuine actresses around, and many of them came from good homes and looked convincing when they played upper-class women. However, it was clear that when it came to the somewhat questionable activities such as performing dance numbers that were meant for the delectation of men (as opposed to an offering to the gods), Anglo-Indians were easier to persuade. After all, Mary Evans had already demonstrated that there was room for a woman who was at ease with her body and used it in ways that could be construed as sexual even if they were not meant to be. From her debut as *Hunterwali* in 1935, Mary 'Nadia' Evans, or Nadia Wadia, as she became after her marriage to her mentor Homi Wadia, wore men's clothes, performed stunts, and drove about in a car, which she called 'Rolls-Royce *ki beti*'. But she was always portrayed as a good woman. She was pro-Indian, pro-poor, anti-British, anti-authority. It is seductive to look at her as the precursor to Helen, for she was not averse to appearing in figure-revealing clothes and exercising for the camera, as she did in *Miss Frontier Mail*. However, as Savita (the character she played in *Miss Frontier Mail*), Nadia only wanted to save her father from a trumped-up charge of murder. She never danced seductively, never smoked or drank. The only time she vamped it up was in *Muqabla* (1942) but that was still a double role in which she was both good sister and bad sister.

Cuckoo was also an Anglo-Indian but was chalk to Nadia's cheese. She was delicate and small boned where Nadia was a statuesque woman, to put it politely. She was petite and pretty while Nadia was presented as an oddity, a macho woman. Yet, in an odd way, the two of them prepared us for Helen.

Helen took the path they cleared, but walked to places neither of her predecessors had shown us. She redefined the grammar of movement for women in Hindi cinema.

~

What we now consider the standards of seduction—the shaking hips, the thrusting breasts—are pure Helen. She brought us the signals of the coquette: the biting of a finger, the full-lipped pout, even the straightforward suggestiveness of the wink. The mixed signals so precious to the patriarchal notion of the woman who never means 'No'—the dismissive gesture and the come-hither walk away—were reprised in song after song. To these were added the movements of abasement: kneeling, lying on the floor on her back, writhing in unrequited passion. There were mime movements too, which brought together the innocence of household activities (fetching water was a big favourite) and the anarchic arrival of romantic love. Helen's choreographers did not let her lip-synch and forget; they also expected her lissome body to reproduce the song.

While she was trained in Manipuri dancing, she was also good at Kathak, although she herself did not seem to think so. In 1964, she told *Filmfare* (ibid): 'As for styles, nothing very classical. I feel more at home doing cabaret, "singing girl" dances, folk dances, cha-cha-cha, twist, and just about everything that can be termed a film dance—a combination of various styles, Indian and Western.' Directors and choreographers could trust her with any kind of dance movement, however sophisticated or ridiculous.

And then there was her face.

My contention is that Helen's face was almost as important in her dancing as her body. Take, for example, that beautiful song of yearning, *Tumko piya dil diya* (*Shikari*, 1963), which she dances with Ragini, one of the Travancore sisters, renowned for their classical training in dance. Ragini's execution is perfect, her body supple. But when you watch the two of them, it is Helen who holds you. Her face echoes the words. Ragini dances well, but Helen's *abhinaya* is much more deeply felt, more attuned to the lyrics. In the last sequence, which is the usual crescendo, Helen's face has the abandon of the born dancer, while Ragini still looks like someone who is smiling because she is supposed to smile.

Thus, it was on Helen's mobile face that sexual desire was first played out. This represented the immediate and most direct change. Generous to the point of caricature, she made great use of her mouth. There are hundreds of Helen smiles. There's the one that suggests playful challenge; the one in which she suggests mockery; the one in which she conveys sensual desire; the one in which she smiles while biting one side of her lower lip in a most suggestive manner. She was almost always smiling when she danced, but this was no mechanical rictus. It was a smile in constant motion, an animated smile. She made great play with her eyes too. She hooded them in half-slumbrous anticipation; she rounded them in mock-excitement; she cocked an eyebrow in erotic challenge.

All this was new to Hindi cinema, even if the idea of the erotic dance was not new to the country—we even have a rasa for it, *shringara*, codified in the *Natyashastra*. But traditionally the look that signifies the erotic has little to do with the come-hither variety of sex. For sex is not mere pleasure, but a variation on the theme of the love of God—the carnal as a route to the Divine. The tantriks explored all conceivable forms of sexual experience only to transcend it. In the carvings of Khajuraho or in the miniatures of the Pahari school, the faces of women and men indulging in every variation of intercourse were not very different from the faces of the lover in waiting or out on a hunt, or the *naayika* combing her hair, receiving a letter or bathing. This led Kenneth Clark, an art critic of western origin and training, to describe them with little understanding as 'passionless'. Helen, he would have understood. If her standard moves were Indian 'film dance' (which is now accepted as a genre of dance in acting institutes), her face was western in its conception of *kama*. It would not have looked out of place in a Toulouse-Lautrec. She was a revolution in Indian cinema.

Finally, of course, there was the sheer transcendence of Helen's personality. Where cinema sought to slot her into a small, well-defined space, she simply burst out of those confines. When she was given silly stuff to do, she did it with huge panache. This must have been especially difficult for Helen, and must count as her greatest triumph, because silliness can be anti-aphrodisiacal. It is not my contention that sex must be a deadly serious business, but impersonal or public sex must take itself seriously. Any hint of irony or self-consciousness can bring the whole structure crashing down. Even laughter can be dangerous to this hothouse.

And yet, how could one not laugh? Take *Sachaai* (1969), a moral tale of good versus evil, where Helen features in a bizarre song sequence. We begin with her dancing inside a liquor bottle. Outside, a slowly revolving dais supports a dozen wine glasses, each large enough to contain a flailing chorus girl. Water isolates them from an audience we do not see. Helen is wearing little more than a bikini covered with cookie-sized sequins. She sings: *Kab se bhari hai saaqi/ Botal sharaab ki/ Aa pee le isme bandh hain/ Raatein shabaab ki* (The cupbearer has long since filled the bottle with wine, come drink of it, for trapped within are nights of passion). The last line is accompanied by a suggestive stroking of the thigh. Against a studio sunset, Shammi Kapoor, dressed as the legendary lover Majnun, rises, holding a glass. He joins in the song and comes to press up against the bottle. The trapped Helen presses against it too. A stock-shot lightning flash and she's out of the bottle. Another chorus joins them dressed in white flamenco outfits. Meanwhile, the bathing beauties in the wine glasses are heaving their chests in and out of the water. Two outfit changes later (the most memorable of which has Kapoor in a blue wig and beard), the song ends with both the lead dancers trapped in the bottle.

In *Tum Haseen, Main Jawaan* (1970), Helen's number begins in a club, with four men clad in tigerskin pants and marigold necklaces playing bongos. Tina (Helen) appears in a silver gown and silver shoes, framed against a ten-foot African drum. She then steps into a fountain and emerges from it, sniffling and shivering. She wiggles a finger under her nose and then sneezes loudly, *Aachhee*. She bends forward to one of the patrons near the ramp and sneezes on him—*Aachhee*—causing him to splash his drink into his face. She dances over to another patron, seizes his handkerchief, explodes delicately into it and returns it to him. Only then does she start singing: *Chhee, meri jaan, chhee* (Yuck, my love, yuck).

At the Hotel Mercanto in *Kaalicharan* (1976), several things are going on while Helen dances. Kaalicharan (Shatrughan Sinha) has come looking for the villains who are hiding in dark corners, waiting to shoot him. Helen, dressed in an Arabian fantasy costume, sings: *Aaj husn par marne ka mausam/ Mujhpar markar jee le* (Time today to die for love, time for you to live by dying for me). The menacing overtones of this song are dispersed—indeed, made ridiculous—when a caricature Santa Claus stomps on to the night club floor, bearing a bunch of balloons, declaring, *Main tera sachcha aashiq* (I am your true lover) and is revealed to be the Police Commissioner (Premnath) himself.

The lyrics to Helen's songs could sometimes be spectacular (some may have suffered from my clumsy translation and some from the inability of the English language to deal with the romanticism of Urdu), but just as often they were pretty pathetic. In *Mome ki Gudiya* (1972), she sang the immortal lines: *Nainon ki gaadi chali, gaadi chali chhuk-chhuk-chhuk-chhuk* (The train of eyes has begun to move, chhuk-chhuk-chhuk-chhuk). These elegant lyrics are attributed to Anand Bakshi who is also introduced as a playback singer in this film. Other lines continue: *Jeevan hai kya, ek rail hai/ Do din jawaani ka khel hai* (What is life? It is a railway line. And youth is a fleeting game).

This was what the original, the best-loved diva of Indian cinema had to contend with.

Nor was she always treated in a manner befitting her beauty, her grace and her ability to dance. But she survived all that as well. One of the most commonly held 'truths' about Helen is that she was never vulgar. This was shored up by the assertion that she always wore a body stocking, which in turn meant that she was never actually showing as much skin as was indicated by the brevity of her clothes. When I told a friend about the strange affection I felt for the Helen figure, he repeated this bit of film lore with the air of a man saying something incontrovertible. 'Helen,' he said, 'was never vulgar.' I agree. But it couldn't have been easy.

In a collaborative enterprise like cinema, the blame for vulgarity is difficult to apportion. It might be the placement of the camera for the purpose of a lewd shot; the costume may be designed to serve the viewer's voyeuristic desire to see female underclothes; it might be the dance director's notion of how the lyrics should be translated into abhinaya; and of course, it might be the dancer herself trying too hard.

Consider *Night in London* (1967), a title that already spells trouble ('London' = The Colonizer = The West = Decadence; and 'Night' of course is a time when all kinds of unsuitable people and emotions are on the prowl). Renu's (Mala Sinha) father has been kidnapped by villains who want her to masquerade as a princess and get hold of a clutch of diamonds in the keeping of a British aristocrat. The diamonds also contain a formula that can spell the end of the world. (Whatever.) In London, three sets of villains, from Hong Kong, from America and from England, pursue Renu. Sue (Helen) belongs to the gang from Hong Kong, perhaps a tribute to her South-East Asian roots. Somewhere halfway into the film she sings the rousing *Aur mera naam hai Jameela*

(And my name is Jameela). In the song she appears in a white raincoat, bearing aloft a white umbrella. She drops both and is revealed to be wearing a sleeveless black-and-silver top that ends in triangular lappets that lap around her hips and black tights. She is soon joined by a group of dark, half-dressed men who pant after her, their chests and stomachs heaving, as she flirts with them, approaching and then withdrawing, dancing towards them and then spinning away. In one shot she throws her arms around two of her plump studs and raising her hips, jerks her pelvis at the camera while throwing her legs apart.

But vulgarity is not merely a function of what is done, nor even of how it is done, but also of how it is received. If it is in the eye of the beholder, my friend was quite right. There was no vulgarity because it was not perceived. We did not see Helen as vulgar and so nothing she did on-screen was vulgar. Perhaps that was because our responses were veined with the affection one might feel for a youngster. In many of her films Helen was called Kitty (*Gumnaam*, *Dus Lakh*, *Hulchul*, *Raakhi ki Saugandh*) or other such diminutive names. This allowed us to be adult because Helen was trapped in a juvenile identity. It was another way of handling all that sexual charisma, all that powerful femininity. We loved her because we knew she could challenge us but she didn't. Everyone watching Helen was allowed to be in charge because *she* was not. But ah the thrill, the underlying possibility, that one day something might snap...

~

By the happy accident of retaining her Western name and inhabiting a space that allowed mobility, Helen created a liberated—and liberating—persona. She belonged totally to Hindi cinema, she was its creation, but she seemed to be slightly apart from it. (This might be, in part, because of that famous aloofness, the complete professionalism she is said to have exuded on the sets. But then, it must have been difficult to perform erotic dances on a set full of men and then hobnob with them.) While most of her dances were meant for mass seduction, turning her into something of an object for the male audience, many women, too, found a lot that was appealing in the Helen figure. And men could also use the Helen persona, as we shall see, to examine their own ideas of masculinity and femininity. There was something for everyone in the way that the Helen figurine was constructed: for the heterosexual man and the homosexual one, for the feminist woman and the patriarchal film-maker. She became everybody's favourite vamp, and sex, I think, didn't have all that much to do with it.

Three

The Woman Who Could Not Care

Lily: Shyam, aaj bahut...pareshan nazar aa rahe ho.
Shyam: Isiliye mein tumhaare paas aaya hoon.
L: Kaash yeh sach hota.
S: Yeh sach hai Lily. Tumhaare kareeb aakar mujhe badi raahat milti hai.
L: Sach? Tumhara koi kusoor nahin. Mard ki fitratein hi aisi hoti hain.
S: Lily, aurat woh haseen paheli hai jise samajhne ke liye insaan baar-baar galti karta hai, magar phir bhi samaj nahi paata.
L: Yeh paheli mein samjhaati hoon.
S: Promise?
L: Pehle galti to karo.
(Lily: Shyam, you look worried today.
Shyam: Which is why I have come to you.
L: If only that were true.
S: It is true. I find peace with you.
L: Really? It's not your fault. Men are made like that.
S: And women are beautiful riddles that men make the mistake of trying to solve, again and again, even if they never succeed.
L [putting her arms around him]: I'll explain the riddle.
S: Promise?
L [pulling him down, right out of the frame]: First make the mistake.)

—An inspiring piece of dialogue from
the 1970 crime thriller *The Train*
(Lily is Helen and Shyam, Rajesh Khanna)

The term vamp has its roots in the word vampire. According to Adrian Room in *Brewer's Dictionary of Modern Phrase and Fable*, it originated around the early part of the last century and came to be associated with the film star Theda Bara who 'first cast her sensual spell in the silent film *A Fool There Was* (1915), based on Kipling's poem *The Vampire*,' from which I have also taken the title of this chapter. In the film version, wealthy diplomat John Schuyler (Edward Jose), a devoted husband and father, has a shipboard romance with a notorious femme fatale (Theda Bara), who lives off a succession of men, all of whom she has ruined. After the resulting scandal brings about his dismissal, he returns home from England where he has been posted, with his seductress in tow, abandoning his wife (Mabel Frenyear) and daughter.

A Fool There Was is a moral tale. By transgressing the order of society, Schuyler has committed an offence for which he must pay. Both the film and Kipling's poem seem to suggest that there is something slightly supernatural about the power that the woman commands over him. In the poem, he makes his prayer to 'a rag, a bone and a hank of hair', bringing to mind totem objects and what might be known in the West as 'primitive religions'. At the end, we are told that the worst shame was to know that she could not care. In the film, the femme fatale has no name. In the credits, she is known simply as 'The Vampire', although she displays no enhanced dentition.

Hindi cinema had little use for a vamp of that kind. The kind of vamp it needed, the kind of vamp Helen became (or was made into) was in part influenced by the historic moment in which she began to dance; in part by the aesthetics, still fluid, that cinema was reshaping from material borrowed from other sources; and in part by the way in which identity was being constructed for women.

Any cinema, to be successful, must give the nation in which it is born what the nation needs. Or perhaps one might say that the cinemas that give the nations of their birth what they need are the ones that can withstand powerful onslaughts from without. India was born in violence and bloodshed on an unprecedented scale. Yet an important part of our narrative of Independence is that we gained our independence through acts of ahimsa and satyagraha. (Thus, perhaps, our discomfort with the bloodbath of Partition, which has never found its way into as many mainstream narratives as one might expect.) Gandhiji may have been morally superior; the nation was not. Perhaps it is not in the nature of a nation state to be. India could have been a moral nation or a statesmanlike nation. It chose instead to try to be both: moral in its tone and position; pragmatic in its dealing with its citizens and neighbours.

A myth was needed to paper all this over. The myth of Bharat Mata or Mother India was perfectly valid while the nation state was still a distant dream or while it could be seen to be in its formative years. But the myth of motherhood allows no taint. A mother must be perfect or she's no mother at all. A lover must be an immaculate *aadarsh Bhaaratiya naari* (ideal Indian woman) or she's not fit for the *jawaan* (soldier) or the *kisaan* (farmer). As sisters, women could offer images of mischief and naughtiness but even this was sanitized of sibling rivalry or the more common sibling malice. The leading ladies who drifted across the screens were presented as perfect, ethereal, admitting no physicality at all. Their clothes were white shrouds for their sexuality. Their eyes were either fixed in the distance or glistening with the tears of the misunderstood woman. Their world was divided sharply into inside (safe), outside (fraught) and fantasy (romantic). To achieve pan-nationality, this idealized figure had to be Hindu, virginal, fair and long-haired.

This in turn meant that the vamp could not be a Hindu. She would have to be an outsider to the mainstream Hindu tradition. It is not clear on whom the title of the first vamp of Hindi cinema should be conferred. It has often been said that Azoori and Kuldeep Kaur were dancing before Cuckoo came along in 1945, and that Cuckoo modelled herself on Azoori. But in the public consciousness, it is the student who outdid the master. Cuckoo is a dim memory for film buffs; Kuldeep and Azoori are connoisseur's curiosities. Helen eclipsed them all and established such a pinnacle of achievement that all the dancers and anti-heroines who came afterwards would look like bad copies.

In 1947, India became independent, Partition divided the British 'possessions' in the subcontinent into two and the dream of the state as all-benevolent mother, Annapurna Devi, Mahalaxmi, began to fade at the edges. It had its last gasp in *Mother India* (1957), a spectacular last gasp in that it was one of the finest Hindi films ever made, but a last gasp nonetheless. When Radha refuses the food offered by the lecherous zamindaar, the applause is thunderous because she has refused to compromise her purity not just for herself, but for all Indian women, in all circumstances. She will sacrifice the hunger of her children on the throne of her principles. This is the Mother Militant, who will send her son to his death. The nation does do this; so does Mother India.

The nation state was not very old when Helen began her first rehearsals. The memsahibs were not yet a distant memory to be retrieved by Raj enthusiasts and professional nostalgists. They had left only a short while previously. And while they were not precisely white goddesses to whom all Indian men aspired (all men, if one is to believe Robert Graves), there was that old colonial hangover of the woman whom you could not touch because she belonged to the ruling class. It was not simply the Indian fascination with white skin, although this played its part; it reached deeper into the realm where the forbidden holds a powerful attraction simply because it is forbidden. If the heroine—and the term will be used when I mean the female protagonist, the woman playing opposite the hero—was the ethereally unavailable Hindu woman, objects of male lust would also need to be devised. For while men are natural worshippers (pedestals maintain a safe distance between the male devotee and the anarchic reality of a sexual woman), they are also men. Someone was needed to satiate the demands of the libido too.

For a nation not old enough to be able to ogle its own women, Helen must have seemed the ideal vamp. What better way of exacting revenge for all those years of frustration than to cast the available white women as objects of lust? Cuckoo was Anglo-Indian; Helen was French-Burmese-British with a touch of Spanish blood somewhere. Azoori and Kuldeep Kaur, it is true, came from less 'foreign', more 'indigenous' communities but they were still not quite mainstream, not Hindu. In any case, neither left much impact, certainly nothing so deep and lasting as that left by Helen. Cuckoo is also remembered. Perhaps we have forgotten the other two because they weren't very good dancers: check out Azoori in Guru Dutt's misbegotten *Baaz*.

While Helen and Cuckoo were not really white, they were white enough, just as Chaani (Ranjana) in V. Shantaram's *Chaani* (1977) was white enough. The child of an Englishman who rapes a tribal woman, Chaani is brought up by another tribal when her mother is ritually murdered to exorcise her sin. She grows up golden-haired, blue-eyed and is introduced to us in the voice-over as '*paapi, bhigadleli, charitraheen*' (sinful, degenerate, loose) simply because she is half-white. In one scene, a woman asks her, 'With your white skin, your yellow hair and your blue eyes, aren't you the image of a malevolent ghost?' Shantaram's sympathies are clearly on Chaani's side, the equivalence between degeneracy and white skin is questioned and in her death at the end of the film her innocence is validated. But it is clear from the way she is portrayed, even appearing with her breasts covered only by her golden hair in one scene, that sympathy does not preclude the deploying of the male gaze. This as late as 1977.

It would be very many years since Independence before a Hindu vamp would be accepted in the form of Bindu, in the late sixties. Until then, outsiders to the Hindu mainstream would be called in to be lusted after, either as Anglo-Indians, Christians, Jews, one or two Muslims, a Sikh. It is also possible to show that outsider status was also conferred on these lust objects within the context of the film. (This would explain the procession of tribals and the number of times that Helen was called Miss Kitty, Miss Lilly—almost always with an extra 'l'—and Miss Rosie.)

So this was where Helen came in. She was the perfect outsider for whom the rules did not have to apply. (If they had applied the rules, Helen might not have been allowed to dance at all, considering that the Indian film censors operated according to a code that forbade exhibition of the human form, 'actually or in shadowgraphs: (i) in a state of nudity; or (ii) indecorously or suggestively clothed; or (iii) in an indecorous or sensuous posture.') It is also interesting to note that in Helen's breakthrough number, the lyrics emphasize her alienness. *Mera naam Chin-Chin-Choo*, she tells us in *Howrah*

Bridge, and later in the song, informs us: *Babuji mein Cheen se aayi, cheeni jaisi dil laayi/ Singapore ka youvan mera, Shanghai ki angdaai* (My name, sir, is Chin-Chin-Choo. I've just arrived from China, my heart is sweet as sugar; my youth is from Singapore, my sinuousness from Shanghai). Thus everything in her physicality has been imported from elsewhere.

But Miss Chin-Chin-Choo has other uses too. She is a signifier who lets us know that the hero has wandered away from the bourgeois respectability of his middle-class trading family and is now in the dark depths of the underworld. This is a tradition that would continue throughout Helen's career, where she would act as a territorial marker, a way of separating light from darkness. Her presence redefines whatever place she is in. She is the instant underbelly; all you have to do is add a dance beat. Now we know the hero has begun his descent into danger; often this descent would be physical, in that he would walk down a staircase or even fall through the surface of the earth into some claustrophobic, subterranean space. However, we understand that this is supposed to be a moral descent.

Since *Howrah Bridge* is one of those rare films in which the heroine (Madhubala) plays a Catholic, Miss Edna, the other dances do not feature Helen, not even *Aaoji* dance *kar lein/ Thoda* romance *kar lein* (Come let's dance, let's indulge in a little romance) and *Aie-ey meherbaan, baithi-ey jaan-e-jaan/ Shauk se lijiye ji/ Ishq ke imtihaan* (Welcome, my lord. Sit down, my love. And if it should please you, feel free to test my love). Were Edna not a Catholic, it would have either needed a tortuous explanation to allow her to dance these songs or Helen would have got them. Had Madhubala been playing Geeta or Sita or Meena, it would have been very difficult to pass her off as a dancer herself and even as someone who helps—however unwillingly—with the smuggling of drugs. For Hindi cinema had no simple equation with the religious communities of India. On the surface, this should have been simple since it should not have mattered. The religious identity of a villain could scarcely matter; there would be bad eggs in every basket.

But the early film-makers knew that they were not simply making films. As the only valid pop culture, they believed that they were creating texts to help build society. Since they were men, these texts were largely patriarchal, probably not out of enlightened self-interest but probably because they genuinely believed that benevolent male despotism was good for society as a whole. The theme of the 'educated wife', for instance, was oft-repeated and each time disaster would follow her inclusion into the family. Later, this theme would change to become the 'westernized wife', anathema in her own right. However, in the fifties, the patriarchs were concerned about the nation that was being crafted. They often sought the blessings of political figures, although a good word from Nehru was not likely to increase ticket sales significantly. They were aware as few others could be of the scars left by Partition. Some had lost their families, their home towns. Others had watched friends depart. Still others had arrived as refugees from the newly formed state of West Pakistan. They felt the need, as a community, to emphasize the importance of coexistence and of mutual tolerance. Muslims would thus be shown in a favourable light as far as possible. Yet there were still some liberties that could be taken with other minorities, specially those that did not patronize Hindi cinema.

If political secularism arises out of arithmetic, the secularism of cinema arises out of commerce. When *Kaagaz Ke Phool* flopped, Guru Dutt went out and made a Muslim social, *Chaudhvin Ka Chand*, although he did not do it under his own name. When he was asked why, he said that he needed a hit. Segmenting the market works. Think of *Coolie* and *Pakeezah* and *Nikaah*, all hits.

(As in everything that one says of Hindi commercial cinema, one might on the other hand point to *Deedaar-e-Yaar*, one of the biggest flops of 1982, but then it had Jeetendra playing a nawab.)

However, there are certain limits to this secularism. For instance, Hindus and Muslims don't marry on screen unless it is an overt act of political significance (*Bombay*). Too many people might be offended and secularism had to be measured against what the audience would accept. Since Hindi cinema, like most popular culture, is majoritarian, it also managed to maintain a subtle power balance within the caste system. When the hero was a romantic and a scholar, he could be a Brahmin, even if it was the Muslim Dilip Kumar playing him. When the hero turned into a warrior, his identity turned kshatriya. Secular gestures had to be similarly calibrated, since a sizeable proportion of the Hindi-speaking audience was Muslim. The Muslim characters were, therefore, honest friends, loyal soldiers, good policemen, bluff Pathans, friendly uncles. That left two communities: the Christians and the Parsi. For one, they were perceived as 'westernized', which was tantamount to sleeping with the enemy. For another, they could be offended without upsetting the box office, since they rarely went out to watch Hindi films.

So Parsis figured as stereotypical eccentrics with walk-on roles. Christians got more screen time but were used in strange ways. In the odd hierarchies that custom and power have established, a heroine could be Christian. Liz (Waheeda Rehman) in *Baazi* (1968), Miss Edna (Madhubala) in *Howrah Bridge*, Bobby (Dimple) in *Bobby*, Jenny (Parveen Babi) in *Amar Akbar Anthony* and Annie (Manisha Koirala) in *Khamoshi—The Musical* all marry their men without trouble. In *Bobby*, the hero's parents only object to her social standing and her lack of wealth, there is no mention of a different religion. There were also some startling positive images of older Christian characters (Lalita Pawar and Nadira, both as Mrs D'Sa in *Anari* and *Saagar*, respectively; Premnath as Mr Braganza in *Bobby;* David as John Chacha in *Boot Polish*), but by and large, the community was seen as degenerate. In *Mome ki Gudiya,* a Christian family has a mother played by the obese Tun Tun, the father played by a midget, and in order to win their daughter and to fit in with them, the hero's sidekick claims that he has started drinking, smoking, going to mujras and *even eating non-vegetarian food* (emphasis from the dialogue delivery).

But perhaps the classic encapsulation of Hindi cinema's attitude to the morality of the young Christian community can be seen in a single song from *Swarg Narak* (1978). Briefly, the story deals with two marriages. The feminist Shobha (Moushumi Chatterjee!) marries college lecturer Vicky (Jeetendra) while the traditional Indian doormat Geeta (Shabana Azmi!) marries playboy and businessman Vinod (Vinod Mehra). The latter marriage fails from the very beginning since Vinod, who, as an act of rebellion against a marriage into which he was forced, spends his wedding night dancing with an unnamed mistress (Komilla Virk).

One night, when Vinod tries to go out, his mother (Kamini Kaushal) stops him. He almost slaps her, then pushes her out of the way. She runs after him and falls down the stairs. Vinod and his unnamed mistress go out dancing. Helen is the floorshow, singing the 'English song' mentioned in the titles. The unimaginative lyrics include lines like 'Love you, come hold me' interspersed with some Aah-ing. However, this is enough to attract Vinod, who callously pushes Virk out of the way and makes his way to where Helen, dressed in High Arabian Fantasy, bathed in red light, is singing, in English: 'I am lonely, come hold me/ Life is so dreary, come, come, come.'

Director Dasari Narayan Rao intercuts this sequence with scenes of Vinod's mother dying, of the doctors giving up, of the dutiful daughter-in-law reciting scripture. At the nightclub, Helen and Vinod are now in a clinch. The scene is bathed in red light as she pours alcohol into his mouth. A church appears in silhouette against the walls of the nightclub, and church bells begin to ring.

It is true that few film-makers have gone so far in their association between degeneracy and Christianity but it was a statement they felt free to make.

Thus, if you wanted a vamp, it would be best to draw her from that 'degenerate' community and to also portray her unequivocally as belonging to that community. It would then be natural for her to sing and dance for men, to be part of a gang, to wave a gun, to show a bit of body, to coquette and pirouette without in any way endangering the patriarchal notions of virginity as an attribute of the Indian woman. If the first female players in film were Jewish or Anglo-Indian, the first female bad girl of any merit, the first loose woman with a taut body, had to be an Anglo-Burmese Christian.

Miss Chin-Chin-Choo was also a *hotel* dancer. As we have seen, the heroine was allowed only a few limited spaces. Her father's home was followed by her husband's home, again as the *Manusmriti* would have it. In between she might be allowed a few moments in a fantasia (which almost always invoked the cosmos) or in the open air, where the beauties of nature added sanctity to the song she was singing with the hero. By contrast, Miss Chin-Chin-Choo and many of the other vamps that Helen would play were to be found in hotels, in nightclubs, in bars.

These were inevitably loci of suspicion. Almost everyone in the hotel business, according to Hindi cinema, is a murderer or a smuggler at worst; an obsequious and smarmy hanger-on at best. Whenever all the doors pop open on any floor in a hotel, as they often do in comedy sequences, only couples come out, usually in their undergarments. Whenever the hero and/or the villain pass through a hotel room in the course of a chase, the inhabitants they disturb are always in flagrante delicto and at some early (clothed) stage of coitus. Villains own hotels as a cover for their activities. Lesser fry check into hotel rooms with their suitcases full of gold, diamonds, drugs or cash. The comedians arrive disguised as room service and the maids are thieves or fair game.

In *Khoon Khoon* (1973), the comedian Asrani plays a voyeuristic police officer who uses the binoculars with which the hero is scanning the city for a sniper to peer into hotel rooms; each one has a woman undressing or a couple in a clinch. In *Kaalicharan*, Hotel Mercanto is the scene for a Helen cabaret, interspersed with a shoot-out with the villains. Up to the nineties, Hindi films looked upon hotels as a dreadful western invention where other 'western inventions'—smuggling, illicit or extramarital sex, the black market—thrived.

This reflects a bourgeois invention of an idyllic India. In this vision, India lives in pristine self-sufficient villages. Everyone has a home and the smaller the home, the purer its inhabitants. This India is rooted, literally, in its soil and metaphorically in its traditions. People who travel always go to their other homes (bungalows in a hill station, and, before the troubles in the Valley, villas in Kashmir) or to the homes of other relatives. While caste is never explicitly referred to, we get the sense (from the names and some behaviour patterns) that this is a kshatriya world, and hence in its ownership and defence of the land, even more connected to it.

The hotel, on the other hand, is full of transients. Who knows who has lived in a hotel room before? And what they did there? *Teesri Manzil* (1966) is played out entirely in a hotel and it is a story replete with murders, suicides and blackmail. Significantly, it is Ruby (Helen) who speaks the first lines in the film: *Rocky, tumhne wahaan nahin jaana chaahiye* (Rocky, you shouldn't go there)—a silken thread of warning, spoken from a swathe of furs and a Gallic shrug, as Rocky (Shammi Kapoor) rushes to the site of a suicide. As late as *Jurmana* (1979), Amitabh Bachchan almost entirely compromises Raakhee's reputation by inviting her to tea in his hotel room.

This is a floating world and thus Helen fits in perfectly. In dozens of films, her arrival is heralded by invoking the name of a hotel. If you are looking for Raakha or Jaggu or Crasto, you will be told that he is to be found at such-and-such hotel where Helen will be dancing. Alternatively, you might be informed more specifically that your quarry associates with a woman who dances in hotel so-and-so. This makes for an easier and more direct lead-in.

Helen's territory within this space was also marked out; it was often illuminated with red light, an easy metaphor, since a 'red-light area' indicates a brothel or an area where women of easy virtue are to be found. The enclosedness was not protective; it was threatening, claustrophobic. When Helen as Monica sings, *Piya tu ab to aa jaa* in *Caravan* (1971), the heroine, Sunita (Asha Parekh) is sitting it out, a stricken look on her face. Sunita has had a rough time of it. She has just lost her father and though she doesn't know it yet, her husband Rajan (Kishan Mehta) has killed him. Even before the marriage can be consummated, she has discovered that Rajan and Monica have been lovers for years. She has survived an attempt on her life and is in hiding. But even if we did not know all that, we would know that the heroine has no business being here. It could only be despair that had brought her here.

Thus, when a film has four hotels to thank before the credits roll—the Sun 'n' Sand, the Ajanta Palace, the Ritz and the Blue Nile—as *Inspector* (1970) does, you know that

Helen is going to have a good time. The first hotel is used merely to establish the lady-killing credentials of Agent 707 alias Inspector Rajesh (Biswajeet), who must now be brought in to stop a neighbouring country's development of a gaseous version of Agent Orange. (A huge amount of the gas seems necessary to kill three weedy plants in a terrarium.) Lilly, one of the lovelies that he has been disporting with, takes him to her home and tries to turn the tables on the lady killer. Inspector Rajesh makes short work of her goon, Hercules, a good supply of pink poison gas and the subterranean crypts of her well-equipped house. There he also liberates another prisoner, Rita (Alka) who sends him off to the Blue Bell Club. As he enters, the lights turn red; Helen, also dressed in red, is all of a piece with the danger of the moment. Her song is not reassuring: *Haai, haai, haai, re tera dil/ Mere teer ka nishaana/ Bach bach bach ke/ Yahaan se mushqil hai tera jaana* (Hey, hey, hey, your heart's in my cross hairs. Getting away may be difficult).

It is obvious that leading lady Alka could not dance. She does heave about in a couple of songs but it is quite clear, after a while, that even the flying-cars sequence (yes, yes) is not going to be enough and Helen comes back for an encore in '*Marhaba, marhaba*'—'Welcome, welcome', in Arabic—a song of such complete irrelevance and choreographed so badly (the dances have been attributed to Surya Kumar), that it need not delay us.

Hotels also come second only to the *kotha*, the den of the dancing girls—or, more honestly, a brothel—as spaces in which heartbreak may be expressed. The hero often takes his broken heart to a bar in a hotel. Brutalized by a woman's misunderstanding—it is rare that his own actions have earned her censure—he is reduced to taking his solace in alcohol and in the company of a woman who is no substitute for his lady love. In *Vaasna* (1968), director T. Prakash Rao spares no effort to establish just how low the young man has fallen. A boy band plays music on a dais in the nightclub. White women puff at cigarettes. Helen appears in shadow-play, dancing behind a screen over which coloured lights pass. Her song asks him to sever his ties with responsibility: *Jeenewaale jhoomke mastaana ho ke jee/ Aanewaali subah se begaana ho ke pee* (If you're alive at all, you might as well live it up. Drink up and let tomorrow take care of itself).

This association between Helen and alcohol is emphasized by the use of multiple images, screen shorthand for the inability of a drunken man to focus his eyes. Once we have established that he is drunk, that his defences are down, that he is now susceptible to her wiles, she reaches out for him to get him to dance as well. This is the final step in his downfall; she now has him in her clutches.

The vamp was therefore constructed out of locally available material, but only that which had some sense of the Other.

Her clothes added to it, again displaced from reality so that she was either dressed as a courtesan (the mujra outfit with its flaring skirt, tight cholis and veil), a western woman (flamenco outfits, tuxedos, trouser suits), a tribal (flowers in hair, grass skirts) or as a belly dancer (diaphanous Arabian fantasy outfits). Only the drenched sari would remain the prerogative of the heroine until the heroine had driven the vamp into extinction.

This is true, one might say, of vamps everywhere. However, the major difference is that the Indian version of the vamp was generally a failure, even at so minor a task as getting the hero interested in her. She might signal her availability in every possible way: the lyrics would reiterate this; her dance movements would repeat her availability with gestures of self-adulation (as when she stroked her own body) or abasement (falling to the floor, rolling on it) or teasing (quick touches, lap-sitting) or even ersatz copulation (lying on her back, jerking her pelvis into the camera). Most of these movements were hybrids that arose from a number of independent sources. There was Kathak, a male dance form that was refined in the Mughal courts and which was later incorporated into the classical tradition; belly dancing, which began in Central Asia as a way in which women trained their stomach muscles for childbirth and which was later turned into exotic/erotic performance; and such ballroom and recreational dances that had found their way into favour with the West, arising from diverse sources. And finally, the camera made it clear that the point of view was always male (more often than not, establishing a dominating point of view, from above).

This physicality was in odd contrast to the relationship between the hero and the heroine. Kissing, as we know, was first banned and then continued to remain absent since directors preferred to use the power of suggestion. Until the turn of the century, almost all physicality had to follow *after* the declaration of love, except where it is punitive. Even up to the time of writing, screen kisses still get talked about. The mark of having achieved success as a female star still seems to be the ability to refuse to kiss on screen. The honourable exception to all this coyness is *Deewar* (1975), where Amitabh Bachchan and Parveen Babi end up sharing a post-coital cigarette in bed, after their first meeting. Both die for this offence against the moral law which states: Hindi film heroines do not kiss several frogs before they find their handsome prince. They allow themselves a chaste cheek on a masculine shoulder only after it has been established that this is the prince.

And yet the vamp was supposed to be a lust object. But whose lust?

The hero almost never was turned from his purpose. Nor was the villain. In *Ek Shriman Ek Shrimati* (1969), Helen sings what is, it must be admitted, an eminently ignorable song—Hey hey hello ho ho my jolly good fellow/ *Dil mein hain jo jo baatein/ Aaj woh keh lo keh lo* (a convoluted way of saying, simply, 'Tell me what's in your heart')—while the father of her unborn child, Ajit (Prem Chopra), to whom she is singing, lights cigarettes, drinks whisky, and plots how to get his hands on Deepali's (Babita) wealth. He's not about to tell Helen anything; he's barely listening. In *Apradh* (1972), a heartbroken Ram (Feroze Khan) has been deprived of his career as a race-driver, his wife Meena (Mumtaz) and his reputation by the machinations of his brother Khanna (Prem Chopra again). When he wants to meet the latter, Helen (unnamed) is sent to 'take care of him'. She sings: *Ay naujawaan hai sab kuchh yahaan/ Jo chaahe le le khushi se/ Tune kahaan/ Dekha jahaan/ Tauba na kar abhi se*...(Hey, young man, everything's on offer here; take what you want. You haven't seen much of the world; don't renounce it all just yet). But to no effect. Ram only begins to reciprocate when he is drunk enough to mistake her for Meena. In *Sholay* (1975), Helen dressed in belly-dancer green gives it her heart-stopping all—including a backbend—in the *Mehbooba, mehbooba* song. While the dacoit Gabbar Singh (Amjad Khan) does express mild salacious interest, the heroes plant explosives without once stopping to glance at her gyrations. In Chandra Barot's *Don* (1978), Sonia (Helen) arrives in the room of the ganglord

Don (Amitabh Bachchan) and begins to sing one of her sultriest numbers, *Yeh mera dil pyaar ka deewaana* (My heart is mad about love). Don goes about his dressing and packing as if hotel rooms come equipped with belly dancers.

The Helen figure only succeeded in her sexual designs when her presence was needed as a symbol of the debauchery of a male figure, generally not the hero. In *Reshmi Roomal* (1961), Manoj Kumar has been sent to rescue a worker who has just recovered from an accident from a bar in which, of course, Helen is dancing, dressed as a Punjabi villager: *Sar pe chunariya kaali motiyon-waali* (A black veil beaded with pearls on my head). The man is unwilling to leave and it is only after a fight involving the ritual breaking up of the bar that he goes home. Similarly, in *Kaajal* (1965), Madhavi (Meena Kumari) waits in full bridal dress on her wedding night, while her husband Moti Babu (Raj Kumar) lounges, drink-sodden, in the arms of Helen, singing, *Yeh zulf agar khulke bikhar jaaye to achcha* (Were your hair to be undone and spread out, how beautiful it would be).

In many of her other films, specially those in which she only danced, Helen was a simple marker of the debauched man, therefore the wrong man for the heroine. In *Heera* (1973), it is not enough for us to know that Balwant is a dacoit, that he has killed two pregnant women and allowed the blame to fall on Heera (Sunil Dutt); we must also see that on the night before he is to marry the heroine Asha (Asha Parekh), he attends a mujra with Helen singing, *Der na karo piya der na karo* (Do not delay, my love), one of her standard songs of erotic torment. In *Khoon Pasina* (1977), when the bonded labourers are starving, Zaalim Singh (Kadar Khan), the local landowner who denies the labourers their wages, is watching Helen sing *Mar jaaoon pyaasi main mar jaaoon pyaasi* (I die of thirst, I die of thirst). Spoilt brats also went to Helen's mujras. In *Phool Khile Hain Gulshan Gulshan* (1978), the petulant young Vishal (Rishi Kapoor) insults his grandfather's birthday gift of a handful of earth from his hometown. When his father puts him on a short leash, he goes off to a kotha where our ready symbol of decadence is waiting in a pastel-blue Kathak outfit, with a blue veil over her head. (It says something about the younger flesh on offer—Zahirra, in a wardrobe of hot pants, halters and micro-minis—that Helen could still be called in to make a case for how spoilt the lad is.) The song, *Kaisa parda hai/ jalwa jalwa hai* (Such concealment, such displays), has a moment in which they dance together, he clapping the hand she has on her rump. When he returns home, he has her veil draped around him. This may be counted as a success for Helen, but we know that it is only a rite of passage. Vishal will be refined into the hero only when he goes to the village under the terms of his father's will, raises a crop successfully and falls in love with the simple village belle Shanti (Moushumi Chatterjee).

Hindi films do not encourage us to identify with any character other than the hero. We must see the villain's lust as disgusting. Thus the vamp, as the object of such lust, is disgusting, even as she turns to offer us her body (it is a different matter that Helen aroused disgust in no one—that was *her* particular triumph). When the heroine turns to the camera to declare her love, we know that the lens is the hero. When the vamp proclaims her availability, she does this for us, the audience. Hindi cinema, by creating gross stereotypes of virginity and debauchery, thus manages to co-opt us.

The virgin heroine would not know lust because all she was allowed to do was to love and wait and suffer. She was not interested in orgasms, since her ideal lay in pleasing her husband rather than seeking her own pleasure. To feel any need for sex placed her outside the pale, made her either a figure of fun (as an older woman) or a loose woman. The only heroine who ever needed a cold bath was Mala Sinha in *Suhaagan* (1964). She was married to a man whose heart was so weak he would die if they ever consummated their marriage. And so he sang *Tu mere saamne hai, teri zulfein hain khuli* (You are in front of me, your hair let loose) while she bathed in cold water to cool her heated blood. Could it be a coincidence that Mala Sinha was a Christian and looked a little different or is this going too far?

Four

'Main Gud Ki Dali'

Helen became the gypsy woman, the courtesan, the nightclub Chin-Chin-Choo, the Arabic belly bombshell, the classical Kathak nartaki, *the fisherwoman in a country-liquor bar, the gangster's moll in a gold-biscuit mall—hell, she was everyone, everything.*

—Khalid Mohamed in a tribute to
Helen for *Man's World*, April 2004

Lagta hai inki maa ne bahut Chinese khaana khaaya hai.
(Her mother must have eaten a great deal of Chinese food.)

—Vijay (Dharmendra) in the film *Pyaar Hi Pyaar*,
referring to Helen, whom he has just met.

In Kedar Kapoor's *Tarzan Comes to Delhi* (1965), there is a scene worth recording, if only for the multiplicity and diversity of its elements. Tarzan (Dara Singh) has come to the city in pursuit of a thief who has stolen a necklace from a tribal deity. The tribe is on the warpath. If Tarzan and Rekha (Mumtaz) cannot retrieve the necklace within a lunar month, Rekha's father will be put to death in front of the totem pole—with the requisite *hoorr-hoorrs* and *haiya-haiyas* with which the tribals of mainstream Hindi cinema sacrifice their victims.

In pursuit of the necklace, the couple go to a bar where Mumbai's renowned jazzman Chick Chocolate of the fifties is playing a trumpet while Helen is singing: *Jhoom re jhoom albele/ Sab se ham hain akele* (Enjoy yourself, my man/ We're different from everyone else). She is wearing a flamenco outfit.

So we have on the dance floor a Franco-Burmese woman (who was known as an Anglo-Indian for the better part of her career) playing a Spanish senorita; a famous Catholic musician from Goa who was popularly known as India's Louis Armstrong (because of his jazz background and dark skin) playing an anonymous bandwala; and a Punjabi wrestler playing Greystoke, Lord of the Jungle. It might have added extra spice if the Muslim Mumtaz (playing the Hindu girl Rekha Suri) and the almost-Olympian cyclist Jankidas, a Hindu (playing a presumptive Goan Catholic and fixer, Mr Pinto), were also present, but one cannot have everything.

The scene is instructive: in this exaggerated tableau of the Other, almost everyone plays a role to which she or he is not suited. Except Helen. She plays herself, which means that she plays a foreign woman who sings in Hindi while remaining an outsider.

The outsider is vital to Hindi cinema, or to all pop culture. By being odd and different, she or he validates the dominant mode. And Helen was always the outsider. She could be any number of outsiders. Often all that was done was to give her a symbolic name, or a dress that reinforced every popular stereotype, and a new version was born.

Take *Ghunghat* (1960), for instance. It is set in a highly traditional, overtly Romantic version of bourgeois India. Here men marry without ever seeing their wives' faces, either at the behest of their parents (as in Ravi's, that is Pradeep Kumar's, case) or to spare a friend the horror of having his sister abandoned at the ritual *pheras* round the sacred fire (in Gopal's, that is Bharat Bhushan's, case). Thus, when a train accident intervenes, a newly-wed Ravi takes the wrong woman, Parvati (Bina Rai), home. When he discovers his mistake, he will not exercise his conjugal rights, which causes Parvati much concern. Her sister-in-law suggests a visit to a show (for its aphrodisiacal properties?) and they go to see Helen singing a warning against love: *Dil na kahin lagaana/ Zaalim hai zamaana/ Pyaar koi jo kare/ Duniya kare haai* (Never give your heart away/ For the world is a cruel place/ It damns those who love).

Helen appears in a variety of Indian costumes in the song, and in each one, she is accosted by a different suitor. Every verse, and the accompanying change of costume and singing style, is prefaced by the introductory line: *Raaste mein mila mujhe ek albela* (I met an interesting man on the road) which introduces, in turn, a South Indian, a Bengali and a Punjabi (all played by Gopi Krishna with suitable changes of outfit). In a highly traditional environment where men do not see their wives' faces until they arrive at the flower-strewn conjugal bed, this free-spirited woman who meets importuning men on the roads is an absolute outsider. There was clearly a moralistic judgment involved.

In 1960, again, in *Mudh Mudh Ke Na Dekh* (the title itself taken from a nightclub song in *Shree 420* picturized on another outsider, Nadira, a Jew), a romantic comedy starring Bharat Bhushan and Anita Guha, Helen performs a dance unconnected with the main story of two headstrong young people running away from an arranged marriage—and, of course, falling in love with each other. Dressed as a tribal gypsy, she sings: *Yeh hai June ka mahina/ Aaye bada re pasina/ Mar gayi garmi se/ Le chal Shimle, babu* (It's the hot month of June/ And I'm in a sweat/ The heat kills me/ Take me away to Simla, my sir). It is a fairly straightforward invitation that can only be issued by a woman outside the straitjacket of sexuality prescribed for the Indian middle-class or upper-caste woman.

This is the trademark of the way the tribal Helen would be presented—as a woman who was liberated enough to be able to declare her desire, but whose desire was almost always aimed at ludicrous males, the only men available to her. In *Inkaar* (1976), her song begins with a man polishing off a shot of alcohol and throwing the glass away. A hand catches it. We know that this is a signal for a 'cabaret' style sequence, another version of the back-to-the-camera pose: for the first thirty seconds, Helen is only represented by her torso, one of the prime locations of sexuality in the male gaze. She is simply dressed by the standards that had been set for her—a high-cut choli in black-and-yellow checks and a bright yellow sari in the Koli fisher-folk style, tied between the legs. (This is also an erotically charged outfit because it brings back the figures of fantasy of middle-class Mumbai: tribal, or aboriginal, fisherwomen.) She traps an ant on the bar beneath a glass and leans into the frame—her face now revealed—and begins the song:

> *Mungda, oh mungda, main gud ki dali/ Mangta hai to aaja rasiya na hi to main to chali* (I am the jaggery, you are the ant/ Come get me, you rake, or I'll be on my way).

All this is aimed at the comedian Keshto Mukherjee, who based his entire career on a series of twitches and tics that were meant to indicate advanced dipsomania.

But to truly understand what tribals, and by extension Helen (except when she was given a sympathetic role), were held to mean, we have to look at the costume drama *Baadal* (1966). Baadal (Sanjeev Kumar) comes from a long line of princes in Hindi films who grow up in hovels, ignorant of their royal lineage. When he comes of age, his mother sends him to the king with a talisman and tells him to follow the king's orders. (We never find out why his mother left the palace, but the ways of kings and queens are now well known. The king misunderstood. The queen left.) In the big city, he meets Bijuriya (Helen), a gypsy of the imagination, and is quite taken by her beauty, though only in the way of the poet, or the knight paying her chivalric honour. This is an oddity because love is generally uncomplicated and monogamous in Hindi cinema. He and the audience have already met the spoilt princess who should be his wife. We know that as a prince he cannot fall in love with a gypsy—unless she, too, is discovered to be a princess, abducted or abandoned as an infant.

Baadal sings to her. This is another departure from the rules which demand that the hero must only sing to his lady love. However, Baadal is obviously a bit of a tearaway. And so, misled by his declaration—*Aap ko jo dekhega, pyaar hi se dekhega/ Ki aap khoobsoorat hain, aap khoobsoorat hain* (Whoever looks at you will only look at you with love/ For you are beautiful, so beautiful)—Bijuriya falls in love with him. Busy making up to the once-spoilt princess (Vijayalakshmi) and fomenting revolution against the usurper king, he doesn't notice Bijuriya's infatuation. Until one day she sings: *Nayan bedardi chhaliya sang lad gaye* (My eyes have caused me to fall in love with the heartless one). Just as the song ends, they are disturbed by an emissary from the princess who is pining for Baadal. He must leave. Bijuriya tries to hold him back, but he dismisses her, saying she is irrelevant.

Driven by her demons—and quite clearly, these arise from the notion that tribals are childlike in their emotions and therefore not to be trusted—Bijuriya betrays Baadal to his enemies.

Another way to look at this 'Othering', this exoticisation of Helen, is of course to see it as a mirror image of Orientalism. If Hollywood could take an ordinary girl from Cincinnati called Theodosia Goodman, smear her with lipstick and mascara, shoot her with leopards and christen her Theda Bara (an anagram, studio publicity machines were eager to point out, for Arab Death), we could take an alien who looked Western and whose name fortuitously rang with resonances of destructive femininity (she even acted as Helen of Troy in Pradeep Nayyar's 1965 film of the same name) and make of her the woman our mothers warned us about. There is a moment in *Anari* (1959) where the Innocent in Hell Rajkumar (Raj Kapoor) finally gets a job painting an heiress. When he is paid, he takes his kindly landlady out to dinner and a show. It is New Year and Helen is performing a song whose lyrics include an immortal countdown, *1956, 1957, 1958, 1959*. At one point, Rajkumar is chosen by the greasy compere of the show to dance. Helen slithers up to him and whispers a 'Hullo' in three distinct syllables. Rajkumar responds with an Oedipally-inflected *Oh Maaaaa!* at the arrival of this threat from the West.

At the heart of Orientalism, too, is the impulse to create an Other; it is not necessarily something that only white, western men do. While not denying the validity of the term 'Orientalism', it is important to remember that it can also be seen as an accident of history. White men came, saw, conquered and Othered. Had men of other colours moved first, I find it hard to believe that they would have behaved differently.

So how would the cinema patriarchs of a newly-liberated nation handle the gift of a white woman? (Yes, Helen was not white, but she was seen as white; in cinema, what you are perceived as is what you are.) Acting on instinct rather than ideology, they would have realized how easily they could turn her into a symbol. Popular discourse monolithizes the West, and rural discourse goes even further and creates 'foreigners' out of everyone from any other geographical region. So Helen could be anybody.

To begin with, Helen played an Anglo-Indian. If the Indian Christian community suffered from stereotyping, the Anglo-Indian community, far smaller, far more westernized, far less of an audience category, was treated even worse. In *Saazish* (1975), meet Peter K. Murray (the comedian Rajendranath) whose name itself is a cross-lingual pun, since the initials, so he tells us, can be read as '*peeke mare*' or 'drank and died'. Murray is Anglo-Indian (he says so), and his singular preoccupation on board the cruise ship on which this smuggle-fest is set, is to try and capture as many bikini-clad white women on film as possible. Anglo-Indian Julie Morris (Lakshmi) in the 1975 monster hit *Julie* loves the Hindu household of the hero because it smells of incense. Her own, she says, smells of alcohol, extinguished cigarettes, meat and fish. It was not until Aparna Sen gave us the indomitable Violet Stoneham in *36, Chowringhee Lane* (1981), that the Anglo-Indians were ever treated with any understanding.

In *Gumnaam* (1965), Helen plays Kitty Kelly, one of seven suspects in a murder. Kitty Kelly is the gold standard for the stereotype Anglo-Indian young woman, and Helen's work in the film was rewarded with a *Filmfare* Award for Best Supporting Actress. In this wildly Indianized version of Agatha Christie's *Ten Little Indians*, the suspects find themselves stranded on a not-very deserted island. We can already tell that Kitty is in some manner involved in the murder of Seth Sohanlal. If we needed further subliminal cues, on the plane that dumps the seven little Indians on the island, she wears red while the heroine Asha (Nanda) wears white. Even when they are warned that they will die for their complicity in the murder, Kitty remains upbeat. *Is duniya mein jeena ho to/ Sun lo meri baat/ Gham chhod ke manaao rang-reli/ Aur maan lo jo kahe Kitty Kelly* (If you must live in this world/ Listen to Kitty Kelly:/ Forget your worries and make merry), she sings on the beach, leaping from rock to rock, kicking up sand, playing with a beach ball in the waves, looking altogether too lovely in a swimsuit with a little skirt.

Surprisingly, she does have at least one 'Indian' virtue that rescues her from being a complete tramp: she does not drink. But the manner in which we learn this doesn't quite redeem her completely: *Mujhe sharaabi pasand hain, sharaab nahin* (I like alcoholics, not alcohol), she declares at one point in the film. She only breaks this rule to forge a bond of feminine solidarity with Asha, when they both broach a bottle of Scotch.

However, when the hired help (Mehmood as a camp butler) shows signs of attraction, she rejects him on the grounds of his dark skin, thus re-ascribing the pan-Indian vice of racism to a specific 'alien' community. Her rejection causes the butler to remark that when a white spot appears on black skin, it's called leprosy; but when a black spot appears on white skin, it's called a beauty spot. This, however, does not prevent him from indulging in a fantasy about Kitty Kelly, presented as a dream sequence in which he sings, *Hum kaale hain to kya hua dilwaale hain* (What if I'm black, I have a big heart).

Kitty Kelly becomes Kitty Williams in *Dus Lakh* (1966). The first time we see her, she is behind a translucent curtain, changing into a swimsuit in slow seductive movements that her beau Jerry (Pran) enjoys. Jerry's suit is hindered because Kitty's mother (Manorama) wants Scotch but he can only provide her country liquor. This strange ménage, completed by Mrs Williams' infantile adult son Willy (Brahmachari), indicates clearly that unlike the coy heroine Rita (Babita in her first film), Kitty is not quite respectable.

To get the money for the Scotch that will make Kitty his

wife, Jerry organizes a scam: Kitty and Rita will dance at a benefit for blind children. Rita dances in blue and saffron in front of the backdrop of a south Indian temple, complete with a *deepstambh,* a column of oil lamps. Kitty in a red and gold pant-suit dances in front of a skyscraper with cutouts of a tuxedo-clad band. The lyrics Rita mouths draw from traditional sources: *Baaje mori paayal chhanana chhanana* (My anklets tinkle chhanana chhanana). Kitty offers a westernized *Twist karoon mein, shake karoon mein, karoon mein rock and roll* (I'm gonna twist, I'm gonna shake, I'm gonna rock and roll).

But it is the collision of the Williams family with the family of the hero Kishore (Sanjay Khan) that foregrounds all the beliefs about the decadent semi-white Anglos. Kishore's father Gokul Chand (Om Prakash) inherits the *dus lakh* (Rs 10,17,753, to be precise) of the title. At first, he organizes a pooja and sings a heartfelt bhajan of thanks. Then he goes off to a hill station. Things begin to go very wrong here, for he meets the Williams bunch. Mrs Williams teaches him to drink, to shake hands, to dance, and finally gets him to pop the question at so unsuitable an age as his. But not before they have sung a pretty duet together:

> Gokul Chand (to a very large and middle-aged Manorama): *Teri patli qamar, teri baali umar/ Teri baanqi ada pe hum qurbaan/ Arre tum bhi jawaan aur hum bhi jawaan* (Your narrow waist, your enticing youth—/ I'm maddened by your matchless charms/ Hey, you're young and so am I).
>
> Mrs Williams: *Yahaan health bhi hai aur wealth bhi hai/ Love ka season, dil mein armaan/ Arre tum bhi jawaan aur hum bhi jawaan* (There's health here and there's wealth/ It's the season of love and there's desire in our hearts/ Hey, you're so young and so am I).

Once they return to the city, Gokul Chand evicts his family through a series of engineered misunderstandings too tortuous to be outlined here. In comparison to their vicissitudes, the

Williams children form a dance troupe and sing a very peculiar number. Willy turns up in long trousers for the first time, but, for no clear reason, with a globe on his head. Helen is rolled in perched on a larger globe, wearing a bowl of fruit for a hat and a flamenco outfit.

> Willy: *Arre du du du*
> Kitty: *Arre ni ni ni*
> Willy: *Arre ya ya ya*
> (If you haven't got it yet, try reading those syllables downwards to get *duniya*, the world.)
>
> Kitty: *Duniya uski sunti hai/ Yeh duniya uski banti hai/ Jo kadmon pe usko jhuka le* (This world listens to you/ This world has time for you/ Only when you conquer it).

As often happened with Helen, there is someone rather nice hiding inside Kitty Williams. Inluenced by Kishore, she connects with her good side. She participates in another dance, this time to bring Gokul Chand to his senses. It is a surreal sequence at the fancy dress party that Gokul Chand throws for his engagement. He himself comes as the mascot of the national airline carrier, the Air India Maharaja; Mrs Williams is Queen Victoria; Jerry is Napoleon Bonaparte and one of the guests is a huge green lizard. Here, Kitty and Rita sing, *Agre ka lala laaya Angrezi dulhan re* (A merchant from Agra has taken himself a British bride). It is a synchronized dance until they take on the role of the henpecked husband and the wife. At the end, they present a tableau of Gokul Chand's impoverished family. Gokul Chand realizes his mistake, repents and takes back his family.

Kitty then becomes a nurse, and thanks Kishore, for she has been saved from a life of degradation. Her adoption of what are presented as Indian values and the consequent willingness to enter a life of service—never mind the Anglo-Indian community's long tradition in education and medicine—saves her from a fate worse than death.

In *Jahaan Pyaar Miley* (1969) an amnesiac Shashi Kapoor's search for love ends with three communities fighting over him, the Hindus, the Muslims and the Christians. The Muslims are represented by an Urdu poet who introduces him to aficionados of music. The Hindus are represented by a famous singer called Lalitaji who wants to cut a record with him. The Christians are represented by the Anglo-Indian Angela (Helen) and her mother. He meets Angela in a hotel—naturally—where he finds a job. Angela dances there, as is her wont, and sings a song that reflects his state: *Baat zara hai aapas ki/ Saari duniya ho gayi meri/ Bolo main hoon kiski* (This is between us:/ The whole world is at my feet/ But to whom do I belong?).

When her mother meets him at the hotel she christens him Richard and invites him home for Christmas. Although his true love (Hema Malini) is ill, he goes because he believes that one should go wherever there is love (hence the title) and in any case, having forgotten his past, he doesn't know himself where he belongs. When he turns up, they are drinking and Angela insists on kissing him. He accepts only the wine, again because he wishes to respect all religions. The equivalence is clear: this is the religion of winebibbers and loose women who kiss on their festivals. Obviously, the hero can have nothing to do with it.

At the next level of alienness is Helen as the girl from China. We know that even if the songs from *Alif Laila* and *Baarish* were her first solo numbers, the Helen story seems to begin by common consent with *Mera Naam Chin-Chin-Choo*. This was to follow her through her career, so that the comment in *Pyaar Hi Pyaar* that forms the epigraph of this chapter was sure to raise a laugh among the cognoscenti, even if the character she played in that film was Indian.

Popular culture is generally xenophobic, since it bases its

assumptions on shared notions about an 'Us'. When it represents the Other, it seeks only to exoticize it, presuming matter-of-factly that the Other as a community are happy to reshape the ordinariness of their lives into the extravagant for our amusement; that they are willing to offer up their culture for our selective consumption, willing to turn their homes into menageries where we can watch strange beasts at play.

Thus it should be no surprise that *China Town* (1962) is full of persons of Chinese origin, evil characters all. The film begins with an invitation to Tangra, the little suburb of Calcutta that was settled by the Chinese who came there after Yong Atchew set up a sugar mill and brought Chinese workmen with him. They were later joined by what were called the Macao ship deserters—Chinese sailors who, virtually kidnapped into service, had deserted ship and were waiting for a 'friendly' vessel.

The titles roll on a nocturnal cityscape and a song begins: *Rangeen bahaaron se hai gulzar, China Town/ Sheherwaalon ki shaam-e-bahaar, China Town/ Aake to dekho ek baar, China Town* (China Town is bright with youth and beauty/ China Town is the place to go for a night on the town/ China Town, you ought to see it at least once). Into the third verse of the song, *Pyaar ka town, China Town* (China Town, the town of love), the titles are over and we are inside a hotel in which Suzie (Helen) is entertaining the customers with her rendition of this song. *Duniya se begaana ho toh aa China Town*, she sings, inviting those disillusioned with the world to a night on the tiles. While she is wearing what might pass for a Chinese shift (it has a dragon picked out in sequins over her chest), the rest of the supporting chorus is in kimonos with knitting needles in their hair. Helen also twirls a paper umbrella, indicating that no one was quite clear where China ended and Japan began. However, the intent is clear. We know that China Town is not an innocent place; that Suzie is part of the underbelly and that there will be dark deeds afoot.

The song ends on the face of the gang leader Wong (the

villain Madan Puri, who, with plucked eyebrows and unconvincing make-up, always played Wong, especially in films made after the Sino-Indian War of 1962). Suzie is in love with Wong's top goon, Shankar (Shammi Kapoor), a violent opium addict. In this shadowy world Suzie may not even be her real name. She may have another, and it may well be Chin-Chin-Choo.

Miss Chin-Chin-Choo would turn up in odd places. In *Singapore* (1960), a secretary is named Chin-Chin-Choo and speaks Hindi in the way that Miss Lilly would always be made to speak it. Ostensibly a murder mystery, the film seems to have been made with the express intention of promoting Singapore as a destination. When Shyam (Shammi Kapoor) arrives to investigate the mysterious disappearance of his friend and agent, Ramesh, he goes out in the night to sing: *Yeh sheher bada albela/ Har taraf haseenon ka mela* (This is an interesting city/ Bevies of beauties wherever you look) with a group of Singaporean girls offering the chorus: *Singapore, Singapore, Singapore.* Later, in the middle of a romantic moment between Shyam and Seema (Padmini), a bunch of girls hop out of the shrubbery and begin singing: *Jeevan mein ek baar aana Singapore* (Come to Singapore at least once in your life).

Helen figures in a dance once the story is well underway. We know that Seema's uncle (K.N. Singh) is after the map that will reveal the treasure hidden on Shyam's rubber plantation. He manages to steal it, but Shobha (Shashikala) sees him and gives the alarm. A fight breaks out and Ramesh and Shyam hide in the coolie's quarters. There's a festivity on and Helen appears, in a vague cross between Indonesian and gypsy clothes. *Raasa sayaang re raasa sayaang sayaang re/ Pyaar ka naam, raasa sayaang sayaang re*, she sings—Raasa sayaang sayaang (as far as I can tell) is the name of love.

The Spanish inheritance, the French blood—that could come in handy too. Whenever Hindi cinema needed a Western woman for a touch of exotica, Helen was at hand. In *Prince* (1969), she played the Countess Sophia who could provide suitable competition to the homegrown princess, offering another polarity of feminine availability, posing flamenco and belly dancing against Bharatanatyam and Odissi. In *Ek Se Badhkar Ek* (1976), she was the Baroness Carolina, a rather ripe cat burglar out to diddle various other claimants to an unlikely diamond found on the battlefields of Kurukshetra. And in hundreds of films she donned a mantilla, flounced her black-and-red frilly skirt and rattled her castanets as a Spanish senorita. This indeed has almost become an iconic image of her now.

~

So alien was Helen that if she was white and yellow, she could also be black. *Bewaqoof* (1960) offers us a blackface Helen, now the complete Other for a racist nation. The film begins with a lawyer, Seth Rai Bahadur, whose mistress and wife both announce their pregnancy simultaneously. Both women give birth. The mistress blackmails the businessman into accepting her child as his own. The nurse, who has been paid to exchange the babies, finds she cannot do it. Rai Bahadur does not know this, and develops a dislike of the child who he thinks is a pretender. He lavishes his affection on the one he thinks is his legitimate son. Soon Kishore (Kishore Kumar) and his mother find themselves on the road. Kishore takes up boxing as a way to earn some money and challenges the boy his father loves, Pran (Pran), to a match. Pran wins using unfair means and Kishore seeks to retrieve his honour by masquerading as a famous African boxer, Bom Bom. (His side kick is I.S. Johar who, unsurprisingly, goes by the name Tom Tom.) At a party thrown in his honour, Helen in blackface, hair au naturel, her body covered in tassels, sings: *Dhadka dil dhak se/ Dekha hai jab se/ Mar gaye hum tab se/ Tauba tauba* (My heart beat so fast/ When I first saw you/ I've been dead since then). A totem pole and another 'Negro' playing an African drum add the finishing touches.

This is probably the only such dance that Helen did. Blackface was never very popular in Hindi cinema. When actors disguised themselves, they generally became Muslims, either nawaabs or Arabs, always bearded. This, along with a bouquet of frightful mannerisms, was seen as sufficient disguise, since the audience had to be kept in the know as well. The only other instance I can remember of blackface is in *Desh Premee* (1982) where Amitabh Bachchan and Hema Malini paint up to penetrate the villain's den in the climax. However, they must indicate their acceptance of lowered status with lyrics like *Gore nahin hum kaale sahi/ Hum naachne gaanewaale sahi...* (We're not white, we accept, we're black/ It's true, we're mere singers and dancers...) The film flopped and blackface died with it.

Even where you would have expected Helen to belong, to claim victory, she was not allowed to do so.

When Helen began her career, Hindi cinema was experimenting with film noir. As a genre, noir focuses on the male in the city. At a time when the agrarian population was an overwhelming majority, the city was still a source of menace. Of the Holy Trinity of Hindi cinema of the fifties and early sixties, Raj Kapoor exuded a wide-eyed innocence when confronted with the city, which would either injure or co-opt him. Dilip Kumar looked past the city at the Elysian fields of pure Romance. It was Dev Anand who gave film-makers in India the confidence to risk noir. Suave and rakish, with mannerisms inspired by the Hollywood star Gregory Peck, he was a product of the city, whether as gambler, taxi driver, black marketeer, jewel appraiser. When Shammi Kapoor came into his own, the two represented the most successful urban heroes: Anand with his almost-effete insouciance and Kapoor with his version of manic nonchalance.

However, film noir in India differed from film noir in the West in one major way: the location of the moral centre of the film. In the west, noir rejected the idea of morality in favour of ethics. The ethical code was located in the hero, and it was made clear, again and again, that it was a code of his own creation. In India, however, until the seventies, when Bachchan as the Angry Young Man brought the first anti-hero into being, few films would try to escape the vice of morality.

The second major departure for Indian noir was the image of the leading lady. Like the hero, the heroine in Western noir was not a repository of moral wisdom either. She might need rescuing but there was a clear sense that the Lauren Bacalls and Veronica Lakes were clearly of the city. By contrast, the Indian film heroine of the late fifties and sixties might have been in the city but she was certainly not of it. She was aloof, distant, offering another moral pole to the attractions of the metropolis.

For instance, when we are introduced to Alka (Waheeda Rehman) in *Kaala Baazaar* (1960), she is tearing up the tickets for a film that her friends have bought from the black marketeer Raghuveer (Dev Anand). Later, in a bad-dream sequence, the besotted Raghuveer sees himself offering her thousand-rupee notes, which she also rips up.

Till then, Raghuveer has negotiated his way through the big city with ease; we have even watched him sing a delightful song in praise of the rupee coin (*Teri dhoom har kahin/ Tujhsa yaar koi nahin*—'You're the talk of the town, my friend/ There isn't another like you'). Now he begins to re-educate himself, so that he can read the poetry Alka loves. This, and the love of Alka, begins a transformation. Helen's song in the film, performed in the equivalent of a speakeasy, is one of forgetfulness but here it is not sorrow but the pangs of conscience that she is asking our hero to forget. She is black-haired, which is unusual for her, but the rest of her outfit and the music show obvious Iberian influences. Even in a noir film, she is the outsider. Naturally, she cannot succeed.

She exults in her own sensual charms: *Jo bhi mera deewaana hua/ Khud se woh begaana hua/ Jo hona hai woh ho rahega/ Sochta hai kya?* (Those who fall in love with me/ Lose all sense of self/ Whatever will be, will be/ Why should you worry?). Through the song, Raghuveer's mobile face reflects the contortions of his conscience. He is horrifed at the moral degradation that easy money earned in illegal ways has brought in its wake. The men paw at the girls; they seem like animals in heat. His choice is clear: the purity to which Alka wishes him to raise himself, or the forgetfulness—the seductions of the world, the loss of identity even—that Helen is offering.

At the end of the song he announces that the gang will no longer peddle tickets. Helen represents his ugly present, soon to be his forgotten past. Alka is the aspirational goal.

If we accept that the lasting image of Helen is a collage of sexual availability, amorality and a marker of menace—that she is the distanced Other—it seems odd to find her in mythological films, which are essentially sanitized versions of stories from the great epics. However, as soon as one accepts that religion can be co-opted into the market, her presence can be rationalized. Kobita Sarkar, who wrote a memoir of her years as a censor, *You Can't Please Everyone—Film Censorship: The Inside Story*, 'discovered that all sorts of sexual cavorting was justified if it was cloaked in a mythological garb'.

That was what Helen was doing in *Sita Shankar Anasuya* and *Bhakta Prahlad* and *Harishchandra Taramati*. She was playing the temptress. The great epics always involve a woman who wields destructive power, which generally arises out of her beauty.

In Homi Wadia's *Sampoorna Ramayana*, Ram (Mahipal) and Sita (Anita Guha) are out plucking flowers. Sita wanders away and Ram chances upon Shurpnakha (Helen in a red-and-gold outfit and wearing a crown that looks like a pagoda), sister of the demon-king Raavan. She sings, *Baar baar baghiya mein koyal na bole* (The nightingale won't sing again and again in this garden). This is an invitation to love.

But Ram wants clarity: *Spasht kaho, devi, kya chaahati ho?* (Tell me clearly, revered lady, what do you want?).

Shurpnakha comes to the point: *Tumhe chaahati hoon* (I want *you*).

Ram replies, unruffled: *Mein vivaahit hoon* (I am married).

Shurpnakha dismisses this with an airy, *To kya hua? Purush to ek saath kai baar vivaah kar sakta hai* (So what? A man can be married to many women simultaneously).

Ram turns her down gently and firmly as the Purushottam, the perfect man, would.

She then offers herself to his younger brother Laxman, who also refuses her. It is then that she metamorphoses into a huge, monstrous figure that looms over Sita. Laxman fires an arrow and cuts off her nose.

Even here, in the righteous world of Lord Ram, Helen represents a sexual threat, a woman who can ask for what she wants. And even here, in a world of magic and sorcery, she will fail to get it.

But in *Harishchandra Taramati* (1970) she actually succeeds. King Harishchandra (Prithviraj Kapoor) is famed for his honesty and moral rectitude. The sage Vishwamitra, however, believes that the king's honesty is only a result of his wealth and position, and decides to rob him of both. He draws Harishchandra's spirit out of his body and into a dream space, a set dominated by a giant statue of Saraswati in the middle of a forest glade. An *alaap* drifts dreamingly. Then Helen erupts from the undergrowth. She is an apsara—covered from head to toe, but the clothes are tightly draped to show off the hourglass figure. Eight women come hopping through the shallow stream. Other women appear by magic with musical instruments in their hands. While Helen dances a mix of Kathak and several folk forms, more statues materialize, all inspired by the divine erotica of Khajuraho. Throughout, Harishchandra seems a little gobsmacked. But at the end he is appreciative.

Harishchandra: *Sunder, ati sunder* (Beautiful, very beautiful).

Apsara: *Mein ya meri kala?* (Me or my art?)

Harishchandra: *Kala ka pradarshan* (The presentation of your art).

He offers the apsara a boon, which is asking for trouble. She asks for marriage. He refuses because he is already married and permits her another try. She asks for the throne of Ayodhya. He argues that a dancer would not be able to rule. At this point Helen disappears and Vishwamitra appears. As a great sage, he is of course more than able to rule. Harishchandra loses his kingdom. This is one of Helen's rare victories on screen.

So there was always a role in mythological films for the vamp, the woman of destructive beauty. But it is difficult to explain Helen's presence in *Karwa Chouth* (1980), a small exploitative film in which the heroine thinks she has given birth to a snake and is eventually blessed for her devotion to her snakechild. (Yes, that kind of film.) The story begins on Karwa Chouth, the day of the fast that women in parts of north India keep to ensure that their husbands will have long and happy lives. It should be the leading lady Mangala (Kanan Kaushal) singing the title song. Instead, it is Helen in traditional colours—saffron yellow and parrot green—and a veil who sings and dances to *Karwa chouth ka vrat aisa/ Jiski mahima hai aparam paar/ O behenon karna baarambaar* (The spiritual blessings of the karwa chouth fast are immeasurable/ O Sisters, perform it again and again). Either Kanan Kaushal couldn't dance or director Ramlal Hans thought the number needed a little more than she could give it.

But you can see the strain. The dancing is traditional garba, but in the close-ups Helen offers us a few facial ticks and coquettish twitches from her more worldly series. It seems like the dilemma from hell for dance directors Badriprasad and Saroj. Here is a dancer whose work is already well known. Her audience will expect her to offer something sensually exciting. But the song is a regressive paean of praise to a fast for husbands. Their way out? A dandiya frenzy at the end of the song.

It is easy to see that Helen's distance from the social order would depend on the needs of the film and the script. Malleability was perhaps the most important quality that her persona and heritage lent her. She could be what was needed and there were many different not-so-good women needed. Helen was exotic as all vamps must be, but the Bombay film industry's somewhat uncomplicated notion of exotica was such that Helen could be made to fit any set of circumstances. As an alien with no fixed place of origin, she could be any kind of foreigner, any outsider.

This malleability can also be seen chronologically. Helen herself maintained that she owed the length of her career to her discipline and her dancing. While this is true—she kept her body in remarkable shape—this was not all there was to it. What is of much greater significance is that the persona she came to inhabit could be moulded to fit whatever was needed.

In the fifties, she was a dancer, but more coquette than seductress. At that point the attraction relied on the tension that her songs generated between presumed innocence and assumed experience. The lyrics presume her innocence, but the fact that she is dancing for us at all leads us to assume experience. Especially since at that time heroines did not dance. They tripped away from the hero, they risked a couple of skips, and very often they would show up cycling—they were rarely allowed any greater mobility than this in their song sequences

In the sixties, the heroines were given a lot more latitude in the amount of movement in a song. The entry of Asha Parekh (whom Shammi Kapoor once accused of imitating him), Babita and Rajshree into Hindi films and of several trained dancers from the South as heroines upped the stakes. This also coincided with the arrival of film noir in India. And Helen went underground. She became the instant underbelly; just add percussion. The broad brush strokes of film noir—Hollywood's way of retrieving melodrama and adding it to what Orson Welles described so well as that 'bright guilty place'—demanded more blacks and whites. Helen's white face and bright sensuality were used to darken the guilty places of smugglers' dens and criminal hang-outs.

In the seventies, when the heroines began to actively seduce the heroes, Helen was as much a part of the landscape as anyone else. The exotic had given way to the notion that every gang comes equipped with one white or semi-white moll. Hotel rooms were similarly stocked with a woman in green Arabian fantasy outfits. The arrival of R.D. Burman's music and Asha Bhosle's voice also gave Helen's career as a vamp a new dimension. The fusion RD infused into Hindi film music demanded a new vocabulary of movement. Who else could dance to Pancham's irresistible beats? Who else could look convincing when executing Western dance steps and follow them up, seamlessly, with some fancy footwork from Kathak?

In *Don* (1978), for example, Don (Amitabh Bachchan) is unsurprised to find that his hotel room comes with all the mod cons, including a belly dancer. Kamini's (Helen) lover was put to death when he sought to leave Don's gang. Now she wants revenge and offers to assist the police. She turns into Sonia, whose job is to find out where Don is and once he has been located, keep him there until the police arrive. She locates him in a hotel and tries to seduce him. 'Not now, baby,' he says, brushing past her, and Helen, just past forty, begins one of the dances for which she is best remembered: *Yeh mera dil yaar ke deewaana/ Deewaana mastaana, pyaar ka parwaana/ Aata hai mujhko pyaar mein jal jaana/ Mushqil hai pyaare tera bachke jaana* (My heart is maddened with love/ A moth drawn to the flame,/ I know how to lose my all for love/ You cannot escape). There is a moment in the bridge between verses when she appears in the door of his bedroom. She stands there and—it is difficult to put this any other way—she *shimmies*. Every inch of her body, liquid, toned, perfect, moves to the music.

On her belly in front of Don, playing with his gun (we get it), she empties it of bullets (we get it, all right), flicking them under the bed. It is possible to read a wealth of Freudian symbolism into this symbolic castration. The delay is, for a moment, successful. The police do arrive on time and Kamini/Sonia has a moment of triumph, but it is short-lived. Don kidnaps her with an empty gun and then kills her. Which is expected—for, were she to succeed at this point, the film would end, but almost as importantly, it would also mean the validation of female sexual power.

And so Helen's brief candle was extinguished once again. Who else could dance like that? Who else could stop you in your tracks with her shimmy in the doorway? If there were no Helen, we might have had to invent her.

Five

Good Girls, Bad Girls

Such women don't have a history.

—Miss Ruby (Helen) to Devendra
(Sanjeev Kumar) in *Anamika*

In almost everything that has been written about the vamps of Hindi cinema, there has been a tendency to reduce the figure of the bad girl to a caricature. Her story is seen as the Progress of the Harlot: she fell, she smoked, she drank, she danced, she snuggled, she smuggled, she died.

This ignores the moral role the vamp played in the films in which she appeared. She was not merely about eye candy,

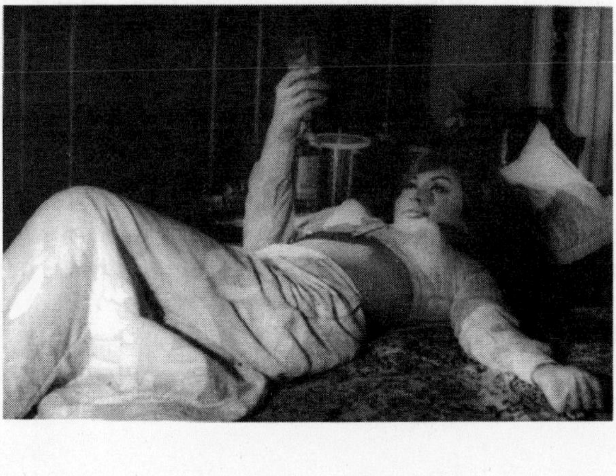

which makes nonsense of the claim that the vamp has returned in the item-number sequences that began in the late nineties. The item-number girl has no other function than to appease the male desire to be voyeur while a woman dances. The name itself—item number—has a cynical quality to it, a revelation of how the industry has adopted film-maker Manmohan Desai's dictum that to be a success a commercial film should offer the viewer a treat in every reel, an 'item' per reel, as it were.

The vamp, however, was not just visual spectacle. Her more significant function was as an alternate moral pole in the cinematic universe whose centre was the hero. Helen performed this role to perfection. As the epitome of destructive femininity, she threw into prominence the virtue of the other women, chiefly the heroine, but also the hero's mother and sister. This also validated the hero's roots, or his origin. The vamp's failure to subvert the hero permanently emphasized not just his basic goodness but also his right upbringing.

Until the advent of the seventies, the hero fitted easily into this moral universe. Even when he was part of the gang, he was on the side of the good. The jewel thief was invariably uncovered as the policeman operating under cover. The hero might be suspected of murder but we knew that the police had got it wrong. If he began bad, he would either see the light or there would be a good twin waiting in the wings. In each case, the vamp, symbolic of his past, would be left behind.

Nor was there a single kind of vamp. Helen played several different kinds, again based on the demands of the script. Some of them were script markers, others had more interesting functions. Take that moment in *Junglee* (1961) when Shammi Kapoor, as Shekhar, has learnt to love and decides to let the world know. In the beginning of the film, we are told that the millionaire Shekhar has never laughed in his life. But once he has been to Kashmir, fallen in love with his Kashmir ki kali (Saira Banu) and learnt to feel fear when she falls ill during a snowstorm, he turns over a new leaf with a vengeance. However, he still has a termagant of a mother (Lalita Pawar) to deal with, and a fake Maharaja who wants to marry his daughter into the family to acquire their wealth. At a party thrown to introduce Shekhar and the fake princess, Helen puts on a show.

The lights dim and we see a single leg first. (The symbol itself is often symbolized by body parts. In Helen's case, it was mostly her legs, but it could as well be her torso, as in *Inkaar*; her rump, in *Bulundi*; her fingers, in *Dil Daulat Duniya*; down to her right eye in *Elaan*.) For a whole minute, she dances alone. Then Shammi Kapoor joins her on stage to exult: *Ai-yai-ya karoon main kya sookoo sookoo/ Kho gaya dil mera sookoo sookoo* (Ai-yai-ya what do I do, sookoo, sookoo/ I've gone and lost my heart, sookoo sookoo). It is an exuberant, uncomplicated song, reflected in the meaningless lyrics and the de-sexualized flirting between Helen (unnamed in the film) and Shekhar. Now that Shekhar has discovered the joy of love, he can shed the straitjacket of his wealth and his stiff dignity. Since Saira Banu was a good dancer, indeed her legs were the first serious competition to Helen's, it seems odd that it should not be the heroine at this celebration of the power of love. But it is Helen, who has no other role in the film, who was called upon to romp with Shekhar, almost in tribute to the energy she could bring to such dances. Besides, the vamp endorsing and celebrating this love gives it far greater currency with the audience, the quality almost of a miracle.

In the hundreds of films that Helen appeared in, it is possible to see clearly the main functions that she performed. The following categories are not watertight compartments, nor is this intended to be a complete taxonomy of the vamp. It is only an attempt to demonstrate that the vamp was not constructed as a monolith of evil.

THE WHITE GODDESS

One of Helen's most famous songs is the slow, smoky cabaret (sung, unusually, by Lata Mangeshkar) *Aaa jaan-e-jaan, mera yeh husn jawaan, jawaan, jawaan/ Tere liye hai aas lagaaye, oh zaalim aajaa na* (Come, love of my life, my beauty and my youth long for you), from *Inteqam* (1969). Helen herself invariably lists this as one of her best numbers. You can see why. It is difficult to think of another song that expresses such a level of heated sexual desire and translates it into such charged visuals. Azad is bound in chains and confined in a golden cage, as if he is a trophy of sorts, or a plaything. He is presented as barely human, a dark, pre-literate Noble Savage who communicates in grunts and snorts. By contrast, Helen is presented as the epitome of the liberated Western woman, her 'sophistication' underlined by her ostrich-feather fan, gold wig studded with rhinestones, blue contact lenses under eyebrows that are also picked out with rhinestones, and leggings under a dark blue bikini bedecked with shiny doodahs. In case we miss the point, she sings, *Door se kitni aayi hoon, tu jaane na* (You have no idea how far I've travelled to be here). She writhes all over his cage, tickles him with a feather, tantalizes him by remaining just out of reach, while a cockatoo struggles with the chain that keeps it on a ring just above the cage. When Azad breaks free, she does not seem unduly troubled, for he is soon back inside it, driven in by slave-drivers with whips. Even today, thirty-five years after it was filmed, there is something seductively dangerous, something outré about the song.

For the Indian audience, the alienation here is doubled: the woman is white, the man black. Placing both the lovers in alien racial identities was efficient in a sense. Tangentially, it made the case for lust being non-Indian while reinforcing stereotypes of the sexual immorality of white women and the sexual degeneracy of black men. It is tempting to suggest that in 1969, this was still a hangover dating back to the sexual unavailability of the memsahibs, but the formula persisted.

In *Mehmaan* (1973), once again the male, in leopard skin this time, and a sheepish grin, is tied up. A golden net is brought on stage which opens to reveal a golden-haired Helen in a pink and silver Arabian outfit. Once again, we have a somewhat primitive man striving to express his sexuality, and the woman liberated enough (because white enough?) to speak for both of them. This is indicative, of course: the strong tribal bound in chains, the sensual white woman who encourages him to sin. The lyrics run: *Tu dar mat dar mat yaara/ Gham kar mat, kar mat yaara/ Pal do pal dhoom machaa le/ Yoon mar mat mar mat yaara* (Do not fear/ Nor be sad/ Enjoy yourself for a moment or two/ Don't suffer like this). In this version of the song, she even unties him herself (and the lights go off, to the consternation of the audience). However, in shadow-play, she tames him and controls him. Then she vanishes.

The version of this theme that we see in *Apne Rang Hazaar* (1975) is a climax-filler. The rich womanizer Sunil (Sanjeev Kumar) seems to be falling in love with the wrong woman (Bindu) but is saved by the connivance of his mother (Kamini Kaushal) and his driver's daughter, Mala (Leena Chandavarkar). But then, he spends much of his screen time being saved. When he is about to be disinherited, his friend Vicky (Danny Denzongpa) kills his uncle. Later, Vicky asks for a return of the favour in a *Strangers on the Train*-style plot development. Vicky wants Sunil to get out of the way while he kills Mala (she is Vicky's long-lost half-sister and will inherit if she lives). The friends fall out and Vicky tries to kidnap Sunil's mute brother Guddu (Master Tito). Guddu escapes and wanders into a theatre where Helen is dancing on stage with a bunch of blackface tribals with feather-flocked spears. The song basically consists of a series of yaaaows and haaoows and c'monbaby-s. It is not clear what this scene was meant to achieve, other than providing an unusual backdrop for the cliffhanger ending.

In 1979, the theme was replayed again, in *Raakhi Ki Saugandh*. A car used in a bank robbery sets Inspector Shankar (Vinod Mehra) on the trail of '*mashhoor* (famous) cabaret dancer' Sweety (Helen). He follows her into a nightclub where a golden cage drops over him and a bunch of *hubshees* (he uses this pejorative term for Africans later in the film when interrogating Sweety) poke at him with spears and knives. Sweety mocks him in song: *Khud hi phas gaya pinjre mein/ Tu shikaari bada anaari hai* (Caught in the trap you set yourself/ You're a fool of a hunter). Only, since this is the hero locked in the cage, he kicks it open himself and beats up the tribals and then proceeds with his quest.

In all four songs, contrasting the white woman and the black or tribal man was a way of maintaining an ambiguity about the lust lives of the Indians. As Aryans (our way of distancing ourselves from the more uncomfortable term 'brown'), Indians could be seen as representing a civilized mid-point between the lust of primitives and the degenerate liberation of white people. That civilized mid-point is Romanticism, an Indian Romanticism with its own hierarchy of acceptable emotions. The alien persona of Helen was ideally suited to keeping these desires at some distance from the principals, whose emotional lives might be dominated by negative emotions such as revenge, anger and Oedipal struggles, but never by lust.

INSTANT DEBAUCHERY

We have already seen that as a dancer, Helen marked the shadowy areas of society into which the hero or heroine had stumbled. Similarly, when it was necessary to establish the villainous nature of one of the players, association with the vamp would serve just as easily. Since a certain group of character actors played villains, there was never any tension as to whom the audience was supposed to identify with. So this further device might seem like over-emphasis. Nevertheless, it was an economical way of enhancing the drama and getting the audience involved in it. In *Taj* (1956), the king crushes a child with his chariot and then drives on, yet a song and dance by Helen is necessary to further underline his decadence. Now there'll be further trouble, we know. In the middle of Helen's performance, the young princess walks in and interrupts it. Enraged, the king slaps his only child and disables her right limbs (until, much later, a singer-mendicant restores them to life with *his* song).

The easiest way to establish the debauchery of the villain—or the villainy of the debauch—was to present him at a mujra or in a nightclub. In that wild romp *Chalti Ka Naam Gaadi* (1958), the arch-villain Raja Sahab (K.N. Singh) attends a mujra at which Helen and Cuckoo perform some extraordinarily fluent kathak. In the very next scene, he will be plotting the seduction of the heiress Renu (Madhubala). But for the moment, a classic feat of economy is achieved. The song, *Hum tumhaare hain zara ghar se nikalkar dekho/ Na yakeen aaye to dil se dil badalkar dekho* (We are yours, just come out of your home and see/ And if you still do not believe, exchange hearts with us and see), changes the tone of the film which until that point has been almost Wodehousian in its light comedy. By presenting Raja Sahab as a silhouette in the first shot and then withdrawing into the kotha, the seduction is aimed directly at the audience. The villain, too, has been successfully indicated and we know that now the drama will turn darker.

In *Ganga Jamuna* (1961), Dilip Kumar plays one of two brothers, Ganga, who turns dacoit; while Nasir Khan plays Jamuna, the brother who joins the police. In her red mujra dress, singing *Tora man bada paapi saanwariya re* (Your mind is a sinner, my love), Helen is clearly a simple marker, emphasizing the debauchery of the zamindaar who has forced Ganga (with all the ironies of that name) into a life of crime. In *Sagaai* (1966), Rajesh (Biswajeet) and Sheel (Rajshree) get together fairly quickly despite the tension between their fathers over the rights to a certain piece of forest. The fly in the conjugal ointment is Kailash (Prem Chopra), and *his* second scene is set in a kotha in which Helen in a pink mujra outfit is singing: *Sajan tori preet raat-bhar ki* (Your love only lasts the night).

Smuggler (1966) tells the tale of Inspector Rajan (Shaikh Mukhtar) who sacrifices his honour to pay for his brother's education. Until the time that he accepts the bribe, the songs are non-threatening: a child's song at a party, a romantic duet. When he accepts the bribe and the action moves to the exchange of diamonds, Helen appears. The song itself has nothing to do with the loss of honour—*Dil ka lagaana is duniya mein/ Poora dhokha khaana hai* (Falling in love is an invitation to disillusionment)—so it is clear that she is only another step on his journey to degradation. In *Aulad* (1968), Helen's song, *Dil dhadakta hai saans rukti hai/ Dekhte ho kis nazar se mujhe* (My heart quickens, my breath stops/ When you look at me like that), is sung for the delectation of a pretender son who has replaced the lost heir. The song cuts between the mujra and the aged father's sickbed.

This continues up to and beyond the tear-jerker *Bikhre Moti* (1971) in which Kamini Kaushal's children are separated after the arrest of her husband, so that one grows up to be Anand (Jeetendra), the son of a respected judge, the other to be Gopi (Sujit Kumar), a criminal. Gopi meets his father on the road—and not knowing that he is related by blood—takes him to his hideout where diamonds are being concealed in dolls. Here four men dressed as Cossacks throw knives into a life-sized statue. They run those knives down the pink plastic of the statue, their faces bathed in red (lecherous) light. The doll falls apart and Helen steps out, singing, *Ek nazar chahoon main halki halki/ Aa yeh keemat hai mere dil-ki, dil-ki* (I want a glance that's light and fleeting/ Yes, that's the price for my heart).

BAD WIVES, BAD WOMEN

The Helen figure could also be called upon to represent or indicate a bad marriage, one that the hero makes out of a sense of duty to some senior figure. It might be acceptable at some level for a man to want to go and see a 'cabaret', but when his *wife* insists, it is a sign that the marriage is in trouble and that the woman is not really a good mate.

In *Dil Apna Aur Preet Parai* (1960), we know that Dr Sushil Verma (Raj Kumar) has been forced into a loveless marriage with Kusum (Nadira), the spoilt daughter of the man who sponsored his medical education. His true love is an

orphan, Karuna (Meena Kumari), a nurse in the hospital at which he works. One night, one of his patients, Girdhari (Om Prakash), falls very ill. This is the night Kusum has chosen to go out and enjoy herself, always a dreadful crime for a woman, especially heinous in a wife. When Karuna calls to speak to Sushil about Girdhari, Kusum hangs up and whisks him off to a restaurant where Helen in a strappy dress asks: *Haai itni badi mehfil aur ek dil/ Kisko doon? Dil kisko doon?* (My, such a huge gathering/ To whom should I give my heart?). That Kusum should choose a show of such blatant licence over her husband's duty is meant to shock us. Girdhari's death and Sushil's anger pave the way for Kusum's death so that Karuna and Sushil may be reunited.

A similar situation was repeated in *Hariyali Aur Rasta* (1962). Shankar (Manoj Kumar) and Shobhna (Mala Sinha) are childhood sweethearts who have grown up together on his father's tea estates. However, Shankar has been promised to Rita (Shashikala), a social worker, who talks the talk but doesn't walk the walk. Shobhna sacrifices her love and is presumed to be dead after an accident—although she is fished out of the river. Shankar marries Rita, who turns out to be a very bad wife. She spends money with both hands, dismisses old servants and even *forgets to send him his lunch*. Instead she spends time at the club where she has invited Miss Dolly (Helen) and party to dance, after which there will be a fancy dress competition with a prize sponsored by her. Thus even as Miss Dolly sings *Parwaanon ki raah mein, deewaanon ki chaah mein/ Jaloon aur Jalaaoon Mohabbat nibhaaoon/ Mera bas yahi kaam hai* (In the way of the moth, in the manner of lovers/ I burn, I inflame, I love/ That's my job), she is not just entertaining the club (and us) but she is also proving that Shankar has married someone unsuitable. The scene is set for Rita to die. She does.

This remains the pattern right up to *Agnirekha* (1973) where Suresh (Sanjeev Kumar), a young widower, is forced by his rich mother-in-law to marry Mohini (Bindu), though he loves Nirmala (Sharda), his children's governess. Helen dances for the engagement: *Babb-babber-loo/ Ek main, ek tu/ Hum dono jo mil jaayen/ To bada mazaa ho* (Babb-babber-loo/ You and me, me and you/ When we get together/ We'll have such fun). Both Mohini and Helen try to get him to show some affection but Suresh remains adamantly, almost caddishly unresponsive. We know, of course, that later events will prove that he was right to do so.

COMMERCIAL SEX WORKER

In all but a few of Helen's roles as the bad girl, there was an implication that her favours were available for money. In *Bairaag* and *Ginny Aur Johnny* (both 1976), for instance, she seems to be available for the price of a diamond necklace. Although Hindi cinema was ambiguous in its attitude to dancers, alternating between the defence that dance was an art mentioned in the shastras and the charge that dancers themselves were generally women of ill-repute, the mass of the evidence was that the woman who danced for the delectation of men did not belong in respectable society.

In *Main Chup Rahoongi* (1962), the unwed mother Gayatri (Meena Kumari), who has voluntarily abandoned her lover Kamal (Sunil Dutt) and chosen to suffer alone, begins a career in private tuitions. One of her young charges is the daughter of a dancer (Helen). A heartbroken Kamal arrives at Helen's house one day, brought by a friend, who thinks that she might be able to cure him of his megrims. She offers him 'chai, coffee or Ovaltine (!)'. The friend explains that he needs stronger stuff and withdraws. Helen sings, *Mere dil, kabhi to koi aayega/ Humdum jo tera ban jaayega* (O my heart, there must be someone/ Who will make you his own). An unsuspecting Gayatri, who is in another room with the little girl, asks the maid of the house about the distracting music. The maid replies, '*Bibi, yahaan to har subah Id aur har raat Diwali hai* (Madam, every night is Diwali here and every day is Id—i.e., night or day, it is time for celebration).

When, as Jenny Francis, Helen tells Ahmad Raza

(Amitabh Bachchan) in *Imaan Dharam* (1977) that she truly has no idea who the father of her daughter is, she is admitting to a life of multiple sexual encounters. In *Raakhi Ki Saugandh* (1980), Inspector Shankar interviews Kitty about her possible involvement in a bank robbery and she tells him: *Shaayad aap bhool rahe hain ki main ek cabaret dancer hoon. Badmaashon ya shareef; har ek ke saath taaluqaat banaaye rakhna hamaara pesha hai* (Perhaps you forget that I am a cabaret dancer; villains or pillars of society, my job requires me to maintain relationships with all of them).

In all these roles, the contrast was between the purity of the heroine and the moral degradation of the commercial sex worker. To move from one to the other was impossible. In *Imaan Dharam*, therefore, Jenny's attempt to go respectable ends in her death. This would happen almost invariably. It was not just a divide between good girl and bad; it was a chasm.

MOLL

Helen endlessly reprised the role of the moll. Through the late sixties and early seventies, where there was a gang, there was Helen. She appeared in every key scene which featured the gang, and was often sent out to offer false friendship to the heroine or to vamp the hero (unsuccessfully). But more often than not, her role was to make appreciative squeaks when something evil was suggested, perform a cabaret as suitable cover for some nefarious activity and then vanish towards the end when the real action began. Whether the gang was smuggling drugs (as Sophie's was in *Jaane Anjaane*), pursuing diamonds with the secrets of world peace hidden in them (Sue's gang in *Night in London*) or setting out to bump off an heiress (Rita's in *Kab? Kyoon? Aur Kahaan?*) or filching fighter-plane designs (Rita's in *Shareef Badmaash*), Helen played the bells and whistles.

However, she could take a hand when she decided on a double-cross, and it is not surprising that she so often did. In

Elaan (1971), for example, Lilly (sic) is part of a gang of spies who wish to acquire an atomic ring of invisibility that has been developed by Indian scientists. Naresh (Vinod Mehra), a journalist, lands on their island to get at the truth. He is caught and tied to a pole and rotated at high speed. Later, he is led into a den decorated in every colour known to man where Lilly, dressed as a matador, is waving her red cape at a man in a bull mask. After a while Lilly throws her cape over the camera. When the red pulls away, we see her face in such extreme close-up that only her right eye is visible. She winks and the camera pulls back to let us see that she has changed, unaccountably, into a Heidi costume: blue pinafore, white blouse and black apron over pantalettes and school-girl shoes. The song is pretty straightforward by comparison: *Dil dena ho to do/ Dil lena ho to lo* (Give your heart away if you want/ Take my heart away if you want). Lilly has designs on the atomic ring of invisibility herself. After her second song, *Janaab ko salaam hai/ Zarina mera naam hai* (Greetings, my lords/ My name is Zarina), she teams up with Ram Singh (Vinod Khanna), another gang member, to chase Naresh (who has by now acquired the ring).

A lone woman in the midst of such a number of men of suspect character, her attempt at double-crossing them, and her inevitable death are routine tropes in almost all films with gangs. Her love was doomed, her acts of expiation insufficient and her fate was death.

THE SKELETON IN THE CLOSET

In *Afsana* (1966), Kamini (Helen) is the cause of Shekhar's (Pradeep Kumar) misogyny. He tells his new lady love Renu (Padmini) about her in grim detail. He first saw Kamini dancing in a club. In a series of odd symbols we follow his proposal (the wake of a boat), his marriage (a chandelier) and his disillusionment (an extinguished candle) when he discovers that she has another lover. He drives her from his house and later hears that she has died in an accident.

However, on the first night of his marriage to Renu, Kamini returns and begins to blackmail him. She comes to his wedding reception and announces, 'All of you have come here to congratulate the married couple, and I want to say...' And then she sings: *Kitni hain albeli, haai zulfein teri, saheli/ Kitna haseen naujawaan hai, jo inse khele, haai, haai* (What beautiful hair you have, my friend/ And what a handsome man he is who plays with your locks).

She and her lover now plan to kill Shekhar since she will inherit as his first and lawful wife. Of course, for this, she ends up falling off a cliff. Only, Shekhar is arrested for murdering her. Obviously even after death she can cause trouble.

Kamini bounces back in *Jab Andhera Hota Hai* (1974), where her mocking laughter drives her architect husband Pratap (Prem Chopra) to homicidal madness. We learn all this in a series of flashbacks as Pratap kills women, one by one. Kamini's father educated Pratap, which gives her a sense of superiority which she flaunts by bringing her lover (Jalal Agha) home to her bed. Finally, Pratap strangles her to stop her laughing at him and then sets off to punish other women too.

In *Anamika* (1973), she represents the possibly unsavoury past of the heroine. The film tells the story of Devendra Dutt (Sanjeev Kumar) who finds a woman lying on the road. Anamika/Kanchan/Archana (Jaya Bhaduri) seems to have many names but no memory other than the strange belief that she is married to Devendra. In the process of discovering her identity, Devendra and Anamika/Kanchan/Archana go to a cabaret performed by Miss Ruby. This is one of Helen's most famous numbers, encapsulating a story within a story: *Aaj ki raat koi aane ko hai* (Tonight, someone will come to me).

Devendra goes backstage to meet Miss Ruby after the show. She is wearing a black slip and smoking. The wig is on the desk, next to a drink. He asks about Kanchan's past. 'You really are a kid,' she says in English, with a sweet, vicious smile. 'Such women don't have a history.'

Later Kanchan tells Devendra her story and it turns out that Miss Ruby was a procurer who offered her shelter when she needed it. A raid disrupted business the same night and Kanchan escaped and ended up in front of Devendra's car. This proves that she is clean, a virgin without a sexual history—although not in quite the way Miss Ruby meant it.

TEACHER

Until the seventies, the hero, too, was assumed to be a virgin. This was even made explicit in films like *Padosan* (1957), where the hero, Sunil Dutt, has not had anything to do with women since he is still in the first stage of the life of a Hindu male, *brahmacharya ashrama*. The idea that a hero should be a sexually experienced male in order to master and guide the sexually inexperienced female only appeared in the seventies, with the arrival of *les freres* Feroze and Sanjay Khan. Until that time, the playboy was still just a young man who drank, smoked and teased young women. He did not sleep with them.

In this setting, the sexually experienced woman who would offer the hero instruction in matters sexual was not treated with much sympathy. In *Chhote Nawab* (1961), the Chhote Nawab (Mehmood) is a thoroughly spoilt brat who refuses to believe that he is twenty, because his birthday occurs on 29 February. This means that he pretends to be five years old, plays with children and rides a tricycle. This might lead one to suspect that he is retarded but after the death of his father, he suddenly grows up when his brother-in-law throws him out of the house. His fiancée Roshan (Ameeta) takes him in and undertakes to teach him the three 'R's, while a friend of the family, Captain (Johnny Walker), grooms him in social graces. Captain owns a nightclub to which he takes the Chhote Nawab. Here, Miss Sophie (Helen) makes her offer in a lovely song: *Matwaali aankhonwaale/ Oh albele dilwaale/ Dil tera ho raha hai/ Gar tu ise apna le* (Hey you with the mischievous eyes/ Hey you of the passionate heart/ I'm falling in love with you/ Won't you accept the gift of my heart?). Although he refuses in song—*Sun eh hasina, main woh to nahin* (Listen, beautiful lady, I'm not the one)—the Chhote Nawab begins to be attracted to her. He buys a horse, begins to throw parties, frequents the nightclub without Roshan and begins smoking. Captain tries to intervene but Sophie leaves his club and takes the Chhote Nawab with her to another. There, she teaches him to drink as well. A song makes this explicit: *Jeenewale muskurake jee/ Khushi ke jaam, muskura, aur pee/ Khabar kisko ki kal kya ho/ Arre yeh do din ki hai zindagi* (Drink up/ Forget your sorrows/ Who knows what happens tomorrow?/ Life is too short to worry). Her duplicity is exposed only when Captain pretends to be an eccentric millionaire on the verge of death who wants to leave all his money to her.

Again, Helen's character had a didactic purpose. The hurt that Chhote Nawab feels when she shows her true colours brings him closer to his family, cures him of his love of upper-class sophistication and validates what the audience already knows: their middle-class values are the only ones that can bring true happiness. The moral outcastes who drink, smoke, dance and generally have a great time will only end in misery.

Ten years later, Helen would still be mocking the inexperience of the young troublemaker Ramu (Raakesh Roshan) in the film *Man Mandir*. His sister Krishna (Waheeda Rehman) has just married the upright taxi driver Deepak (Sanjeev Kumar). He pawns her jewellery on the pretext that there is illness in the family and takes his friends out to dinner. Here, for his troubles, Helen asks in a chant: *Kahiye-ji kya loge?/ Dil loge?/ Kho doge!* (What will you have?/ My heart?/ You'll lose it!). Then she begins to sing: *Tum abhi kamsin ho, tum abhi nadaan ho* (You're still innocent, still naïve), lines that more traditionally would be addressed to a woman.

But perhaps the most explicit example of Helen's pedagogy can be seen in *Bhai Behen* (1969), the story of two brothers, Suren (Sunil Dutt) and Mahen (Diwakar), who live in the paternalistic regime of their father (Ashok Kumar). Mahen is caught dancing in a public place, dragged home and is about to be beaten when he has a heart attack and dies. Heartsick, Suren walks out of his home and falls in with Ratan (Pran) who, it is clear to us, simply wants to milk the family for what he can get.

Ratan organizes an education in a form-fitting red gown and feathery boa. Helen sings: *Hai dil karoon mein kya/ Saamna tera hoga/ Pehloo se jaana nahin/ Tu hai meri zindagi* (What should I do?/ Do not leave me/ You're my life). At the end of the song, Suren and his tutor collapse behind a pillar on to the floor, and Ratan smiles victoriously. We may safely assume that the intended lessons are coming along well.

The educative role could also include initiation into a life of crime, a life that is always presented as westernized. In *Aaj Ka Ye Ghar* (1976) Mala (Jaymala) appears as the linchpin of the poor household into which she is married. The opening scenes are full of a hurried domesticity, establishing the husband (Shriram Lagoo), the young brother-in-law Vijay

(Romesh Sharma) and the in-laws (Lalita Pawar and A.K. Hangal).

Vijay likes money a little too much. He is shown in bad company, being encouraged to smoke and drink. His gang takes him to see Miss Roohi (Helen) who wants him to organize five thousand rupees so that they can make a profit of a lakh. Then it is time for her show, a hot number in which she appears as a Rajasthani gypsy, singing about being bitten by scorpions at night and so, wanting his company. Vijay tries desperately to look sophisticated but fails miserably. Almost all the flirtatious gestures are aimed directly at Vijay, which means the song must be read as a metaphor for his seduction not merely by the woman whose hand he will take in the end, but also for a way of life.

In a few short reels, Vijay has fought with his family and walked out, taking his mother with him. He warns her that she had better not complain about the way he lives. Then Miss Roohi comes over and looking for a light for her cigarette, finds the diya lit for the gods. A storm erupts but Vijay takes Roohi's side against his mother. Later, when his mother is trying to sing a bhajan to Lord Krishna, *Darshan do Nandkishore*, she is interrupted by Vijay and Roohi dancing to a truly dreadful rock tune, 'Come on darling, love me more'.

Finally, Vijay kicks the mother out and keeps going downhill until he ends in jail and repents his ways. Through the film we do not know much about Miss Roohi (women like her have no history, after all) but it is safe to suggest that she represents the world at its wickedest. The lessons she teaches are not likely to do a hero any good.

Six

The Cure of All the Sorrows of the World

Sharaab nahin hoon magar ek nasha hoon
Main saare zamaane ke gham ki dawaa hoon.
(Alcohol I am not, but I am an intoxication
I am the cure of all the sorrows of the world.)

—Lyrics from Helen's song
in *Adhikaar* (1971)

I must have danced my way through more than a thousand films in various languages, including Marwari and Bhojpuri.

—Helen, to *Filmfare*, on receiving a
Lifetime Achievement Award in 1998

With the exception of a few very silly films (*Aap Beeti*, *Maya*, *Khoon Khoon*, *Jab Andhera Hota Hai*), Helen's name on the marquee meant that she was going to dance, which in turn generally meant a song. Not always, again, for there were some dances without songs as well (*Hulchul*, *The Great Gambler*). These sequences were primarily intended as eye candy but that was not the only function they performed.

The song in Hindi cinema has been paid much attention, most of it dismissive. It is regarded as a hold-over from older art forms such as folk theatre and the *Raas Leela* and thus excused on the basis of its antiquity. It is scorned for its lack of realism, decried even by its exponents as 'running around trees'. However, a more reasonable way of looking at the song would be to see it as unreal in the rational sense—no hundred-piece orchestra plays when two people fall in love, nor can a woman walking through a cemetery be audible to everyone simultaneously in a huge mansion—but certainly not meaningless in its symbolic reality.

Helen's songs generally are described as cabarets. Historians of dance and other forms of public entertainment might cavil at the use of this term. For cabaret was born on 18 November 1881, when Rudolphe Salis opened his 'Chat Noir', a cabaret artistique, on Montmartre, Paris. His intention: 'We will satirize political events, enlighten mankind, confront it with its stupidity, cure those creeps of their ill-temper...' The original purpose of cabaret, therefore, was to shock the middle class (*epater les bourgeois*). It was more than a bunch of ladies showing off their frilly pantalettes or lack thereof. Skits were performed that lampooned authority; there were also other 'acts', from contortionists to sword-swallowers to magicians. It was vaudeville with its underwear showing, a variety programme that teetered on the verge of being explicit, while never actually getting there. The frisson arose out of that unfulfilled promise.

Helen understood that. In *The Britannica Encyclopaedia of Hindi Cinema*, she says, '...cabaret doesn't mean just wriggling your body as people think—it's narration in dance. Paris nightclubs like Foley's and the Crazy Horse had these great cabarets.' Indeed, this was what she did in her best cabarets—*Aa jaan-e-jaan* from *Intequam*, *Piya tu ab to aa ja* from *Caravan* or *Aaj ki raat koi aane ko hai* fron *Anamika*—where a narrative is contained within the ambit of the song.

However, the word cabaret in the context of Indian cinema has come to mean a sexually suggestive dance performed by a woman for an audience that is either actually shown or is evident in the film. It is in this sense that the word will be used hereafter.

The usual codicils apply. This is not an exhaustive list and analysis, nor is it a defence. It is an attempt at rescuing the songs in which Helen featured from the charge that they were only about titillation. Some categories are based on the content of the lyrics and others on the role the song played in the story. It might seem that one should play into the other but this is not always so.

Often, categories spill into each other. The song of misdirection is sometimes also a song of seduction, as in negligee-clad Vera's number in *Shikar* (1968). Helen's song in *Kaala Baazaar* (1960) has elements of both the song of forgetfulness and the song of self-adulation.

And there are anomalies, too. For instance, how to categorize Helen's Holi song in *Biraadari* (1966)? It serves no purpose in the story, which is about an old lady (Lalita Pawar) with a sharp tongue and a heart of gold who can never collect the rent from her impoverished tenants, thus denying her daughter Seema (Faryal) the finer things of life. When the old lady decides to renounce the world and go on a pilgrimage, Seema prepares to get some goodies and sell the property. So we have Helen dancing as a Koli tribal, which is easy enough to understand; she's the Mumbai fantasy we crafted out of the aboriginal fisher-folk while squeezing them out of their homes. But why does she have a blonde wig?

Later, when Seema does sell the property, there's another celebratory dance, a mujra, again performed by Helen minus the kiss-curls. She isn't just a replacement for the heroine. Faryal could dance; not as well as Helen could, to be sure, but she too made a career out of vamping. Perhaps Helen was called upon to add firepower to the cast. Perhaps it could be that for this—and many other inscrutable, irrelevant songs—we have to thank the modus operandi of Hindi film directors until recently. In many films, she suddenly turned up, danced and disappeared. In *Parasmani* (1963) her song is an add-on, nothing more than a divertissement, before the action of the film. On the occasion of the Raksha Bandhan festival (yes, that *is* odd), she sings: *Oui maa, oui maa, yeh kya ho gaya/*

Unki gali mein dil kho gaya/ Bindiya ho to dhoond bhi loon main/ Dil na dhoonda jaaye (Oh dear, oh dear, what have I done?/ I've gone and lost my heart/ If it were a bindi, I could have found it/ Hearts aren't easy to find). Once that is over, no more Helen. More's the pity.

Amitabh Bachchan once remarked that he had never received a bound script until 2003. Thus when there is no script but only the skeleton of an idea, when the dialogues are being written as the shot is being readied, when producers impose their suspect commercial wisdom on 'the talent', you might have a song or two that has no function, no relevance at all. In all the 'celebration' that attends commercial cinema these days, this fact tends to be glossed over but it can't be ignored: most of Hindi commercial cinema is B-grade trash.

What follows, then, is my sitting duck. It is a taxonomy that has been created to be shot down. It has been created as much to suggest that Helen's songs were important within their context as to generate some discussion about the function of Hindi film songs. If it also manages to suggest that the songs did play some role in both determining the moral universe of the film and the trajectory of the story, that would be a pleasant side-effect.

SONG OF SEDUCTION

In some senses, all of Helen's songs are songs of seduction. Their underlying theme was erotic, regardless of the other functions they performed. Almost all her songs in her role as 'Teacher' and 'The White Goddess' (see previous chapter) can be seen as songs of seduction, for instance. And even in later aspects, the seduction of the audience was implicit in her dancing, since the underlying morality of the script would not allow the hero to be seduced and every plot point would involve him in songs. Thus this subset contains only those songs which have an explicit function of seduction within the storyline, the seduction of a male member of the cast.

How good a job did Helen make of seduction? A great one for the viewers—her fan base hasn't diminished much in close to fifty years. But within the framework of the Hindi film? That's a different story.

In the costume drama *Halaku* (1956), Parvez (Ajit) and his revolutionary friends seek to send dancers who have been primed to poison the evil Halaku (Pran). *Aji chale aao, aji chale aao,* sings Helen with Minoo Mumtaz for support, *Tumhen aankhon ne dil mein bulaaya* (Come to me sir, come to me/ My eyes invite you into my heart). As we expect, they fail at their task, since it would be ludicrous for the villain to be removed so easily. As in all popular culture, the villain can only be conquered by the hero; personifications of evil can only be defeated by the personification of good.

In *Harishchandra Taramati* (1963), Helen plays an apsara who has been sent to beguile the pious king Harishchandra into parting with his kingdom. She succeeds, but only because the king appreciates her art, not her—a subtle difference to be sure, but a difference nonetheless.

In the game of one-upmanship *Ek Se Badhkar Ek* (1976), she tries to vamp the jewel thief Shankar (Raj Kumar) with *Ek se badhkar ek/ Main laayi hoon tohfe anek/ Zulfon ki shaam laayi/ Dil tere naam laayi/ Mazaa aayega mulaaqaat ka/ Kya programme hai aaj raat ka?* (One better than the next/ My gifts exceed each other/ There's a night of dark tresses/ A heart marked for you/ This meeting promises to be fun/ What's your programme tonight?). She has disguised herself as the rather overwhelming Baroness Carolina, but he sees through her, and she fails to divest him of the prized diamond that is in his possession.

As Sonia in *Don*, Helen attempts to slow down Don (Amitabh Bachchan) with *Yeh mera dil yaar ka deewaana* so that the police can arrive and arrest him. She succeeds only because he seems to have an inordinate amount of packing to do and the police move with remarkable alacrity. She fails because Don eludes the police again.

She almost always failed, which was perhaps the secret of her success. In failing she kept the moral universe intact.

SONG OF REFLECTION

Often, lesser characters would be called upon to define plot moments, to reiterate in song what had transpired already in dialogue and action. This is a way of heightening the emotional content of the moment, a way of indicating a turning point.

In *Aag aur Daag* (1970), Raja (Joy Mukherjee) loses his parents when they commit suicide after his father loses everything in a crooked game. Raja is brought up by another gambler (Madan Puri) who urges him to take revenge. As a renaissance criminal (thief, gambler, safe-cracker) Raja is in a good position to do so. But he falls in love with Renu (Komal), the daughter of the man who cheated his father. It is when he discovers this that he arrives at the hotel that his father-in-law owns, and Helen underlines the turning point in his life with her song: *Aaj ki raat faisle ki hai/ Aaj ki raat ka jawaab nahin/ Chaahe jitna gunah kar daalo/ Aaj uska hisaab nahin* (Tonight will be decisive/ Tonight will be unique/ Break all the rules/ Tonight no one's keeping score).

When Helen sings *Chale ladkhadaake, kadam dagmagaake/ Nahin hosh humko kisi baat ka* (I stumble, my steps falter/ I'm not in my senses) in *Parwaana* (1971), she is not just suggesting the erotic intoxication of love, although that is the ostensible intent of these lyrics sung by a dancer who does not know any of the protagonists. We can tell that she is actually underscoring Kumar's (Amitabh Bachchan) mental state. Asha (Yogeeta Bali), the woman he loves, has just told him that she loves Rajesh (Navin Nishchol) whom she met on holiday. He has tried everything up to that point: emotional blackmail, self-inflicted violence, physical threats. He has begged her and begged her uncle (Om Prakash). Now in the bar, the song reflects his moral disintegration, for he is planning a murder that will implicate Rajesh. The presence of Helen, a symbol of immorality, also underscores his drift from the moral world he has inhabited so far.

It also often fell to those lower in status to declare the love between the principals. Constrained by social obligations, duty or whatever the plot had in store for them in terms of obstacles, the hero and heroine were often unable to express so socially anarchic an emotion as love. It would take a tribal, a gypsy or some common or market entertainer to articulate their feelings for the audience. When the Brahmin son of the village priest (Bharat Bhushan) falls in love with the princess (Nimmi) in *Angulimala* (1960), they cannot give vent to their feelings. They make much use of the lip quiver to indicate repressed love but if this is not enough, Helen, bedecked in peacock feathers, swathed in a leopard skin print, wiggles and sings: *Bade aaye shikaari shikaar karne...* (He thinks of himself as a great hunter). It is evident from the way she is dressed and the attendant musician who dances with her that she is meant to be a tribal. This is another layer of distancing from the upper-caste lovers.

Their uncertain position on the fringes of society is

supposed to give the 'outsiders' more licence to love and to follow the dictates of their hearts. If this is an accurate reading, their presence constitutes a critique of middle-class values in which duty, family, status and all the other reasons not to love are given primacy over the heart. So this sort of song is generally Romantic, putting love over everything, thus expressing the philosophy of Hindi films, which put an idealized form of love at the top of the pyramid.

Another reading could be that the outsider is seen as farther away from civilization (and its somewhat daunting restraints and social encumbrances) and so is closer to an earthy, sensual nature. If you look at these songs, it is generally the woman who is sexually desirable while the man is fat, comic, balding, graceless. The same outsider status was conferred—until the time of the blockbusters in which stars took over all the leading roles—on the comedian and his love interest, usually the 'supporting actress'. As we will see in a later chapter, this second heroine was generally Helen.

However, the vicarious declaration was not always required only in so obviously hierarchical a setting. In the madcap *Bombay Ka Chor* (1962), it was deemed necessary that Kishore (Kishore Kumar) and Mala (Mala Sinha) should use the good offices of the dancer at a wedding in their bustee to reflect their love for each other. Kishore has come to the city in search of funds for an orphanage. Mala's father is the nasty heir who is closing it down. She, on the other hand, dances for charity (under the auspices of the indicatively named Indo-Western Women's Association). A rift between father and daughter means she moves into the tenement where Kishore is living.

At a wedding in the bustee, Helen arrives to reflect the amour growing between the principals. *Dekha kisine kuchh aise, hoy aise,* she sings, *Hum to ghabraake pyaar kar baithe* (He looked at me in such a manner/ I fell in love out of fear). At the end, Mala smiles and Kishore's cap levitates.

SONG OF FORGETFULNESS

Right up to the Selfish Seventies, the underlying moral of Hindi cinema was that the Self came last. First came the nation, then society, next the family, and the caste unit after that. It was therefore meet that the vamp should offer forgetfulness. *Jeenewale muskurake pee/ Khushi ke jaam, muskura, aur pee* (Drink up/ Forget your sorrows) sings Sophie in *Chhote Nawaab*. *Gham chhod ke manaao rangreli* (Forget your worries and make merry), sings Kitty Kelly in *Gumnaam*. *Jeenewaale jhoomke mastaana ho ke jee/ Aanewaali subah se begaana ho ke pee* (If you're alive at all, you might as live it up/ Drink up and let tomorrow take care of itself), sings Helen (unnamed) in *Vaasna* (1968). *Main saare zamaane ke gham ki dawaa hoon* (I am the cure for all the sorrows of the world) sings Rubiya (if that is her name, for this song is her only appearance and the name is hummed by a couple of knockdown Beatles as the chorus) in *Adhikaar*.

This oblivion to which Helen's song lured the hero or the protagonists was often personal. The songs came at a point when the hero was at his nadir: misunderstood, abandoned, cast out. However, underlying this call to forget was a larger message—that a life lived without responsibilities was the easier life. In this sense, the song of forgetfulness could also be read as anti-social, anti-State.

Each of these songs underscored the vamp's outsider status. Lest some mistranslation occur, lest the audience suspect that this was a lesson that was being offered, the song of forgetfulness always took place in suspect territory, such as a bar or a den. The tunes were generally western and the dancer was also dressed to establish that she was from the fringes. In *Chhote Nawaab*, Sophie wears a white shirt with Cossack sleeves, becomingly unbuttoned to show some cleavage, and a dark skirt, while the heroine wears saris throughout the film. In *Gumnaam*, Kitty Kelly wears a swimsuit while Asha is in a cream salwar and churidhar. In *Vaasna*, Helen's Arabian outfit gets some help from Mexican sidekicks and a pink woman puffing on a cigarette, all placed there to emphasize that this is firmly outside the ambit of Indian culture. In *Adhikaar*, she is wearing a backless black dress with a blaze of silver and purple sequins on it as Shyam (Biswajeet) downs alcohol to forget the grief occasioned by what he thinks is Radha's (Nazima) betrayal.

What the vamp describes as pain—gham, bekhudi—is the real world. Her solace is illusory and temporary and she admits it, but also points to the illusory nature of the world, to the fleeting pleasures of existence. The equation in the vamp's world is clear: the nation, society, family, all demand that we suffer to maintain the social fabric; western culture offers the impermanence of pleasure and the cult of the self. We must choose between the two. Popular cinema in India has never left us in any doubt about what we must choose. Helen was the reward, in advance, for that choice.

SONG OF MOCKERY

The lust object knows that she is lusted after. She knows that the men who have gathered to watch her are stripping her with their eyes. This means that she has power over them and this translates into a certain kind of mockery. Nowhere is this clearer than in Tina's (Helen) first cabaret in *Tum Haseen, Main Jawaan*.

The song has Tina, dressed in a silver gown and silver shoes, walking into a fountain. She emerges shivering, and bends over one of the patrons near the ramp and sneezes, *Aaachee*. She dances over to another patron, grabs his handkerchief, sneezes into it and returns it to him. Then the song begins: *Chhee meri jaan, chheee* (Yuck, my love, yuck).

Mockery was also often directed at the institution of love. In *Kathputhli*, Helen as Roma sings of a variety of lovers, none of whom are willing to do much more than make extravagant promises. Although the song begins with the usual paean to the power of love—*Jeena kaisa? Oh pyaar bina jeena kaisa?* (What is life without love?)—the narrative between the verses talks of the bank manager who has fallen in love with her bank balance, the metaphoric Majnun who is willing to die for love of her but will not risk getting wet in the rain.

In *Anamika*, the *Aaj ki raat koi aane ko hai* number offers a story within a story in which Miss Ruby awaits her lover in an European square, an echo of the *Piya tu ab to aa ja* song in *Caravan*. She is wearing a mackintosh and a hat and a pink dress over pink panties (which we see when she twirls excitedly). She is stalked by an enthusiastic hood who tries whipping her with his mac. She is rescued by the police, but then it starts raining. Wet, she splashes water and sings: *Aisa na ho loot jaaye re tera pyaar* (Beware, you might lose your love). The hood returns and forces her into a telephone booth. The camera cuts away but when it returns, Miss Ruby is lying inside the booth, post-coital, drunk, a little battered but satisfied. And when her love arrives, they dance together again, as if she is suggesting that a little rough use does her no harm, and she is willing to return to the arms of the lover she was waiting for before the hoodlum had his way with her.

A more direct song of mockery occurs in *Dus Lakh*, where Helen as Kitty Williams mocks the ageing Om Prakash for his choice of wife in *Agre ke lala*. However, this kind of song was comparatively rare because it meant that the Helen figure would have to ally herself with the beliefs and values of bourgeois society. In this case, the song presages the conversion of Kitty Williams into a nurse who rejects all that is bad about her Anglo-Indian roots (which is just about everything) and serves humanity.

SONG OF SELF-ADULATION

If no one else would praise the attractions of the vamp, either in words or in verse, either by giving in to her charms or noticing them, it obviously fell to her to call attention to them. Since this type of song was also a reflection of the vamp in the eyes of the world, it also fell to her to execute the motions of an admiring male audience. Hence most of these dances use a certain repertoire of sexual gestures, from coyness (her hands splayed and folded over the crotch) to self-appreciation (stroking arms or hips) to simulated stimulation (hands in hair, at lips, near breasts).

In the costume drama *Insaaf* (1956), Helen entertains a band of revolutionaries who have turned against their rulers. Her song extols her own virtues: *Jab se aayi jawaani/ Hui duniya deewaani/ Mera ghar se nikalna mushqil hua* (Ever since I grew up/ The world has been in love with me/ Now leaving the house has become difficult). In *Faisla* (1965), she performs a dance while the hero (Jugal Kishore) is being initiated into the rites of manhood (smoking and drinking) by an enemy (Jeevan). He is also in the process of falling in love—not with Helen, of course, though she'll have him know that nothing compares to her: dancing to an all-female orchestra, she sings,

Ee-aa-ee-aa-oh/ Ee-aa-ee-aa-oh/ Mein hoon madam baawri/ Surat meri saawri/ Sabse haseen sabse judaa (Ee-aa-ee-aa-oh/ I am carefree, I'm unique/ I am more beautiful than anyone else). And in the *Aur mera naam hai Jameela* number from *Night in London*, she is even less modest: ...*main jis gali se bhi guzree qayamat hui/ Log nazren bichhane lage* (I caused a sensation in every street that I walked/ The world had eyes only for me).

Right up to *Jhootha Kahin Ka* (1979) she was still at it. Ajay (Rishi Kapoor) is a poor mechanic. He pretends to be a millionaire when he meets Sheetal (Neetu Singh) who is extremely wealthy. He takes her to see a cabaret and here, among bodybuilders lifting weights and flexing muscles in strobe lights, Helen comes sliding down a ramp, her knees crossed like a Varga girl. She sings: *Dekho mera jaadu/ Pal mein kar doon bekaabu/ Aankhen do paimaane/ In mein doobe deewaane* (Watch me work my magic/ In seconds, I'll make them lose control/ My eyes are wine glasses/ Men drown in my eyes). Through the song, she strolls among the bodybuilders, her eyes full of admiration. The refrain strays into double entendre territory: *Bade bade loot gaye/ Khade khade loot gaye* (The big have been defeated/ The erect have been deflated).

SONG OF MISDIRECTION

These are songs generally sung when the moll wants to distract the hero from his purpose, which is generally to find out something about the gang for which she works.

Her misdirections never did work sufficiently. Certainly not at the club in *Night Club* (1958), a front for gold smuggling. A young police officer planted there by Kishore (Ashok Kumar) has been murdered and his sister, Bindu (Kamini Kaushal), decides to try and work her way into the gang so that she can destroy it. Kishore disapproves but cannot stop her and so decides to go and investigate himself and finds Helen dancing: *Kahaan phir hum, kaahan phir tum/ Kahaan yeh raatein/ Dhadakte dil se ho jaayen zara do baatein* (Who knows where we'll be tomorrow/ Where such nights again/ Let our hearts converse tonight). She has hardly any effect on him.

In *Shikar* (1968), as Vera, Helen tries to seduce the policeman (Sanjeev Kumar) who has come to her home to search for incriminating evidence of her involvement in the murder of her boss. She strips off her pink negligee (so suitable for a single girl at home), and reveals a glittery blue dress (so suitable for distracting a policeman). The song is overtly seductive—*Mere paas aa, kidhar khayaal hai/ Aankh se aankh to mila, kidhar khayaal hai* (Come to me, why do your thoughts wander?/ Let your eyes meet mine, why do your thoughts wander?)—but it fails.

In *Deewangee* (1976), she has an even more evil purpose. Shekhar (Shashi Kapoor) has got hold of a stash of diamonds from a gang. The gang kidnaps his wife Kanchan (Zeenat Aman) and his son. He has left the diamonds with his friend Harry (Ranjit) who is in love with Kitty (Helen). Kitty has always rejected Harry because he is poor. When she discovers that he has the diamonds in his possession, she subverts him, throwing herself into his arms, telling him that he and his diamonds have won her. Shekhar is waiting for the bag when Kitty sashays in, telling him that Harry has gone for the keys of the locker and that he (Harry) has told her to entertain him (Shekhar) in the interim. *Meri jawaani kare ishaare/ Tujhe bulaaye, tujhe pukaare* (My youth beckons you, calls out to you) she sings. This is a classic song of misdirection, a distraction while Harry gets away with the diamonds. Not for long, of course.

The only exception to this rule happens in *Ram Balram* (1980), in which Helen, who had by then been dancing for thirty years, matched steps with someone at least thirty years her junior. She is only the mother of one of the heroines, but when push comes to shove and three of the principals have been locked in the hold of a ship by a deranged criminal on crutches—Jagatpal (Ajit)—she gamely tucks her pallu in and begins to dance. The song? *Balram ne bahut samjhaaya/ Ram ne dhokha khaaya/ Ab Ram hi jaan bachaaye/ Beda paar lagaaye*

(Balram advised caution/ But Ram was deceived/ Now Ram alone can rescue us). Through a crack in the ceiling we see that it is the reformed kothewaali Tara (Helen) who offers the men the glad eye and then a big deliberate wink. Madhu (Zeenat Aman) offers a flying kiss but it is Tara's cleavage we see through the portholes, a tribute to her agelessness. The intention of the song is made explicit with *Jab tak Ram ki seh na aaye, gaate raho yeh gaana* (Until Ram brings help, keep singing). This is one of the odd times when Helen is exclusively on the side of right, but then, it was already the beginning of her iconization—she is even given grey hair.

THE CLIMACTIC SONG

In *Jaali Note* (1960), a feast of Helen songs despite the presence of Madhubala, Miss Lily makes her last appearance framed in a doorway. She switches off the lights to announce her presence, thus also symbolically announcing the comeuppance of the gang of counterfeiters. She sings: *Nigaahon ne pheka hai/ Panje pe chakka/ Balam tera mera/ Pyaar hua pakka* (My eyes have trumped you; my love, you and I are now an item), though we can't be sure to whom this is addressed. The song serves only to introduce the final battle between good and evil.

The climactic song was more than a punctuation mark announcing the end of the film. Often it was used to emphasize the evil of the villain who would bring on the dancing girls at the point at which the hero was suspended between life and death, thus providing an interesting contrast between Eros and Thanatos and underlining his sadism. Besides that, it filled out the contours of the climax, allowed time for ropes to be gnawed through, police to be called or diversions to be organized.

Khel Khilari Ka (1977) has two brothers separated after a village fair, although they have matching Shiva tattoos. Their father is killed and their sister raped as they watch. They grow up into Raja (Dharmendra) and Dhruv (Uday

Chandra). United by their common quest for revenge, they arrive at the rapist's den. They are both captured. Dhruv is dangled over burning coals and Raja has to keep the pressure on the pulley or he dies. The doors of the den open and Helen comes dancing in, asking: *Pyaar bada hai ya jaan badi hai/ Baazi ab dono ki ladi hai* (Which is greater, love or life?/ Today, the two must compete).

Towards the end of *Besharam* (1978), all the villains who have conspired to rid Ramu (Amitabh Bachchan) of his father, his sister and his mother are having a meeting. Ramu has infiltrated the gang as a South African millionaire interested in smuggling diamonds. The police need the meeting to go on past two a.m., for reasons unknown. One might assume that Ramu would do the honours here but for some reason this is where Helen, assisted by another dancer, makes her appearance: *Tum kitne bhi chehere badlo yahaan/ Tum ban jaao beherupiye/ Hum ko dhoka nahin de sakoge magar/ Arre humne khud jaane kitnon ko dhokhe diye* (However many faces you change, however much you try to hide/ You won't be able to fool us/ We've lost track of how many we've fooled). Strangely, the obvious inference of this song—that he has been unmasked—escapes Ramu. Perhaps this is in unconscious tribute to Helen, who has stopped smiling but is in superb physical shape under the black and silver outfit.

THE REPLACEMENT HEROINE

This may only be guesswork but it is often possible to spot Helen dancing where the heroine was unable to. In *Karwa Chouth*, as we've seen, Helen extols the virtues of the fast for husbands when by every logic the heroine should have done this. In *Jalan* (1978), the story revolves around Ambika's (Ambika Johar) relationship with her father Seth Deendayal (I.S. Johar), who has just abandoned her mother for a life of glamour. He even runs a magazine called *Glamour*, staffed entirely by his women. At the end, Ambika has to shock him by turning herself, suitably masked, into one of the women he lusts after. When she dances *Mere hothon ka jaam* (The wine of my lips) in a nightclub where he has brought his bevy of beauties, it becomes painfully clear that she cannot dance, and Helen does most of the moving and shaking.

In *Awaara Abdulla* (1963)—a film that can only be called a costume drama if you account for the fact that costumes ranging from Zorro to Ancient Rome are involved—the heroine Shahnaz (Praveen Chowdhury) was once again unable to dance. The film centres round Shera (Dara Singh) who is a prince in exile. When he learns that he has the right to the throne, he dresses up like The Lone Ranger and heads into town to wrestle with John de Silva (Wrestling Champion of Europe) and Ad Rod Goa (Wrestling Champion of the West Indies). He is arrested and made to support a huge circular platform on which Zarina (Helen) dances for the younger prince (Chandrashekhar): *Kahaan se laayega yeh husn yeh shabaab koi/ Zamaane bhar mein nahin aapka jawaab koi* (Where will we find such beauty/ There is none to match you in this world). This is fairly standard. But it is odd that when Shahnaz is asked to dance to save the life of her beloved, Shera, she needs support from Helen.

In *Noor Jehan* (1967), Helen, as Dilruba, gets to sing two songs that reflect the love between Mehr-un-nissa (Meena Kumari) and Salim (Pradeep Kumar). In the first, she has introduced the idea of love to the Prince in *Mohabbat ho gayi mere meherbaan ko/ Kisi na-meherbaan se* (My patron is in love with someone who doesn't care). She engineers further meetings with Mehr-un-nissa and when the palace turns against them, she also sings their defiance: *Aa gaya lab pe afsana-e-aashiqui/ Ab kisise fasaane ki parvaah nahin/ Hum unse mohabbat kiye jaayenge/ Ab is zamaane ki parvaah nahin* (I will tell you a story of love/ I will tell it with no thought of the consequences/ I will love him with not a care for what the world thinks). It is likely that Meena Kumari was unable or unwilling to dance at that stage in her career, so dance directors P.L. Raj, Sohanlal and Satyanarayan had to make do with Helen, who also dances when Mehr-un-nissa recites at the spring festival: *Sharaabi, sharaabi yeh saawan ka mausam/ Khuda ki kasam, khubsoorat na hota/ Agar is me rang-e-mohabhat na hota* (This intoxicating summer would be without beauty, were there no love in the air).

Seven

She Was Dying to Become a Good Girl

Shaayad in baazuon mein hone ki keemat maut thi. Dekho—maine keemat chuka di, Rocky...Rocky...Main mujrim nahin hoon, Rocky...mera jurm...sirf tumhaara pyaar hai.
(Perhaps the price of your embrace was death. Look—I've paid the price, Rocky...Rocky...I'm not a criminal, Rocky...my crime... was only that I loved you.)

—Helen as Ruby in *Teesri Manzil* (1966)

Helen is presented as Manoj Kumar's fiancée in the first few scenes of the 1964 thriller *Woh Kaun Thi*. And the audience already knows, at some instinctive level, that this is some kind of mistake.

It isn't just that it is Helen; it's the way she is presented. For starters, she seems to dance for a living. If she has a pressing reason and is shown to refuse money and gifts from greasy bounders, the audience might still allow itself to believe that she is a virgin. But this Helen is also Catholic—her name is Jenny. Again, as we have seen, this is often but not always a mortal sin. However, when all this is coupled with the fact that she wears skirts and shirts and has short hair, our sense of wrongness increases. The heroine of the pre-1990s Hindi film never has short hair. She can wear a short wig for purposes of deception (to play a prank, to infiltrate the villain's den). She may also sport it for a song or two in early scenes when she is an unreconstructed young woman, but not after she has experienced the immediate alchemy of love and is about to be married. Even shoulder-length hair is permissible. But a pageboy combined with shirts and skirts? Something is certainly wrong.

Besides, even before Jenny makes her entrance, we have been given a clue that Manoj Kumar is meant for more hirsute things. The opening scene has him driving through a storm when his car is stopped by a woman in white with long hair (Sadhana). When she gets into his car, his windscreen wipers stop. Later, she asks to be let off at a cemetery and the gates open magically for her. She then vanishes among the graves, singing the big number, the leitmotif in the film: *Naina barse rimjhim rimjhim* (Tears fall like rain).

In contrast, Helen has two fairly ordinary songs. There's *Tiki riki tiki riki ta-turi* (Nonsense syllables) and *Chhodkar tere pyaar ka daaman/ Yeh bataa de ke hum kidhar jaayen* (Were I to lose your love/ Tell me, where would I go?). When in the latter song she sings, *Hum ko dar hai ki teri baahon mein/ Hum khushi se na aaj mar jaayen* (I fear that in your arms/ I might die of joy), we know what's going to happen. And it does.

She dies.

In *Pagla Kahin Ka* (1970), everyone at the nightclub where Jenny (Helen) dances stresses that she is a good woman. Sujit (Shammi Kapoor) assures us that she is as loyal as she is beautiful. Shyam (Prem Chopra) says it too. However, Jenny herself does not seem quite sure. In an early scene, on the beach, she rises from a dark bed of sand, rises obviously from Sujit's embrace. She wants to leave; he pleads with her to stay a while longer. This is standard romantic stuff, but it is soon escalated when he proposes marriage and she puts him off on the tenuous grounds that as a nightclub dancer she may not be good enough for him. Tenuous because Sujit works in the same nightclub and is an orphan to boot, which in a caste-ridden society gives him only the edge of gender over her.

She then asks what would happen if she left him, if she were to turn unfaithful. He replies that she would not be able to. In a delightful fit of female perversity, she walks away, prompting him to sing: *Tum mujhe yoon bhula na paaoge* (You will not be able to forget me). She is allowed only a single verse of this serenade before we return to the nightclub for the New Year celebration and the title song of the film, *Aashiq hoon ek mehjabeen ka/ Log kahen mujhe pagla kahin ka* (I am in love with a beautiful woman/ So much in love that the world calls me mad).

Later, after Sujit has committed murder to defend Jenny's honour and been acquitted on grounds of an insanity that he fakes, she does turn 'unfaithful'. But only because Shyam has raped her while he was away. This drives Sujit truly mad and he ends up in a mental asylum.

In the asylum, psychiatrist Dr Shalu (Asha Parekh) is at hand to rescue him with some trips to a lake, a faked Jenny, and the complete version of *Tum mujhe yoon...*, as befits the leading lady. When Jenny explains to Dr Shalu the circumstances that forced her to abandon Sujit and marry Shyam, the good doctor has no sympathy and tells her what she should actually have done: Jenny should have killed herself. It may be disconcerting advice from a psychiatrist but it is good advice from a long-haired heroine. All of Jenny's saris—and from the moment of Sujit's arrest she is decorously clad in them—cannot wash away the guilt of her short hair.

So she pays.

She dies.

In *Teesri Manzil*, Helen had a bigger and more significant role than usual. The film begins with a suicide, a woman screaming as she jumps off the third floor of a Mussoorie hotel. Bathed in dark aqueous light, the ghouls gather. A distraught young man runs past the reception. He is stopped in his tracks by a lisped warning from Ruby (Helen), the hotel dancer: *Rocky, tumhen wahan nahin jaana chaahiye* (Rocky, you shouldn't go there)—a warning made more potent by being the first line in the film, by the knowingness of Ruby's tone and the expensive fur in which she is swathed.

A year later, Sunita (Asha Parekh) comes to Mussoorie to take revenge for her sister Rupa. She believes Rupa was seduced and then cast off by Anil Kumar Sona alias Rocky (Shammi Kapoor), the drummer in the hotel's jazz band, causing her to kill herself. Rocky learns of her intentions and disguises his identity. Even as the two begin to fall in love, the story takes an unexpected twist when the police discover that Rupa did not jump off the third floor of the hotel but was pushed.

A love triangle has been set up inside the murder mystery, one in which Sunita's youth and vibrancy will be pitted against the sexual allure of Ruby. (Ruby's allure is showcased in R.D. Burman's brilliant composition—and one of Helen's best songs—*Ai haseena zulfonwaali jaan-e-jahaan*—O beauty of the dark tresses, the love of all the world.) While the mystery does have its moments, we know that Rocky/Sona will choose Sunita. For we know that Ruby is a fallen woman. But her own 'dying confession' at the end, which forms the epigraph of this chapter, is chilling in what it reveals about our attitude to women.

Mujrim? Criminal? Ruby eavesdrops on conversations, intercepts letters, dances in a nightclub and wears black gloves. All these may be social solecisms but do not indicate criminality. We are never sure whether she knew who killed Rupa; if she did and did not reveal it to the police, she might be guilty of obstruction of justice. She certainly does not blackmail Rocky to keep his 'secret', which is not even much of a secret.

Mujrim? Or is that just wrongdoer, moral offender?

Among the other truisms with which Hindi cinema works is the belief that truth sits on the lips of dying men. Or women, even women on the fringes. This, then, is a moment of truth. Helen calls herself a *mujrim* because she is a fallen woman, and as a fallen woman, she must die. Sunita herself says as much earlier in the film: 'When a young woman crosses certain limits in love, the only future she has is death.' The limit here is the loss of virginity. In this archaic moral view, respectable Indian women are either virgins or married. The nightclub dancer who throws herself at the hero is neither, so she must die.

By being constructed as an outsider, the Helen figure had much to say about how we constructed our notions of ourselves.

~

The vamp's world is a fringe world—hence the French appellation of *demi-mondaine*—and from the shadows she blows smoke rings at the status quo. Her womanhood is not linked to her womb; it is linked to her sexuality. The easiest way to establish the heart of gold within the prostitute/dancer is to give her a child as the reason for her to sell her body (Shabana Azmi in *Bhaavna*; Suchitra Sen in *Mamta*; the nameless courtesan who appears briefly in the song *Yeh mahlon, yeh takhton, yeh taajon...* in Guru Dutt's *Pyaasa*). When, without child or other pressing social need (dying mother, ill father, sister to be married, brother to be educated), she offers her body for sale and does not choose death immediately afterwards, she is perceived as cocking a snook at the building blocks of our society: the ordinary heterosexual couple, whose fidelity to each other is, in civilized societies, only an ethical contract. The basic unit of society—the monogamous marriage—is besieged.

The vamp brings in her trail the threat of disruption. Rehabilitation is not an option, for the reformed bad girl is an even bigger problem: what is society to do with her? It is easier, all round, for the bad girl to die or disappear. Thus, death would become a recurring theme in Helen's career.

There are two kinds of death that Hindi films offer. There's death as a reward for stardom—since a death scene is generally a crowd-pleaser and allows for amplified histrionics. In *Roti Kapda aur Makaan*, Manoj Kumar had an interminably long death scene. In *Sholay*, Amitabh Bachchan dies with a panache that makes the remaining few last scenes of the film a let-down. In *Muqaddar ka Sikandar*, a deathfest, first Rekha, a courtesan, kills herself to deny Amitabh contact; then Amitabh kills her other suitor, Amjad Khan; and finally Amitabh himself dies spectacularly, leaving the pallid Raakhee to the second-string Vinod Khanna.

The bad girl's death was never in the same league. It was of the other kind. She didn't get a speech or suitable weepy music with which to end her screen time. She was simply cleared away by a bullet other such quick device.

It should be apparent by now that there is only one type of bad girl: the sexually fallen woman who did not have the moral fibre to kill herself. In *Bombay 405 Miles* (1980), Helen dies because she abandons her child and her husband for a life of ease as moll to a rapist, kidnapper and killer. Of course, Pran, the husband she abandons, is no saint either. He blackmails people by calling them up and telling them that he knows their secrets. But then, in the clearly defined morality of Hindi cinema, redemption often awaits the man who sins, should he repent in time. Bad girls have no such luck. They are either effaced by a careless script or die.

But even here it is possible to discern two separate kinds of death.

The first kind of death was simply Nemesis catching up with the wrongdoer. In these films, the Helen character was portrayed as unequivocally evil. Through the course of the tortuous plot of *Love and Murder* (1966), we gather that Helen (who does not even merit a name) belongs to a gang which is run by a psychedelic eye. One of the members of the gang helps rob a bank and then makes off with the money. The gang assumes that his sister Gita (Jaymala) has it. Since Gita has protection in the form of Ranjit (Ramesh Deo), they send Helen to vamp him, which she duly does, singing: *Mere dil, meri jaan/ Tu keh de to kar daaloon/ Main dil ka haal bayaan* (My love, just say the word/ And I'll tell you what's in my heart). In turn, Ranjit joins the gang and romances Helen to get information. It becomes obvious that Helen is the kind of woman who wants the money for herself, and is willing to double-cross the gang *and* Ranjit. Eventually everything is sorted out, but not before Helen has died, tortured by Ranjit who ties her to a strange contraption that administers shocks and asphyxiates her simultaneously. One might say she had it coming: a gang member, a double-crosser both in love and commerce.

In *Nasihat* (1967), Pinky (Helen) claims that not only can she dance, she can also make others dance to her tune. This dull film, which has Dara Singh playing the villain who dies and is replaced by the lookalike hero, could not even be rescued by Helen's red gloves, her supporting chorus of orange miniskirts and the song *Boy-oh-boy/ Mujhko deewaana na kar/ Aa mere kareeb aa* (Boy-o-boy, do not madden me/ Come, come close to me). A gang-member, Pinky makes the fatal mistake of keeping a diary with which she blackmails the uber-boss (a cut-price version of the villain from *Diamonds Are Forever*) and gets killed for her pains.

Likewise, in *Preetam* (1971), Helen plays Sarita, with not a single redeeming feature, not even the excuse of being an outsider—Catholic, Anglo-Indian. Preetam (Shammi Kapoor) has been adopted after his murderous and abusive father was arrested and his mother died. He grows up into a good-natured wastrel while the true son of the family, Anil (Vinod Khanna), grows up into an intelligent and studious young man. Only, he isn't intelligent enough to see through Sarita, his lady love, a cabaret artiste and part of a gang run by Preetam's biological father who wants to destroy the family.

Anil dies before he and Sarita can be married. Quick on the uptake, Sarita claims to be carrying Anil's child and threatens suicide. Preetam agrees to sacrifice his love for Sharan (Leena Chandavarkar) to keep the family honour intact, especially since he owes the family for adopting him. On the wedding night, Sarita should be sitting demurely on a flower-strewn bed, covered in her red sari. Instead here she is, stepping out of the bathroom wearing a red robe. She throws it open with a flourish—for us, because Preetam is asleep—and reveals a short red nightdress, the breasts accentuated in black sequins. She turns, again for us, and unzips her nightdress until we are quite sure that she is wearing nothing else underneath it. Then she climbs into bed with Preetam and awakens him.

When he turns her down, she urges: *Come darling, aaj ki raat bhi koi sharam karta hai?* (Who feels shame on a night like this?). She tells him the truth: Anil never touched her. She tells him a lie: she hated Anil and loved him (Preetam) from the first. He slaps her but she persists and gets in the last word. 'Leave the door open, in case you change your mind,' she says. 'I'll be waiting.'

Sarita harasses the family, smoking, drinking, refusing to divorce Preetam with an unanswerable question to her mother-in-law: 'For an Indian woman, isn't it a crime to even think of divorce?'

Here is the crime then: a sneaky attack on the ideal Indian woman and therefore on marriage. Naturally, she deserved her death.

Instances can be repeated endlessly. In *Mere Jeevan Saathi* (1972), Kamini kidnaps the hero when he is unconscious, keeps him captive in her palace, whips him when he will not play the piano for her, and tries to turn him into a toy boy. Many of these acts may be criminal but the real crime is her early declaration in the film that she is a hunter and that the more intelligent and dangerous the prey, the more the kill excites her. The temporary softening in the delirious panting of *Aao na gale lagaalo na* (Come hold me) is nullified by her exhilaration at the idea of pursuing on horseback a blind man who is on foot. When she plunges to her death off a cliff, it is clear to anyone that she is being punished for her sexual predatoriness.

The second kind of death reserved for the bad girl was expiatory. Here the vamp was generally portrayed as a good woman gone astray. For instance, in *Pyaar Kiya To Darna Kya* (1964), Nisha (Helen) is only a cat's paw in a larger game of revenge being played by Jeevan (Pran). She is a dancer in his hotel and is in love with him. He wants her help in taking revenge against the rich boy and spoilt brat Rajesh (Shammi Kapoor) who, he wrongly believes, has insulted him by helping his sister marry a servant.

After they've succeeded in their plan, Nisha reminds Jeevan of his promise. He refuses to marry her and so she spills the beans to Rajesh. In a rage, Rajesh beats Jeevan up. Nisha arrives after Jeevan has been thrashed senseless and revives him with a glass of water. He shoots her, but she has already called the police. Her death here is an expiation of her connivance against the hero; it is not punishment, for she acted out of an honourable motive: love.

In *CID 909* (1967), we're in James Bond territory, with Feroze Khan playing the code-numbered secret agent of the title. Indian scientists, Lord love 'em, have invented a formula that will maintain international peace (?) and which has been pinched by a gang of spies (?!). The only problem is that the formula is in code. Sophia (Helen) tells her fellow gangsters that only two people can decode it: a famous professor and his daughter Reshma (Mumtaz), coincidentally and fortunately, Sophia's friend.

And so Sophia arrives at Reshma's house and invites her to her last performance in the city. CID 909 also turns up to watch over Reshma, which is part of his duties. Dressed in High Arabian Fantasy, Sophia kisses a glass and lilts: *Yaar badshah, yaar dilruba/ Kaatil aankhonwaale/ Oh dilbar matwaale/ Dil hai tere hawaale* (My lover, my king/ Your eyes are deadly/ My heart is your captive).

Later, Sophia tries to get hold of the formula herself. She is shot by the gang leader for this temerity, but not before she has released CID 909 and Reshma from captivity—last-minute proof that she was not entirely black-hearted. Again, therefore, she dies in expiation.

In *Hum Tum Aur Woh* (1971), Anita (Helen) leaves her poor husband Mahendranath (Ashok Kumar) because she wants a better life. Naturally, that very night he is offered a job in Singapore where we know he will make his fortune. We also know that Anita's new life will founder. It does. She turns into Lily, further evidence of her descent, since the new Catholic name indicates not just her new profession, that of a dancer, but also a renunciation of her mainstream identity.

The film revolves around an attempt to kill off Ashok Kumar who wants to share his profits with his workers. When he is bundled off to Shimla, the gang follows and so does Lily, now inveigled into the scheme of murder. As part of the gang's ultimate plan (too complicated to explain here), the heroine of the film, Aarti (Bharti), has also been kidnapped; she is the love interest of Mahendranath's nephew Vijay (Vinod Khanna), the hero. Aarti is about to be disfigured when Lily—who has by now discovered that the marked man is the husband she so thoughtlessly rejected—arrives in a frightful wig, white boa and red dress at the top of the stairs, waving a whisky bottle and singing: *Husn agar zid pe aa jaaye/ Baat kisiki na mane, na man* (When beauty turns stubborn/ Nothing will turn it aside).

She gets the men drunk, cuts the heroine loose and in so doing seals her own fate. The gang now knows that she has gone over to the other side. She dies in Mahendranath's arms. It is thus made clear that she was not an entirely mercenary woman without a heart. She is not even a fallen woman—earlier in the film we have seen her refuse a suspicious 'dinner appointment' with an admirer. However, she was misguided enough to abandon her husband. We are allowed to feel sorry for her but forgiveness and rehabilitation are more than can be expected.

In *Upaasna* (1971), Julie/Lily kills but she does so out of a moral reason. When we meet her, she is Lily, and doing one of her most sexually outrageous dances while Mohan (Sanjay Khan) is trying to drown his sorrows in her nightclub—he has been publicly dumped by the love of his life, Kiran (Mumtaz). Lily begins in a bathtub, blowing foam away. Then she steps out in a bikini, dries herself, gets into a pink dress with two panels held together by strings and begins the impersonal seduction of the cabaret.

Hi sweetheart, she breathes at a random drinker and then laughs. *Sharam aati hai*? (Are you shy?)

To Mohan: *Aao darling, mere saath* dance *karo* (Come and dance with me, darling).

To the accompaniment of flickering strobe lights and high-pitched squeals, she goes into a spectacular frenzy that ends with her in a heap on the floor. A huge brazen image of an uber-man wearing a loincloth appears. She has lost many of her clothes again and is in another bikini with a blonde wig and a feathery head dress. The song is also provocative: *Oh meri jawaani pyaar ko tarse/ Ang ang se masti barse/ Mujhko bana le mehboob* (My youth yearns for love/ Mischief pours from my body/ Make me your love). Most of the song is spent courting this bronzed statue, stroking its body, squirming on the floor in front of it, thrusting her pelvis up repeatedly until the statue cracks and a man steps out.

Later Lily takes the drunk Mohan home. There she reveals that she was in college with him, where she was known as Julie. She has had a rough life, she tells him, but adds that she is still fighting, although she is now a single mother with a child in boarding school. Inspired by this, he promises to try and put his life together. She offers to pray for him, and church bells ring.

In a situation that prefigures *Imaan Dharam,* which we shall discuss shortly, Mohan offers to play father. This works out rather nicely for everyone until Mohan sees Julie's picture in the house of the ganglord.

Dressed in a white sari (clearly, to inspire our confidence in her story), Julie confesses that the ganglord is the missing father of her child; he promised her marriage, got her pregnant and then abandoned her. She also confesses that she killed him sometime later in order to protect a girl he was trying to rape. We know already that Kiran was forced by the same ganglord to smuggle diamonds and dump Mohan. We also know that he tried to rape her, and that she stabbed him and believing herself to be a murderer, has taken shelter in the house of Mohan's brother Ram (Feroze Khan) who is well on the way to falling in love with her.

This is economical. At one stroke, it clears Kiran of her guilt and sets the stage for the reunion of the lovers. Here it is also interesting to contrast the way Julie dies with the way Ram dies. Julie is on her way to court to give evidence that will clear Kiran. She is shot outside the court and dies with a quick choke and gasp. Ram and Mohan give chase. Ram fights the smugglers and dies in Mohan's arms after a long speech that makes everyone cry.

Imaan Dharam (1977) was supposed to be Helen's big number, playing heroine to the One Man Industry. It is likely that Salim Khan, who co-scripted the film—and with whom Helen was then involved—managed to get this past the film's producer because there were two other couples—Shashi Kapoor/ Rekha and Sanjeev Kumar/Aparna Sen—offering star support to this unlikely combination. Besides, after *Deewar*, it was accepted that sexual transgression could be part of the Bachchan persona. Also that it little mattered who the heroine was in a film that starred Amitabh Bachchan.

In the film, Ahmed Raza (Bachchan) is a small-time hood who earns his living by playing witness for hire. One day, he is hired by Jenny Francis (Helen), a drunken prostitute, to play father to her daughter who wants to know who her father is—'*Sawaal jiska jawaab mere paas sachmuch nahin hai* (A question to which I truly have no answer).' This makes it clear that the child is not the cause of the prostitution but a by-product of it.

The relationship with the child civilizes both of them, which is in keeping with the rest of the film, where everyone seems to ascend to virtue, except for Sanjeev Kumar and Aparna Sen, who are already atop Mount Righteous. Jenny gives up drinking; Ahmed swears off lying (she is wearing white when he does so).

He offers to marry her but just before that can happen, she falls ill. He is sitting by her bed, regaling her with stories that are making her laugh. She laughs herself into a seizure caused by spurious medicines that have been created by the very people Ahmed Raza defends with his lies. She leaves him in charge of the child and pays for her sins. However, here Helen's death is elevated to star status. She gets a proper scene, a little irony and a touch of pathos.

Perhaps because of the failure of *Imaan Dharam*, a flop that rocked the industry, or because of the whims of the editor, *Dostaana* (1980), the other film into which Salim wrote Helen, had her dying a quick death again—unsplendid, unremarked.

We first meet Sylvia leaning on a golf club and applauding prettily as the smuggler makes his shots. *Beautiful shot!* she coos. *Main mar gayi*! (I just died!)

Inspector Vijay Verma (Amitabh Bachchan) is hot on the trail of the smuggler and his men. His informant is John D'Souza (Pran), a man with a grudge against smugglers. As an honest checkpost official, he had once refused a bribe; the smuggler sent his men to kill his wife and cripple his son. Sylvia is his sister, who has infiltrated the smuggler's gang. For all her goodness and courage, when she is caught at it, she has time enough only to give us this nugget of information before she dies.

Most of Helen's other deaths were retributive. They became something of a habit, so that her halfway decent (sympathetic to heroine's jealousy), halfway decadent (willing to sacrifice her love for the hero for a diamond necklace) character Lucy in *Bairaag* ends up dead almost as an afterthought. But then, there were three Dilip Kumars (a father and two sons) also cluttering up this messy film.

Helen was dying right up to *Sannata* (1981), where her end comes in a bathtub, but only after she finishes singing an abysmal song, its refrain in English: 'Superman, Superman, you know how much I love you, you know how much I care for you.'

It would take iconic status, as we shall see, to restore her to a death that was cinematically significant.

Eight

The Comic Comes Courting

Kaisa mulga hai re sharmila!/ Tujhse to mulgi bhali.
(What a shy little boy you are!/ A girl would be better than you.)

—Lyrics from Helen's song
in *Inkaar* (1977)

In one of those scenes that stick in your head, Vijay (Rajesh Khanna) walks into his borrowed bedroom in *Dil Daulat Duniya* (1972) and begins a conversation with a statue of Cupid. He asks the Prem Devta—as he refers to the chubby cherub—whether 'she' loves him. He means the woman he loves, Roopa (Sadhana). A female voice answers that she does. He looks around and finds Rita (Helen) perched on his cupboard. Since she has already shown signs of infatuation—on meeting him, an image of Rajesh Khanna the superstar pops into her head—it is safe to assume that in her reply she is referring not to Roopa but to herself.

'What are you doing on my cupboard?' Vijay asks reasonably enough.

'If Romeo can climb on to Juliet's balcony, why can't Rita climb on to your cupboard?' she retorts. As a logical answer, this leaves something to be desired. She compounds the confusion by announcing that she has read his love letter.

'What love letter?' he asks, since he has written none, not in this film anyway.

'Your song,' she says. '*Gaana to dil ka postman hai, postman* (A song is the postman of the heart).'

But perhaps we should begin at the beginning. Udhaarchand Shikaarpuri (Om Prakash) meets Vijay and Raju (Agha) who have just spent the night in a park after being evicted for not paying their rent. He takes pity on them and brings them to the house in which he is squatting. Raju brings in his family, which includes his wife, his child and his sister, Rita.

Roopa, whose house it actually is, comes home and discovers the intruders but chooses to pretend that she too is poor and had only entered the house to steal some clothes for a job interview. She persuades her parents to join in the charade as well—but that's a separate, convoluted story. What should concern us here is that Vijay and Roopa fall in love with each other. And Rita falls in love with Vijay.

Almost as soon as she has moved into the house, Rita has a bath. We only see her fingers first, playing in the water spurting from the showerhead. Her hair is done up, her shoulders bare and her toes are kicking up a froth in the water. All these are sexualized actions, meant to establish her as a good-time girl. She begins to sing.

Rita: *Masti aur jawaani ho/ Umar badi mastani ho/ Aur dil mein beimaani ho/ To phir pyaar hoga* (Where there's mischief and youth/ An age without a care/ And a heart that is a rascal/ There love will blossom).

Vijay: *Bilkul* (Of course).

He seems to be sitting in a swivel chair next to her bath tub. This seems bizarre, till you realize it is only a split screen meant to tantalize.

Rita: *Ikraar bhi hoga* (A promise will be made).

Vijay: *Bilkul.*

Rita: *Deedaar bhi hoga* (A glimpse will be snatched).

Vijay: *Bilkul.*

Roopa joins the song in her bedroom. The shift takes

place so that Helen is reduced to a couple of intercut shots after the first verse and we get a lot of Roopa spinning in front of a mirror. The song ends with the screen split three ways, Rita and Roopa echoing '*Bilkul*' simultaneously.

This is the *dil ka postman* to which the lady on the cupboard has referred.

Although Vijay, suave in a seventies' fashion, assists her off the cupboard, she is obviously not meant for him, nor he for her.

Punnoo (Jagdeep) is a neighbour. To establish his stupidity, we meet him fishing in the swimming pool. When he hooks Rita on his line, he falls in love with her and begins a surreal pursuit that involves handcuffing her to himself, hiding in another cupboard, wearing a Groucho Marx mask and demanding that she come to his birthday party which is to be held in another swimming pool.

In the sixties and the seventies, Hindi cinema invariably used swimming pools to establish the youth, the sexual availability and/or the westernization of the characters. Here it is the locus of a confrontation that would be part of Helen's career.

Framed by Jagdeep's arched legs, she begins to dance in a one-piece swim suit covered by a man's white shirt. He leaps, she kicks and thus do they address each other: *Oh meri laraloo/ Main teri puppyloo* (Oh my laraloo, I am your puppyloo).

They waltz and twist in one fell dance step. He tries to bite her thigh, falls into the pool and somersaults underwater. Since this is a comic sequence, as indicated by the lyrics, the movements are jerky, staccato to the point of caricature.

Here, then, is another conundrum: the luscious Helen with her pretty face, shapely body and lovely legs paired with Jagdeep, whose entire repertoire of acting consisted of widening his bulbous eyes, violent grimaces and a series of erratic jerks. Or with Johnny Walker, whose face could never have been described as handsome and whose body never rose above the weedy. Or Mehmood of the broad gestures and broader dialects. Or Rajendranath, who almost always wore shorts, Freudian shorthand for underdeveloped male.

The classic vamp in western cinema made room in her life for men of her choosing: the alpha male, the man she could not have, the strong and silent man or simply the man *she* chose. Her power lay in the power she could wield over these men coupled with the suggestion, subtle or otherwise, of insatiability arising partly out of biology and partly out of psychopathology.

With Helen, things were a little different.

In *O Tera Kya Kehna* (1959), Helen (unnamed) describes mockingly practically all the men who would woo her as second lead: *Hero-cut baal hain/ Aawaara-cut*-pant;/ *Reshmi roomal mein/ Chavanni-waala scent* (His hair is cut in filmi fashion/ His trousers are Chaplinesque;/ He carries a silk handkerchief/ Soaked in cheap scent). In the song, she exercises her power over her male admirers in a direct manner: she dismisses them with a slipper.

Ironically, Hindi cinema allowed the vamp this power only in the metaphoric dreamscape of the cabaret and that too only where it did not touch the lives of the principals. Cardboard men (the male extras and dancers) would routinely be felled by the power of Helen-as-femme-fatale. Right from *Baarish*, which started her off, she was knocking men over. The lyrics were generally self-adulatory, the sorceress exulting in her own power and the helplessness of men confronted with it. And yet we have seen that in her relationship with the only male that counted—the male lead—she always failed. She also often failed with the villains. Her successes were among the figures of fun.

But if the figure of fun were to occupy centrestage—as the comic genius Kishore Kumar often did when he was acting—she would again be relegated to the sidelines. In both the songs that she shares with Kishore Kumar that I know of, she is eclipsed by his manic energy. In *Jaalsaaz* (1959), her song appears to have no connection to the rest of the plot, which involves murder, misplaced heirs, pretenders to a fortune and suchlike. Sunderdas (Pran) wants to acquire a fortune by transplanting a boy from the streets as the heir in a family that has had the not uncommon misfortune of misplacing a son. He decides that Shankar (Kishore Kumar) would make a good pretender to the throne despite some regrettable tendencies such as wearing a hen as a hat. He colludes with a faithful retainer of the family, who needs money for his sick mother's medicines. The retainer also has a sister, Meera (Mala Sinha), with whom Kishore falls in love. Later Sunderdas reneges and does not pay the retainer. In the ensuing scuffle, Sunderdas's partner gets shot. Sunderdas encourages the man to escape but plants his wallet at the crime scene so that he will be identified.

Poof.

Helen springs up, literally out of the bottom of the screen, with two balls of fluff in her hair. For some reason Kishore Kumar is also present, cuddling his coat. He sings: *Hip hip ho ho hurrah/ Tera har gaana kansura/ Kare koi nahi na pyaar/ Sur badle hazaar* (Hip hip ho ho hurrah/ All your songs are always off tune/ No, no one will love you/ Even if you change a thousand tunes). Through the song, he plucks the dagli (headgear) off a Parsi, grabs a piggyback ride on an innocent bystander, pretends blindness, squeaks and whirls, thoroughly, totally, upstaging Helen.

This continued in *Half Ticket* (1962) in which Vijay (Kishore Kumar) and Helen (unnamed in the film) share a stage. Masquerading as a child so that he can pay less on a train (hence the title), Vijay must elude the villain (Pran) who has slipped a stash of stolen sparklers into Vijay's pocket as a safe place to keep the loot, at least until the train pulls out of Bombay station. In the course of a madcap pursuit that involves several songs and much hopping in and out of railway compartments, Vijay escapes into another escapist space, a stage on which Helen and her 'Cossack' troop are performing a dance to the song *Woh ik nigaah kya mili/ Tabeeyatein machal gayin* (Just a glance from you/ And my heart is running wild).

Vijay is in the archetypal disguise used by generations of Hindi film stars—he turns into a Muslim simply by slapping on a moustache and a beard and wearing an achkan. The disguise does not work, although it is not the moustache that falls off, as it normally does. Here Pran leans down from the rather sturdy rocks of the set and peels it off. Undeterred by discovery, Vijay continues to dance with Helen. A new twist is added in which her stage lover—fat, with a big moustache—starts pursuing him. It is tempting to imagine that both her lovers are faintly ridiculous—one cavorting around the stage and not really intent on her, the other with a huge paunch—but it is useful to remember that fat men at the time were seen as menacing. No one had much use for muscles in cinema before the eroticization of the male physique began with the likes of Sunny Deol in *Sunny* and Salman Khan in every other film. Whenever menacing masculinity was required, the fat men came out of the woodwork, folded their arms and expected respect for the size of their bellies. Here, at least, the lover is not a comic figure, but he is certainly deficient in the looks department.

~

In the old, old story of a pair of lovers rebelling against a wicked tyrant, *Changez Khan* (1957), Helen and Johnny Walker sing in turn:

> Helen: *Husn jawaan ishq jawaan/ Jhoom rahe dono jahaan* (The earth and sky sway/ With the beauty of youth and love).
> Johnny: *Zindagi hai tere liye/ Kuchh to maza le le* (Life is for the living/ Let's have some fun).

While the lyrics may suggest that Johnny Walker is encouraging a young woman to cut loose, her body language implies that she is willing to cut loose with anyone but him. Dance director Badri Prasad gives her a lot of coquetting: delicate shoulder and hip movements, come-hither glances, but also as many avoidance manoeuvres whenever Johnny Walker approaches.

Even when she was not actually paired with the comics, Helen was often called upon to contrast her femininity against their lack of masculinity in a song. Much comedy arises out of the eagerness of the comic for sex, or for a woman. This implies he is a virgin, and therefore that he is immature, since sex is taken as a rite of passage into masculinity. Hence too the way in which the comedians were made to dress: heightened colours, shorts, knickerbockers, all associated with childhood.

In the filler cabaret that comes towards the end of *Aap Ki Khatir* (1977), Sarita (Rekha) lands up at an ersatz or Hindi-film-version of a Goan party. Her obsession with money has got her mixed up with a gang of thieves and she must repay the money she has borrowed to gamble on the stock market in services, here a diamond drop. In the middle of a car-chase, we stop awhile so that Bhola (Asrani, the popular seventies' comedian) and Shola (Helen) may dance on a table:

> Asrani: O *meri Shola, oh meri Shola*
> Helen: O *mere Bhola, oh mere Bhola*

The names are also significant. Shola means flame. Bhola means naïve/innocent. The Othered couple is sexual (she) and retarded (he). The man is Asrani, comedian; the woman is Helen, sex symbol. The man is to be laughed at. The woman is to be leered at (for she, conveniently, belongs to no man, or to a virgin fool). The man represents impotence, and his impotence is underlined by the sexual availability of the object of his desire. Helen's clothes again reflect popular stereotypes of Goan clothing, lots of frills, red and black polka dots, cleavage and leg show. Her hair is a mass of frothing curls. Most of the song is in mid or long shot, with a single close-up in order that she might bite her lip at Asrani.

The implication of this is clear enough. It validates every man in the audience, for all of them, any of them, would have a fair chance if all that stands between them and the flame on the table is a parody of masculinity. And if someone like Helen could love such a twitching mass of nerves, there must be room for every man.

In film after film, comedians ranging from the effete to the unspeakable wooed Helen with frenetic desire, a dreadful parody of the 'real' thing. (Here reality is to be taken as Hindi film reality, which means romantic songs and heroic deeds.) Mehmood as the butler with the odd hair and odder accent in *Gumnaam* would woo Helen, flapping his lungi, in the song *Hum kaale hain to kya hua dilwaale hain/ Hum tere tere tere chaahne wale hain* (What if I'm black, I have a big heart/ And I love you, you, only you). To her, Agha, morose of face, would present his heart in *Maya* (1961). In *Noor Jehan*, Johnny Walker would make clumsy love to her while Mehr-un-nissa and Prince Salim sigh and moan love songs to each other on the banks of the Jamuna. In *Intequam*, she would be paired with the infantile Rajendranath as part of a revenge plan (but the subplot isn't even worked out fully). In one of her most famous numbers, *Mungda mungda, main gud ki dali*, she aims her seductions at the twitching Keshto Mukherjee. Even she doesn't believe he's worthy of her. *Kaisa mulga hai re sharmila!/ Tujhse to mulgi bhali* (What a shy little boy you are!/ A girl would be better than you), she sings.

In *Baazi* (1968), tables are turned. Both Suzie and Lucy Fernandes (Chand Usmani and Helen) are in love with Joe D'Cruz (Johnny Walker) and squabble over him in a dream sequence song: *Ek anaar, do beemaar/ Kaisi uljhan main hai pyaar* (One pill and two patients/ Love is strange). We never know which one he chooses. The love triangle simply gets lost in the action.

~

In a way the world of the comic was also a fractured one. The figure of the comic was borrowed from other traditions—folk theatre, Bombay's Parsi theatre, circus acts involving dwarfs and fat ladies—without any major modifications. Every aspect of the comic had to be funny: his clothes were infantile, his speech was mannered, his face mobile to the point of contortion. The comic could never throw away a line; each one had to be punched in and often underlined with illustrative gestures. The tradition of the vidhushak or decadent Brahmin, whose comic effects were produced by a surface absurdity that masked deeper social comment, had been jettisoned. It was only when a few comedians (I.S. Johar, O.P. Ralhan, Mehmood) achieved some measure of success at the box office and could headline their own productions, that the comic was briefly retrieved from pathetic idiocy.

Often the comic was presented as someone alienated from his Indian roots, a wannabe white man lost in an Indian world. In *Aulad* (1968), Mehmood plays Chamanlal Charlie, an Anglophile. He falls in love with Shobha (Aruna Irani) whom he first sees at her bath in the river. Their first duet together has some interesting moments:

> Mehmood: *Jodi hamaari jamega kaise jaani/ Hum to angrezi, tum ladki Hindustani* (How will it work between us?/ I am British, you're an Indian).
> Aruna Irani: *Tumko bhi mushqil, hamein bhi pareshaani/ Baat maano saiyaan, ban jao Hindustani* (It's difficult for you; it's tiresome for me/ Listen to me, my love, become an Indian).
> Mehmood: *Angrezi mulk mein kitna* romance *hai/ Baahar ka chhokri kitna* advance *hai* (In the land of the

> English, there's so much romance/ Foreign girls are so advanced/forward).

In terms of its sources and in its construction, the vamp's world was different from that of the typical Hindi film comic this song portrays. Her alienation was a different one altogether. But there was much to be said, in terms of economy, for putting these outsiders together.

The comic, by courting the vamp, denied her any real sexual power. It is impossible, for instance, in *Saazish* (1975), to take Madam Lola's (Helen) sexual credentials seriously when she is being wooed by P.K. Murray (Rajendranath) who has the intensity of the truly shameless. He calls her his 'bambina', his '36-26-38', his 'sweetheart', while she lounges at the rail, smoking a cigarette in a long holder and smouldering out at the ripples in the swimming pool. He compliments her with the panache of the puerile: *Tu to gori madam hai/ Chalnewaali tum tum hai* (My white-skinned madam/ You're a horse carriage in fine fettle). However, it turns out that *he* is the carriage, for he gets down on all fours and lets her ride on his back (a position of debasement), a favour she rewards by chucking him into the pool at the end.

Since she gets nowhere with the hero Jai (Dharmendra), has Murray for a beau and even *shares* the only cabaret (a peculiar song whose refrain goes 'How sweet *Dadaji*, how sweet') with the heroine (Saira Banu), she is pulled off any pedestal on which she might have been set by male lust. By giving her Rajendranath as her only swain, it was made clear that he who fell in love with such a woman must be desperate in his lust; it was also made clear that this could be any woman. Classical feminism would maintain that this is true of gender relations: first, elevate the woman into an object of desire and then pull her back down to earth, where she belongs.

The vamp could be importuned at will. Whereas the heroine might slap the face of the importuning male, the characters Helen played rarely responded in this fashion.

They were only allowed a few squeaks of disapproval, a few 'Stupid's, 'Idiot's and 'What nonsense's. The second leads played the game of love but they played it for laughs.

In *Ustadon ke Ustad* (1963), Rita (Helen) belongs to a gang of bank-robbers. She is entrusted with moving the loot but her bag and Dinesh's (Pradeep Kumar) bag get exchanged. He is arrested for the theft and with help from a friend, Pyaare Babu (Johnny Walker), attempts to trace Rita, identifiable by a scar on her hand.

Pyaare spots her and pretends to be a rich African businessman, Hoomba Loomba, who has come to India to find his dream girl (a 'chikki-chikki'). Most vamps were presented as credulous creatures, whose credulity was a concealed moral tale; it generally arose out of greed. Rita is no exception and so off they go, out into the open air, to sing a duet. Since we know that Pyaare is faking love, the natural surroundings do not confer sanctity on the song; rather, they underscore the pretence.

Johnny Walker: *Mere dil ko jiski talaash, maine woh sitamgar pa liya* (My heart has found the sweet torment it sought).

Helen: *Meri har ada pe jo jaan de, maine woh sikandar pa liya* (I've found the conqueror who will give his life for my charms).

Pyaare fails to get her to take off her gloves and so has not seen the scar.

This means another song, but this time in a nightclub which in turn seems to be set in an island paradise with men selling bananas and papayas. Rita appears with a basket in a tree house and descends the stairs, crying, 'Coconuts, coconuts.' She is not pleased to see Pyaare.

Helen: *Maine kahaa tha aana Sunday ko Sunday ko/ Monday ko aaye kyun?* (I told you to come on Sunday, on Sunday/ Why then have you come on Monday?)

Johnny Walker: *Milna jo chaahe dil tumse ji tumse ji/ Tumse to bolo kya karoon?* (My heart longed for a meeting with you, with you/ Tell me then what was I to do?)

Johnny Walker's light-heartedness made nonsense of the lyrics. This was not about a man eager to meet a woman; it was skilful mockery that allowed the audience to participate in the joke against a woman of no substance, a light-skirt whose primary interest in a man was the size of his wallet.

Another reason for this pairing of vamp and comedian lies in the way films were constructed before the age of the multistarrer. The hero and heroine in a film left very little space for anyone else. But even so, what space they did leave was filled by the hero's sidekick and his love interest.

The hero's sidekick was always a professional comedian. In this role, he could offer advice, either good or bad, follow a woman, deliver a letter, tell us a little about the hero's earlier life, and perform all those little jobs for which he had been preparing in folk theatre for several years. The relationship between the two is difficult to define. It was not friendship; it was too unequal, it had far too many elements of condescension in it. The sidekick's prime function was to underscore the hero's masculinity with his own inadequacies. The hero was always brave; the sidekick always ready to give up and dart under the nearest bed or table at the first sign of danger. The hero was always personable; the sidekick either had a tick or a twitch or a squeak or a deformity or all of the above. The hero was always casual about the opposite sex (a casualness that, we should understand, arose out of the calm certainty of being sexually attractive) until the heroine came along; the sidekick was obsessed with his own sex life or lack of it and was willing to take whatever came along. This meant in turn that the sidekick's love interest could be just about anyone, from the fat comedienne Tun Tun to the luscious Helen.

In *Khoon Khoon* (1973), Inspector Anand (Mahendra Sandhu) chases the serial killer Raghu (Danny). His sidekick Pancham (Jagdeep) romances Julie (Helen), the daughter of a constable known here by the pejorative appellation Pandu

(Asit Sen). Her role consists entirely of bemoaning the loss of a sari Pancham has bought for her but which Anand whisks away for his mother. She doesn't even get the dances; those are left to the more frankly sexual Faryal and Padma Khanna.

In terms of the plot, the second leads had different and distinct functions. In *Zindagi* (1964), poverty forces Beena (Vyjayanthimala) to join a dance troupe directed by Gopal (Raj Kumar). The lascivious owner abducts her. She is rescued by Rajan (Rajendra Kumar), a rich young man, who falls in love with her. Jaggu (Mehmood) is his servant: effete, idiotic, the Fool. On Rajan's birthday, the people of the village turn up to dance for him, led by Chameli (Helen). The song, *Ghoongharva mora chham chham baaje* (My anklets beat out a rhythm), allows us to see that Rajan is wealthy and establishes various other characters in the film, including his father and his servitors. Later, when Rajan and Beena have been married and Beena is pregnant, Chameli announces the happy news in a song, *Ek naye mehmaan ke aane ki khabar hai* (A new guest is expected in the house). After Rajan abandons Beena, uncertain about her relationship with Gopal, Jaggu and Chameli try to reunite the lead pair (although it is finally an earthquake that does the trick).

The second leads could also help the hero get revenge, as Rajan (Rajendranath) and Lajwanti (Helen) do in *Dhadkan* (1972). This is a confused story in which the villain Kewal (Rupesh Kumar) kills the lost heir to a fortune and then impersonates him. The heir is reincarnated as a child called Dobby and reveals the truth. Suraj (Sanjay Khan) then decides to drive Kewal mad, and to aid him in this Hamlet-like plan Lajwanti acts out the murder in a cabaret sequence, stopping only to prod Kewal in the shoulder and sing in a syrupy-sweet voice: *Jab tune kuchh na kiya/ Deewaane kyon darta hai?* (When you have done no wrong/ Why are you afraid?)

But most often, the sidekicks were needed to lighten the tone when the melodrama between the leads was getting too heavy. In *Dil Ne Pukara* (1967), for instance, Jyoti (Helen) and Bansi (Mehmood) play comic second fiddles to an elaborate love triangle between Rajan (Sanjay Khan), Asha (Rajashree) and Prakash (Shashi Kapoor).

During the early part of the film, there are high spirits all round since they are in Kashmir. Bansi hides under Jyoti's chair whereupon she pushes him into a lake; Rajan pretends to be a boatman and whisks Asha off for a song. All familiar tropes and figures of Hindi film romance. But unbeknownst to Asha, her father wants her to marry Prakash, an orphan and friend of the family. However, when he hears of her love, Prakash withdraws his suit as a gentleman would.

The drama gets heavy here, so, even as Rajan is trying to get Prakash to disclose the name of the woman the latter loves, Bansi has rubbish emptied on his head by an older man, fights with him and loses. Filthy, he arrives at Jyoti's home to find that her father is the man whom he has fought and lost to.

Some reels beyond this, Rajan has an accident at sea and is given up for dead. Asha's father dies of shock, and Prakash offers the distraught lady consolation and marriage. Then Rajan returns. Heavy drama again, so Bansi provides comic relief by knitting up a sweater with which he pursues women, hoping that it will fit the woman he wants to marry. Which means, any woman. Jyoti and he cavort by a pool, singing a song whose lyrics are completely at odds with their antics: *Is kadar zaalim-o-kaatil, is tarah toda mera dil/ Main kehta reh gaya zaalim—Mera dil hai!* (In such a brutal manner did you break my heart/ I was left pleading: that's my heart you're breaking!).

Later, when Asha has taken poison and is on the verge of death, Bansi gets a job in hospital. Jyoti objects to Bansi's style of dressing. A song follows in a children's park—another infantilization—with life-sized tea cups and saucers: *Oh yoon na tan-ke chalo/ Oh yoon na ban-ke chalo* (Oh, don't strut like that/ Don't dress up like that).

Still later, when *Prakash* wants to kill himself, Bansi is pretending to be blind and raising laughs.

Second leads lived in Cloud Cuckoo Land, in a state of

a perennial youth, a Wodehousian space where only love mattered and deceptions, masquerades and comic sequences were the stuff of life. If they ever wept, it was a loud burst of shrieking tears.

~

Among the few exceptions to this rule were the films made by the producer-director-comedian O.P. Ralhan. As producer-director, he could ensure that he got a fair deal even when he was dealing with such big stars as Rajendra 'Silver Jubilee' Kumar. When Helen was paired with him, she sometimes got a fair deal too.

Talaash (1969) centres on Raju's (Rajendra Kumar's) confusion over being in love with a mountain lass, Gauri (Sharmila Tagore), and then meeting his boss's daughter Madhu (Tagore again) who looks exactly like Gauri, except that she has blue eyes and is much less coy than the woman to whom he has already pledged his troth.

Ralhan is Lachhu in the film, Raju's college buddy and general advisor. He is the son of a cloth merchant. Raju meets the woman of his dreams in an idyllic mountain setting; Lachhu meets his fantasy, Rita (Helen), when she comes to his clothing shop and asks for a dress and then asks him to help her zip it up. So strong is the attraction that she causes him to faint when she chucks him under the chin on leaving. His father takes this as a sign of weakness and sends him and his buddy, Raju, on a long vacation. On board the plane, Lachhu finds himself next to Rita and cosies up to her. She seems to be happy to accept his advances and tells him that she is a dancer at a certain hotel into which, predictably, both boys book themselves.

In a short blonde wig decorated with ostrich feathers and a bikini over a body-stocking, Helen sings: *Kar le pyaar, kar le ke din hain yahi* (This is the right time to fall in love). She is in full form, pouting, mocking, patting the sweat off the men's foreheads, chucking them under the chin, et cetera. Lachhu leaps on to the stage, landing on her knee, and suggests: *Aa main tujhe batla doon yeh pyaar ka raasta chalna* (Let me teach you what it means to walk in the ways of love).

Truly Smitten, Lachchu proposes to Rita. Her father refuses.

Rita dances again. This time it is a cabaret veined with sorrow, which is a strange animal, but since we know her circumstances, we understand: *Mera pyaar, meri khushi hai tumhaari/ Arre hanste ho jab tum, muskuraati hoon main/ Peete ho jab tum, dagmagaati hoon main* (My love, my joys are yours/ When you laugh, I smile/ When you drink, I stumble). She is joined by the standard male attendants but they are much more aggressive than usual. They manhandle her, lift her up, drop her down, roll her about. They stand for the world that interposes itself between the lovers. There is also a shot in which we see her reflected in a thousand small mirrors, a reference to Madhubala as Anarkali in *Mughal-e-Azam*, who also struggled against the world. Ralhan intervenes, dances with her, and for a moment there is happiness.

While this is more serious than most other romances in which Helen found herself, it is still quite clear that Lachchu is a figure of fun.

When other directors tried to shift things around, they were punished at the box office. In *Pyaar Hi Pyaar* (1969), a couple of unwed mothers have their babies exchanged in an ashram. As if that were not bad enough, a third baby gets involved. The three children grow up to be Vijay (Dharmendra), a millionaire's son; Gogo (Mehmood), who becomes Vijay's driver; and Satish (Pran), the bad guy.

For a comedian, Gogo has a surprisingly large and somewhat significant role in the film, and, by association, so does Chamcham (Helen), the girl he falls in love with. To impress her, he asks for his boss's help in masquerading as a rich man's son. In Vijay's clothes, then, and with Vijay as his driver, Gogo goes to meet his beloved, who in a white mini and large square-framed glares, is dancing at an alfresco party

by a lake. Breaking many of the respected conventions of cinema, Vijay *also* makes a play for Chamcham. When Gogo embraces her, Vijay reminds him that they had promised in childhood to do everything together and embraces her too. The hero desiring any woman other than the heroine was unusual; him desiring the comedian's love interest was unheard of.

Worse, at the end of the film—after several involved subplots and after Helen has danced for us in red-sequinned leotards and done a haystack sequence in a mustard-yellow ghagra-choli—it is revealed that Gogo, not Vijay, not Satish, is the real son of the millionaire. Chamcham, too, as a result, is now a rich, respectable woman.

It should not come as a surprise that these transgressions were rewarded with failure at the box office.

And finally, another stick-in-the-mind scene: At the end of *Dil Daulat Duniya*, the heroine Roopa (Sadhana) asks Rita (Helen) whether she still loves the hero, Vijay (Rajesh Khanna). Helen says she wrote his name in her '*prem ki* diary' in pencil and then erased it and wrote Punnoo's (Jagdeep) in ballpoint.

'Tis meet.

Nine

Rolled Gold versus Gold

Mardon ki basti mein murde bankar nahin jeeya jaata.
(One shouldn't live like a zombie in the world of men.)
—Kitty Kelly (Helen) in *Gumnaam*, to Asha (Nanda)
as they begin to broach their first bottle of Scotch

During the Golden Age of Cinema, as it is often called, when Helen began her career, there were only good women and bad women. Good women might wear 'modern' clothes until they married but thereafter they settled into saris and did not clamour for glamour. Bad women never wore saris and when they married—as they sometimes did—they still wanted to drink and go out to nightclubs. Good women had long hair restrained in sedate 'Indian' styles; bad women had bobs or wild hair blowing all over their faces. Good women were interested in love and the nation and the family and children; bad women were interested in the joys of the moment and in themselves. When good women were required to be sensually arousing, Nature had to play a part by drenching them with some timely rain; bad women used artifice to be sensually arousing, and they were not even allowed to disguise this artifice: they wore revealing clothes, outrageous make-up and tasteless costume jewellery. Good women didn't want sex, even after marriage. When their husbands wanted to assert their conjugal rights, they always made protests about waking the children and it being the wrong time (of the day and month) and the wrong stage in life. Bad women seemed to think about nothing but sex, mouthing lyrics that pretended to be about love but actually addressed lust.

The moments of overlap between these two kinds of women produced an interesting range of relationships.

THE MANGALSUTRA VS THE JEWEL IN THE NAVEL

In any contest between the demi-monde and the bourgeoisie, the demi-monde loses. Working strictly in the overstated contrasts by which melodrama in Hindi cinema operates, one might assume that there would be ample opportunities for black to be placed against white but that didn't happen much. Once in a while, as in *Caravan*, a hunted gazelle of a heroine might turn up alone in the same space as Helen but generally the two were kept apart by the way in which they were constructed and the spaces to which they were assigned.

In the fifties, Helen's space was clearly delineated from the heroine's. The latter's normal habitat was her father's home. She emerged from it with a bevy of friends, all on bicycles, in order to express in song her joie de vivre and muscular virginity. After she had fallen in love with the hero, whom she would have met on just such an expedition, their songs would again be set in the open air, thus invoking Mother Nature to sanctify the love so expressed or to establish its 'naturalness'. 'Running around trees', the pejorative term that the English-speaking middle class often uses to dismiss Hindi film songs, was as much about strategy as it was about scenery.

Helen's spaces were the enclosed public spaces of nightclubs and hotels, spaces defined by transients, criminals and visitors from the West. The heroine came to hotels properly escorted by her father or her husband; she was a little girl on a special treat. More often than not, she retreated from it in distress, in a mess of tears and chiffon, running for the safety of her home. Helen, on the other hand, rarely had a home. When she did, it was presented as an extension of her immoral life. Decorated in red plush and leather, it was equipped with hidey-holes in which diaries could be concealed (*CID 909*; *Nasihat*). It had a bar since a woman like her must drink and offer alcohol and a mirror that would turn upon her, revealing the Mickey Finn she was about to slip into the hero's drink (*The Train*; *Shikari*; *Hum Tum Aur Woh*). It has a bathtub in which a song could be sung or a murder committed (*Sannata*). The only references to a religious life were Catholic references but most often these were done away with and the whole was given the impersonality, and therefore the identity, of a hotel room with all the immoral baggage that we have seen such a room carried. She generally lived alone, ripe for murder (*Woh Kaun Thi?*; *Sannata*). If she had children, they were stashed away in orphanages (*Imaan Dharam*, *Upaasna*) where they yearned for their fathers who were always missing.

While the figure of the heroine was generally so rooted that even her orphan status became part of her identity, the Helen figure was a free-floating signifier of any number of meanings. The two figures made strange companions but there were times when they were found in the same frame.

In *Aansoon Ban Gaye Phool* (1969), Vidyanand (Ashok Kumar), is a college principal of great integrity. When he falls foul of a builder's lobby, he is framed for corruption and goes to jail. After his release, he refuses to contact his wife Sumitra (Nirupa Roy) and descends into a life of crime, aided by his friend Shambu (Pran), a good-hearted scoundrel. In the world Vidyanand now inhabits, a world determined by his desire for revenge, Neelam (Helen) is co-conspirator.

As a hotel dancer, she gets the standard song, *Oh suno to jaani/ Oh meri kahaani/ Arre duniya hai tere peeche/ Aur mein teri deewaani* (Listen, my love/ Listen to my story/ The world chases after you/ And I am mad about you). But of greater interest is the moment in which Sumitra discovers her husband's whereabouts and comes to seek him out. Forewarned, Vidyanand asks Neelam for a love song that should cause him to forget everything except love. Fortunately, she is dressed for the occasion in an off-the-shoulder red dress with black sequins, yellow and blue accents and a feathery boa. Another standard song with standard lyrics follows: *Meherbaan mehboob/ Dilbar jaan-e-man* (My benefactor, my beloved/ My sweetheart, etc.)—and as the last words of the song fade, Sumitra enters, pulling her white sari over her head, a gesture that nicely combines respect for her husband and fear of the new space in which she finds him. Vidyanand tells her that she has no place in his life. When she runs away, crying, he asks Neelam to take care of her 'didi'. Neelam, the golden-hearted dancer, protests. She says that each tear shed by Sumitra will become a curse and burn him and that he had no right to involve her in such a sin. It is clear that here again the Helen figure fails, because her lush loveliness poses a challenge to Sumitra's solid middle-class acceptability and the uncontested fact of her *mangalsutra*.

However, there is always the odd exception. Helen does not quite win in *Taxi Driver* (1973), but she does not lose either. Rai Saheb (Ashok Kumar) has a very dutiful wife, Laxmi (Nirupa Roy), whose idea of touching her husband's feet on the first day of navraatri involves intimate contact between her forehead and his toes. She is pregnant and he is unfaithful with the connivance of his driver, Shankar (Bhagwan). He is cheating on her with Sitara (Helen) whom we meet singing in her kotha, *Pyaar badnaam mera/ Naam bhi harjaai hain/ Zurm gairon ne kiya/ Maine sazaa paaee hai* (My love is infamous/ My name is mud/ Others sin/ I take the blame). Just as she breaks into the antara—*Jinhen ho pyaar sanam/ Bin bulaaye aate hain* (Those who are in love/ Need no invitation)—Rai Saheb walks in.

When the song ends, and the audience departs with its *waah-waahs* and *subhanallahs*, the lights dim. There is a moment of silence and then a candle flickers to life and the song continues, intimately, for a one-man audience. At this second ending, just as they are settling down to a night of love, Laxmi bursts in and offers divorce. Rai Saheb tells her he is the master of the house, that he will do as he chooses and that she has no business to follow him like a detective. Laxmi calls Sitara a prostitute, is slapped by her husband and walks out. Sitara urges Rai Saheb to go after his wife but he refuses, saying he will spend the night with her, as he had planned.

Laxmi leaves home. Their child, Ashok, grows up to be a taxi driver (Vishal Anand) and after several false alarms, the family is reunited but only after Ashok has saved Rai Saheb from the clutches of a conniving manager and his floozies. But since we hear no more about Sitara, we must presume she has lost him too.

Where her husband had actually strayed—or where she was offered evidence of this betrayal—it becomes clear that the wronged wife feels no animus/jealousy towards the Helen figure. The overwhelming emotion is pain at her husband's betrayal, at his disrespect for the sanctity of the marital bond.

So Helen can be allowed a heart of gold, she need not be all black. But she won't get the man.

JEALOUS WIVES

If wives were actually allowed to feel jealousy, it was only where we, the audience, know that the husband or hero is blameless. Otherwise, the Kittys and Sophies are incidental in the wife's scheme of things.

In *Pyaar Kiya To Darna Kya*, Nisha (Helen) is set upon Rajesh (Shammi Kapoor) by her lover Jeevan (Pran). Jeevan wants to avenge an imagined insult to the honour of his family; he suspects that Rajesh helped his sister marry beneath her.

In the beginning of the film it is clear that Rajesh has been spoilt by his father (Prithviraj Kapoor). He is reformed when he falls in love with Savita (B. Saroja Devi). He wins a gold medal in academics which becomes something of a token of their love. When he insists on marrying Savita, he is thrown out of the house. To celebrate Diwali, he pawns the gold medal to Jeevan who gives it to Nisha to help her wreck Rajesh's marriage. And so Nisha turns up at their home, drags Rajesh away on imaginary errands, calls him Raju, shows Savita the medal and drives her to a state of jealousy in which she starts some retaliatory flirting with Jeevan. When Savita discovers that she is pregnant, Rajesh is unsure of the parentage of the child.

This might seem like some pretty successful vamping on Helen's part, but we are never given any indication that Rajesh is attracted to Nisha. When she sings *Bahaaron ki kahaani/ Sunaati hai jawaani/ Tu nazrein milaake/ Deewaane zara sun, sun to* (Youth tells the story of Spring/ Meet my eyes/ Listen to me), Rajesh is unresponsive. He drinks himself into a heap on the floor and only when Nisha morphs into Savita does he try pulling her into his arms.

In *Benaam* (1974) Amit (Amitabh Bachchan) and his wife Sheila (Moushumi Chatterji) go to an office party where

Helen turns up. Her trademark wide suggestive beam is emphasized by a red dress slit up to the thighs, red shoes and bangles in her ears. (Sheila is dressed in a pastel sari.) She is Amit's college buddy. She suggests that she will dance only if he sings. She takes a couple of quick spins, her hands whisking outwards and begins: *Aa raat jaati hai, chupke se mil jaayen dono/ Jalke kahin apni aag mein jal jaayen dono* (Evening approaches, let us meet in secret/ Let us draw close and burn in our own fire). Amit is sitting with his wife, both smiling, as if in middle-class agreement of the inappropriateness of this behaviour. The other guests begin the peculiar two-step that passes for 'ballroom dancing' in most Hindi films. Helen practically drags Amit onto the floor and then he begins to sing. She leans her head on his shoulder, as though reminding him of some earlier intimacy. Her fingers mesh with his. He excuses himself and goes back to his wife, who is now sitting in the informal zenana of Indian parties of the seventies, and asks her to dance. But she is already in a pet (and Moushumi could do pets very well). Helen winks and calls him back. Angry with his wife, he picks up a glass and offers it to Helen. They dance cheek-to-cheek. His wife fumes.

A similar scene is enacted in *Aaj Ki Taaza Khabar* (1973), only this time the theme of a wife's needless jealousy is worked out a little further. The film opens at a party where Sunil (Kiran Kumar) and wife Geeta (Radha Saluja) bump into Helen who is in a pink and silver sarong and halter. She seems to recognize Sunil although he does not recognize her. Later she chats with him while Geeta, too, fumes.

The next night, Geeta goes to bed alone since Sunil is late. She dreams her way on to a studio set. She is still wearing a night dress but Sunil, in a suit, ignores her; he is transfixed by a painting of Helen. The painting turns into the real thing. Helen comes to life, in a yellow pant suit with more than its fair share of frills and with a fruit basket on her head. She laughs mockingly and holding out a bunch of grapes from her head, begins to sing: *Aaja khilta hua shabaab hai/ Aise mein kuchh kaho/ Mausam bhi laajawaab hai/ Aise mein kuchh karo* (Come, my youth is in bloom/ It's time to make a declaration/ The weather, too, is beyond compare/ It's time to do something). She leads him to a bed in the middle of the set. He follows willingly. Geeta runs to the bed but they vanish.

This continues with Helen appearing at the beginning of each sequence as a painting (of a Harlequin, of Cleopatra), turning into the real thing, drawing Sunil away. Each time, Radha follows and tries to intervene but never manages to make contact. As a nightmare sequence, it is fairly psychologically accurate with its evocations of jealousy and helplessness.

Aap Beeti (1976), is a tired love story in which rich boy Ranjit (Shashi Kapoor) falls in love with poor girl Geeta (Hema Malini). At one point in the story, she teases him, pretending to have a twin sister. In response, he brings 'Rita darling' (Helen) to visit the shoe store at which Geeta works. Rita is wearing a hat and very little blouse and very little skirt. Ranjit then tells Geeta that Rita darling and he are getting married on Sunday.

'Is this your girlfriend?' Rita asks, an odd question for a fiancée.

'I'm a rich man's son so poor women always try to befriend me,' he says.

'Where do we go for a honeymoon?' asks Rita, mistress of the non sequitur, stroking his arm.

'From Liverpool to swimming pool, wherever you want,' he replies, to her strange delight. Geeta stalks off in a rage—she has already expressed her disbelief in his love in a song on a surreal set populated by humongous shoes and sandals in primary colours.

Obviously such jealousy was always misplaced. The hero would not fall. However, the vamp's tricks could be used to show how much the heroine loved her man and how easily she could fall prey to jealousy, which is another demonstration of her unworldliness.

THE DANCE COMPETITION

The contest between vamp and virgin was sometimes outlined directly in terms of a dance competition. Vamps rarely competed with each other. The closest brush may be in *Twelve O'Clock* (1958), a murder mystery in which a man (Rehman) tries to do away with his wife. His mistress is played by Shashikala, a dancer in the hotel he owns. Since she is pregnant, she has been packed off to Delhi and Helen in a dark sequinned pantsuit takes her place for the number *Arre tauba yeh teri ada/ Hansti bijli gaata shola* (Goodness gracious, these charms of yours/ Like lightning that laughs and flames that sing). At the end of the dance, the hotel owner's business associates ask about the other dancer (Shashikala) who was better. It was not the last time Helen would lose, but she generally lost to the heroine.

In *Dr Vidya* (1962), the tearaway Shanta (Helen) and the good girl Geeta (Vyjayanthimala) are students at the same college. Shanta is already married; her husband Jagdish has returned from England but retains his Indianness: he touches the feet of his elders and wears a bandhgala to Geeta's birthday bash. When Shanta's friend Kundan (Prem Chopra) suggests a drink, he refuses. Kundan remarks that two years in England should have given him a liking for alcohol. Jagdish replies that people who think in such a manner have never been to England and do not know that the British have values too—a fairly revolutionary statement in its lack of parochialism.

Geeta dances for the guests at her birthday party, on a stage set as a village. She sings a semi-classical song (*Pavan deewaani, na maane/ Udaaye mera ghunghta*—The naughty breeze refuses to listen/ She plays with my veil) and performs a semi-classical dance. By this time, it was acceptable for the heroine to dance (it may be remembered that it was in 1936 that Rukmini Devi Arundale had founded Kalakshetra and begun the process of retrieving Bharatanatyam from its 'unsavoury' past and making it a suitable skill for the middle-

and upper-class girl to learn). There was, however, a codicil: she could only dance for charity or as a polemical display of skill. For dancing as a profession was still looked upon with suspicion in Hindi film scripts. Just a year before *Dr Vidya*, in the film *Zindagi*, the same Vyjayanthimala, as Beena, had had to face the horror of her family when she elected to dance for a living. The acute poverty that drove her to this was emphasized several times in the film.

At the end of the *Pavan deewaani* song, the political nature of the dance is underlined by a little bit of business between Shanta and Geeta. Shanta says that she had come ready for a ballroom dance, only to find Geeta doing an '*ut-puta* (graceless)' item. Geeta counters that it is the dance of the gods, mentioned in the Mahabharata. Shanta says that she hasn't read it because she does not read Hindi—a rejection of the epic on so many levels, that it can only mean that she has been completely alienated from India. Geeta underlines this when she says that if Shanta is ashamed of reading the Mahabharata in Hindi, she can read it in English.

Geeta's marriage is arranged with the rustic Ratan (Manoj Kumar). He has already had a run-in with Shanta and Kundan, when at a picnic in his village they flirted openly with each other and were rude to the villagers. After this, he is convinced that educated girls are shameless, a theme that Hindi cinema still cherishes. At the wedding, Shanta and her friends mock Ratan's baaraat, which they say seems to have come from the zoo. Ratan also overhears Shanta telling Geeta that she was wise to marry a rustic since he will serve her; had she married someone educated, the boot would have been on the other foot. The proud groom sets his face against Geeta and, rejected, she returns home to pursue a career in medicine.

Shortly afterwards Shanta and Kundan come to invite her to a charity show. Shanta also tells Geeta that she has separated from Jagdish, for, 'if a coat doesn't fit, what is the problem in changing it?' This leads to a predictable argument that culminates in the song they sing at the charity show: *Ai dilruba, tujhko kya pata/ Har dil ko jeetkar jeena hai zindagi* (Beloved, what do you know of the world?/ Life means winning every heart). Both women sing the same kind of lyrics and execute roughly the same kind of coquettish movements, but clearly in the mouth of each woman these lyrics are supposed to have a different meaning.

The climax runs for at least two minutes and ends on Geeta, as it must, since Vyjayanthimala is the star. A piece of dialogue in English that follows makes this clear:

Kundan: You were gold.
Another: Shanta is rolled gold.

Much later, after Geeta has set up a dispensary in Ratan's village under the name of Dr Vidya, Shanta and Kundan come to the village for a fair. After it is over and the two are driving back, Kundan tells her the car has broken down. This is a ploy, for he has accepted money to make her available to another man. Aghast, Shanta protests that she thought Kundan wanted to marry her. Kundan laughs and hands her over. It is almost unnecessary to say that Ratan rescues her, for she must be made to see that the values of the village triumph over the values of the city and the Western world.

Shanta thus realizes how women who leave their husbands are seen by the world. At the end, she turns up in a sari, though we are not told whether Jagdish accepts her back.

In Lekh Tandon's *Prince* (1969), a similar collision of values takes place, although it takes a little more work to see Amrita (Vyjayanthimala) as the perfect Indian woman since she is royalty and does not care for commoners to win over Blue Bloods even in so small a thing as a snowball fight. This was around the time that the privy purses promised to the Indian princes who had joined the Union of India were suddenly abolished by the 24th Amendment to the Constitution, so it is possible to detect some Establishment-pleasing going on. However, as soon as she marries Shamsher and settles down to an agrarian life, Princess Amrita gives pretty socialist speeches to her father.

But this happens later.

At the start of the film, we see that the prince of the title, Shamsher (Shammi Kapoor), is a debauch, until he is converted by an encounter with a sadhu (the essence, one might say, of Indian values). He then fakes his own death and takes a job in another kingdom as a syce in the royal stables—all in order to 'find' himself.

Impressed by his skill at polo, Amrita's father appoints him aide-de-camp. That's when the Countess Sophia (Helen) turns up from Europe in a russet wig, a white suit and a huge white bag. She approves of Shamsher, in English: 'Quite a *charming* ADC.' The competition that follows has no location in the script but we know what it is about. It is about winning the hand of the prince, even if neither woman knows yet that he is of royal blood. (But what of it? *We* know that he is of royal descent. And dance-seductions are aimed at us.)

Amrita starts with Bharatanatyam, in a red costume. Sophia wears tights and an orange-and-yellow top and does a modern dance. The song emphasizes the competition: *Muqabla humse na karo/ Hum tumhen apne rang mein rangaayenge ek hi pal mein* (Don't take me on/ I'll change you round in a

second). Amrita shifts to Kathak and then to Odissi, while Sophia does flamenco and belly-dancing. The competition here is not entirely value based; it is also a version of the fantasy of a prize male being fought over by women.

Amrita wins, her victory a confirmation of her latent Indian values—despite all her faults, she does classical Indian dances—and a reflection of both the trajectory of the story and the star value of the competitors.

Another competition worthy of mention is the one between Waheeda Rehman and Helen in *Baazi* (1968). It redounds to Helen's credit that she was pitted in direct competitions against the best dancers of the time: Vyjayanthimala and Waheeda Rehman, even if very little use is made of the latter's dancing skills in this instance. *Baazi* is interesting because Waheeda Rehman is not a good Hindu heroine in the film. She is Elizabeth D'Silva, whose uncle has died under mysterious circumstances that are being investigated by Inspector Ajay (Dharmendra). She is an orphan, which is lucky for her, or she would have been saddled, as we have already seen, with a family of magnificent dysfunctionality such as in *Dus Lakh* and *Julie* and other such films.

Since Liz, as a Catholic, cannot represent Indian culture, the competition-cum-charity-show is turned into a contest between love and lust, with her room-mate Lucy Fernandes (Helen) representing lust. The clash is presented as a contest between Snow White (Sameena in the Indianized version) and the Ugly Stepmother.

This is an unusually long sequence, lasting more than ten minutes. Helen (as the Stepmother), dressed in red and green High Fantasy Arabian with a russet bouffant announces: *Main ek haseena, nazneena/ Koi mujhsa nahin* (There's no one as lovely as me). Waheeda, dressed in bridal white with a white rhinestone tiara sings: *Main Sameena, mehjabeena/ Mujhme kya kya nahin* (I'm Sameena and I'm a paragon of virtues). While Lucy whirls, drops onto one knee, arches in a backbend and wiggles her hips, Liz only trips *en point* and sometimes whirls a 360-degree whirl. By the second verse, she has switched to a shorter white dress, though she retains the tiara. On the floor, writhing, Lucy announces: *Main qayamat ki pahchaan hoon/ Bijlee hoon, toofaan hoon* (I am a sign of the apocalypse,/ I am lightning, I am a storm). To which Liz replies: *Main mohabbat hoon, imaan hoon/ Ek aashiq ka armaan hoon/ Jo mere paas aaye/ Sukoon-e-dil paaye/ Phir jaaye na kahin, kahin na* (I am love, I am honour/ I am the ideal of the lover/ He who comes to me finds his heart's ease/ And has no need to look elsewhere).

No prizes for guessing who wins.

A KIND OF SORORITY

There were moments when the Helen figure could be used to good effect in the heroine's life, a reworking of the 'fallen woman with a heart of gold' trope (the classic version requires the fallen woman to demonstrate her cardiac worth to the hero; here she demonstrates it to the heroine). Veera in *Shikar* (1968) and Lily in *Upaasna* are fallen angels who turn into Nemesis-figures. Both these characters, played by Helen, kill off villains who are threatening the heroine with their lascivious intent. By some coincidence the heroines in both films (Asha Parekh and Mumtaz, respectively) are called Kiran.

In *Raakhi aur Hathkadi* (1972), it is the Helen figure, leaning heavily on a walking stick and therefore out of the sexual stakes, who offers the beleaguered heroine, Asha Parekh, a job in her hotel. However, her role as a mentor to the heroine is best-developed in *Kathputhli* (1971). Although she has the somewhat ambiguous name of Roma, owns a hotel in which she dances, and unknowingly even throws some seduction at the already-married hero, she is portrayed as a well-intentioned person.

When her husband Vishal (Jeetendra) is incapacitated in an accident, Nisha (Mumtaz) goes to her boss for help. Bad move; he rapes her instead. When Nisha tries to end it all, Roma rescues her. When Roma hears Nisha's story, she makes three remarks, all of which mark her as a woman of substantial clichés. She says: *Zindagi aur maut ka faisla sirf Bhagwan ke haath mein hai* (Life and death are in God's hands) and *Zindagi sirf shareer ke zinda rehne ka naam nahin, yeh to aatma ke jaage rehne ka naam hai* (Life is not only about the body staying alive, the soul must stay alive too) and *Zindagi aag hi mein jalne ka naam hai* (The meaning of life is suffering). Then she tops all of this with a final *Asli jeevan wahi hai jo doosron ke liye jeeya jaata hai* (A life lived for others is the only real life). She offers Nisha a way out: a new job and training in Delhi where she can give birth and send the child to an orphanage. Unfortunately, Vishal finds out, thinks Nisha has been unfaithful and spurns her. He turns to Roma (who does not know his true identity) and is about to emigrate with her when the truth comes out and the happy ending excludes the do-gooder.

In *Inteqaam*, Gita (Sadhana) is framed by her employer Seth Sohanlal (Rehman) after she refuses to have sex with an important client, Murlidhar (Asit Sen). She goes to jail, her mother dies, and she swears revenge. When she returns, Giriraj (Ashok Kumar), whom she has helped earlier (hiding stuff for him from the police), offers assistance in getting revenge since Sohanlal cheated him as well.

Giriraj and Gita set up a casino, Casa Egyptiana, where Rebecca (Helen) is the dancer. Her first song, *Aaa jaan-e-jaan, mera yeh husn jawaan*, causes Murlidhar to fall in love with her and write her incriminating letters. He is punished by being blackmailed delicately by Gita and Rebecca. Next, Giriraj sets Gita on Seth Sohanlal's son, Rajpal (Sanjay Khan). He wants her to marry him and destroy the family. Rebecca is set on the tracks of Rajpal's buddy, Pyaare (Rajendranath) but the subplot gets lost in the film.

No indication is ever given of why Rebecca is so willing to take part in all these farces. When Gita and Rajpal do get married, and she sets out to defame him and his family, Rebecca pours the alcohol that Gita demands in the song *Kaise rahoon chup ke maine pee hi kya hai, hosh abhi tak hai baaki/ Aur zara si de de saaqi, aur zara si aur* (How can I stay silent when I have drunk so little?/ Give me some more, wine-bearer, some more). Rebecca does no dancing here. Nor, actually, does Sadhana, who lurches her way through the song. At the end she is led away by Rebecca and Giriraj. Care is taken to establish that she was not drinking alcohol but cola in water (?).

Even when Helen was not cast as a mentor, she could offer some solace in sorority with the heroine. For instance, in *Tum Haseen Main Jawaan* (1970), Ranjit (Pran) wants to do away with a child who has inherited the money that formed the basis of his great expectations. His lover Tina (Helen) is aghast at this cold-blooded attitude and does her best to help the child's aunt Anuradha (Hema Malini) foil Ranjit's plans for infanticide.

TWO WOMEN AT PLAY

Until the time of the song mentioned in the epigraph, Kitty Kelly in *Gumnaam* has been a teetotaller. It is safe to assume that Asha (Nanda) has also never got drunk in her life, since she barely dances, wears white or cream throughout the film and, above all, is the heroine. Kitty's abstinence, though, is unusual, since she wears red, dances in swimsuits and suggests that the only way to live is to forget one's worries and live it up (*Gham chhod ke manaao rangreli*). But as we have seen in the chapter 'main gud ki dali', she damns herself anyway by saying several times: *Mujhe sharaabi pasand hain; sharaab nahin* (I like alcoholics; not alcohol).

Under threat of death, things change a little, which is not surprising. What is surprising is that Kitty manages to get Asha, the heroine, to drink too, and together they cavort about a bedroom quite happily, singing, *Peeke hum tum jo chale aaye hain is mehfil mein/ Ek naya rang jama denge is mehfil mein* (Drunk, we have arrived at this celebration/ We will bring new colour to it [with our behaviour]).

The oddest thing is that this is only 1965. At the time

of writing, in 2004, heroines still don't smoke or drink. If they do, they die (Meena Kumari in *Saahib, Bibi aur Ghulaam*; Parveen Babi in *Deewar*; Hema Malini in *Aas Paas*). Nanda lives to tell the tale of her hangover! But then, perhaps she does that because this is Hindi cinema's way of playing out the male fantasy of watching women at play with each other.

This old tradition, a woman dressed as a male and then 'romancing' the heroine, is a fairly well-established one. In *Aab-e-Hayaat* (1955), for instance, Helen's dance sequence is performed in the middle of an inn in Fantasyland, somewhere in the Middle Ages, where the hero Jalaal (Premnath) and the villain As-Silah (Pran) and the heroine Scheherazade (Shashikala) have gathered. Scheherazade is the only surviving princess; two others have been whisked away by a wizard with evil designs on their fair persons. Scheherazade, who has a yen to emulate Haroun al-Raschid and keep tabs on the State of the Nation in disguise, turns up at the inn in drag. At a dive, a round-faced and pretty Helen arrives—dressed suitably for once—in billowing harem pants and sings, *Maara re maara re maara maara re maara re woh maara/ Aankh kataar, dekho mera vaar/ Tera dil kiya hai paara-paara/ Tera dil kiya paara-paara* (A hit, a most palpable hit/ My eyes are daggers/ I've sliced through your heart). She flirts with As-Silah and with Jalaal and then, most outrageously, with Scheherazade, who makes the appropriate comically shocked faces.

In *Taj Mahal* (1963), Helen plays Gulbadan, emissary and catalyst for Prince Shah Jehan (Pradeep Kumar) and Arjumand Bano (Bina Rai). Towards the end of the film, when Empress Noor Jehan looks like she is going to get her way and marry her favourite, Laadli Bano, to Shah Jehan, Gulbadan and another female dancer, dressed as a male, sing: *Na na na re na na, haath na lagaana/ Tose baar baar kahoon, mohe na sataana/ Doongi gaariyaan* (No, no, do not touch me/ I have told you often, don't tease me/ Or I'll abuse you).

A similar performance is repeated in *Kab? Kyon? Aur Kahaan?* (1970). Helen plays Rita, part of a gang run by the evil uncle of the heroine Asha (Babita). The gang's mission seems to be to bump off Asha so that her uncle can inherit her money. Rita is strictly ornamental; the song she sings equally pointless, if one is only concerned with the trajectory of the film. However, in terms of feeding the male fantasy, the hotel dance which presents Miss Sujata and Miss Rita playing out the yearnings of a bride on the wedding night has a clear function. The lyrics are also predictable: *Yeh aankhen jhuki-jhuki-si/ Yeh saansein ruki-ruki-si* (My eyes, lowered/My breath, halting).

The voyeuristic fantasy reaches its apotheosis in *Shareef Badmaash* (1973), a lame-duck spy thriller starring Dev Anand as Rocky in the title role. Both Rita (Helen) and Seema (Hema Malini) are dancers. Indian scientists, those whizkids, have some new fighter-plane prototypes and a bunch of spies want to get hold of them to sell them abroad. Seema is an unwilling pawn in this game and Rita, a mercenary. Their first dance together does not have a song attached. Rita does a modified striptease—one blouse conceals another. Seema doesn't strip, though she pole dances. Rita loses her yellow sarong and has a blue skirt (mini bikini) underneath. She flirts with Rocky, sitting on his lap and stroking his face. Later, as Rocky watches them in their room, a debate begins:

> Seema: *Mein naach rahi thi; tu kapde utaar rahi thi* (I was dancing; you were stripping).
> Rita: *Nahin, kyunki tu buzdil hai, darpok hai, kaayar hai* (No—[that was] because you're a coward).

Rita dares her and Seema drinks the large part of a bottle. They challenge each other to win Rocky's affections, each extolling the other's attributes.

> Seema: *Tere hothon mein to duniya bhar ke phoolon ka rang hai* (Your lips are full of the colours of all the flowers of the world).
> Rita: *Tere hothon mein to sharaab hai* (Your lips are intoxicating as wine).

Rita encourages Seema to go to Rocky's room and '*bijli ki tarah gir; baadal ki tarah baras* (fall upon him like lightning; pour down on him like rain)'. But Seema chickens out and Rita puts her to bed.

In all this, Rita is the catalyst. She allows Seema to drink and express some sensuality under the guise of alcohol. We know that this is not how Seema would behave in ordinary circumstances.

Many male fantasies collide in the scene. There's the homoerosis of the scene in which the women sit on the bed, admiring each other; the voyeurism of Rocky watching through a peephole; and the competition of two women over the same man.

The only catfight that I know of in the whole Helen oeuvre occurs in *Parmatma* (1978), and, coming at the end of a song, it is completely incidental, not even in the conventional way that songs can sometimes be unrelated to the plot. After singing a climactic song (*Aankh lad jaati hai, lad jaane de*—'Our eyes convey messages of desire, let them') she observes a young deaf-mute being molested by one of the gang-members. She wrenches her away from him and begins slapping her, saying, *Aaj tujhe sabak sikhaana hi padega* (I will have to teach you a lesson today). A catfight ensues, which ends just as it gets gruesome with Helen pinned between the deaf-mute's legs, grabbing at her breasts and then pulling the blouse off her shoulder.

It is left to our imagination why the deaf-mute is being punished for actions that are not hers. It seems as if the Helen figure (unnamed) is running interference here, redirecting blame at the victim in order to save her a fate worse than being raped. But this might be inferring a little too much from too little material, since we know nothing about her character or why she should be presented as an upholder of female virtue at all.

Ten

Fade Out, Fade In

Bade-bade loot gaye,
Khade-khade loot gaye...
(The big have been defeated,
The erect have been deflated...)

—Lyrics from the Helen number
in *Jhoota Kahin Ka* (1979)

By its nature, the exotic has very limited options. It must either reinvent itself, endlessly distancing itself from what is perceived as normal, or be eclipsed by other ways of seeing. Once a certain limit has been reached with the audience, a mind-barrier crossed, a taboo violated, the search must start again.

It is easy to see the 1970s as the time when Helen's career began to decline. By this time, she was an old lady in cinematic terms. Twenty years into her career, the industry should have been looking—in that ugly phrase—for fresh meat. A hungry new bunch of women had invaded her space and were competing for the same roles, with or without body stockings. So the industry should have been sending out a cruel message: take things the way they are or pack up and leave.

It could be that simple.

It rarely is. The industry, one of the few genuine meritocracies we have, even if a nepotistic meritocracy, has no time for circumlocution. If it had no need for Helen, the offers would simply have dried up. Instead, she went on dancing, went on appearing—even if the roles she got were generally abbreviated to a single dance sequence, or less. But the length of the role does not always determine its impact.

For Helen managed to retain some of her luminosity. Aided by the arrival on the musical scene of R.D. Burman and assisted by the silken voice of Asha Bhosle, she did more than just survive.

This was the time I was growing up, and although I know I am making a wild generalization here, for my generation,

she was far more than just a dancer. She had transcended that; she had become a category, a type, even an archetype. We spoke of Helen-type songs; we called beautiful women Helens, half mocking our own susceptibility, half in awe of the power they wielded over us.

And yet the seventies were a contradictory decade. She was still playing heroine in some B-grade films. She was still to dance some of her most memorable numbers: *Piya tu ab to aaja* (*Caravan;* 1971), *Aaj ki raat koi aane ko hai* (*Anamika*; 1973), *Mehbooba mehbooba* (*Sholay*; 1975), *Mungda mungda* (*Inkaar;* 1977) and *Yeh mera dil yaar ka deewaana* (*Don*; 1978).

Sensuous impatience; the sordid made sexy; the sex bomb who doesn't give a damn—she danced the best of every possible bad-girl routine. None of her challengers—and there were many through the seventies—can claim to have done half as much.

And few actors were so badly wasted in trite rubbish.

While it is true that women have a shorter shelf life than men, peripheral women can go on much longer. It is not impossible to conceive of a forty-year-old Miss Lilly or Madame Lola preying on a twenty-something hero. It would simply be further proof of her degeneracy. Vamps do get older, but for a while their added years represent added sexual charge.

In *Mere Jeevan Saathi* (1972), for instance, Helen's cinematic seniority to the hero, Rajesh Khanna, added an edge to her pursuit of him. Prakash (Khanna), an artist, accepts his millionaire father's challenge to make his art pay. He fails until he bumps into Kamini (Helen), the princess of Ramgarh, who undertakes to be his patron. Before the first party she throws in his honour, she also offers herself to him. When he refuses, she tells him that she knows artists have moods and that she is willing to wait for the right mood. At the party, it is obvious that he is being assessed for his good looks rather than for his artistic abilities. The titles roll on his evolution into a society painter and a playboy (the background score underlines this with a slimy male voice oozing: 'He's a playboy, a sexy playboy').

Prakash meets ophthalmologist Dr Jyoti Varma (Tanuja) and falls in love with her. Kamini hears of this and comes to visit him at his studio one evening. Since no model seems to be present, she starts to take off her clothes, the camera zooming in for a close-up. He rejects her but she throws herself at him. Jyoti witnesses what seems like a love scene and walks out. Prakash tries to explain but she drives away. He returns to his studio and slaps Kamini, to bring her to her senses. He tells her that he cannot love her; that only a man more debauched than her could.

She returns the next day to warn him. She is a hunter, she says, *Jaanwar jitna khatarnaak ho, jitna chaalaak ho, use maarne mein zyaada maza aata hai* (The smarter and more dangerous your prey, the greater the fun of the kill).

When Prakash is blinded in an accident, Kamini kidnaps him and holds him hostage in her palace. She whips him when he will not play the piano for her, but also throws herself at his feet. This has a dual purpose: his enslavement is atonement for his debauchery; her abasement plays to the eternal male fantasy of the nubile woman desperate for a man. The song *Aao na, gale lagaa lo na/ Lagi bhuja do na, oh jaan-e-jaan* (Hold me, put out the fires you've ignited in me) is one of the classics of feminine seduction. Asha Bhosle delivers it with an added breathiness to her voice, the rhythm of the song broken into short erotic gasps. And Helen cuts loose. She throws herself into it, abases herself, rubbing her face against the hero's feet, kneeling in front of him, pushing herself into him.

Kamini fails. Prakash will not succumb. When he tries to escape on a horse, she follows, hugely enjoying the chase. It's a shame when she plunges off a cliff; the rest of the film is

the usual grinding melodrama without the Rani of Ramgarh to give it an edge of sexual danger.

Mere Jeevan Saathi would not have worked as well had a younger woman played Kamini. The power equations between struggling artist and patron, princess and commoner, but especially older, experienced woman and younger man, make her temporary control acceptable and limned with forbidden charm.

However, such roles were few and far between. Already by the end of the sixties, she was being given much less screen time than before. And the camera had begun to take liberties. In *Yakeen* (1969), Helen has a single cabaret with a second-rate song. This happens when a fake Rajesh Verma (Dharmendra), a spy, has replaced the original Rajesh Verma (also Dharmendra), a nuclear physicist. The fake one is from Mozambique, where a gang of international composition (some Arabs, a few Whites) seeks to steal the nuclear science formulas that the original Rajesh Verma has been developing. The Indian intelligence forces (represented by that gnome David) suspect the impostor when his dog doesn't recognize him and his servant ends up dead. They take him to a bar to get him drunk, and Helen sings: *Bach – bach – bach – bach ke/ Bach ke kahaan jaaoge/ In nigaahon se, in adaaon se/ Bach ke kahaan jaaoge?* (How will you escape from my gaze, from my charms?)

The song is a series of low shots, some with her holding her crotch. In one shot, she is framed by men's legs, a shot that would begin to be repeated since it defined her status as a sexual object, trapped in a world of men.

It was almost as if there was a multiple personality at work throughout Helen's career, but this was accentuated in the seventies. For, when, in 1972, she was getting respectable films like *Mere Jeevan Saathi* and *Apradh*, and even a heroine's role in *Sultana Daku*, what was she doing in *Do Gaz Zameen Ke Neeche?* This begins as a horror film but ends as a fairly tame revenge story. After the death of his first wife, scientist Raghuvansh (Surendra Kumar) has led a monkish life. One day, after visiting his wife's grave, he sees a group of men attacking a woman. He rescues the woman, Anjali (Shobhna), and takes her home. In the night, she snuggles up to him and they make love. Naturally, as an honourable man, he marries her.

All this is actually a ploy, devised by Anjali's Mamaji (starting with the Mahabharata, the evil uncle is almost always the mother's brother) to get money out of Raghuvansh. When they think they have finally succeeded in killing Raghuvansh but can't find his money, things begin to fall apart. Mamaji begins to drink and goes to a bar. Helen is partly herself (russet hair) and partly a tribal (green and purple half-sari and a nose-ring the size of a bangle). She half dances, half mimes the words of the supremely forgettable song *Peeke aaye gharwa bedardi aadhi-aadhi raat* (My thoughtless lover comes home drunk to me in the middle of the night). Then she vanishes.

It could be argued that Helen's career was a case of mismanagement. She was still associated with P.N. Arora at this time. When the relationship finally ended, she was left penniless. In a profile of notorious gangster Karim Lala, journalist Saswati Bora quotes an insider, Zaffar Khan (*The Age on Sunday*, 17 March 2002): 'Zaffar Khan recalls the time when the actress Helen came to Karim Lala for help. "Helen's friend P.N. Arora had taken away all her earnings and was refusing to give her any money. A desperate Helen went to Dilip Kumar, who told her to go to Karim Lala. Helen came to meet Karim Lala with a letter from Dilip Kumar. Lala mediated in the matter and Helen got her money back," says Zaffar Khan.'

Financially insecure, it would have been natural for her to take anything that was available. It may also be that Arora's control of her career extended beyond the monetary. Perhaps she was thus forced to accept roles that did not fit with her stature. Or perhaps that stature is only one we have established in retrospect and Helen had no such notions about herself.

Whatever the reason, there she was in *Ek Nanhi Munni Ladki Thi* (1970), a Ramsay Brothers production, which means B-grade schlock. Shamsher Singh (Prithviraj Kapoor), some kind of has-been royalty, believes that a bejewelled dagger and a statue of Vishnu that are in a museum belong legitimately to his family. And so, he steals them. He eludes the police and goes underground but in the process, manages to misplace the Vishnu idol. In his renewed pursuit of the statue, which is being smuggled to Portugal via Goa, Shamsher bumps into Helen in a blue Arabian fantasy outfit.

Ai nazneen ai gulbadan, a way-past-his-prime Prithviraj Kapoor sings to her, and offers her 'bageechas' and his heart. You can see her face slightly confused at times, as though she is not quite sure what she is doing in a film like this. The willing smile has faded, her mouth a parody now, her teeth always gritted. The camera is savage in its inspection of her body, lingering on her pelvis. This is not the spirited dancer who always seemed to be enjoying herself. And it is not age either; seven years later she would still be vamping up a storm in *Inkaar*.

The relationship with P.N. Arora, as we have seen, might also be the reason why Helen did not get her fair share of media attention at that time. After the coming of *Stardust* in October 1971, the central theme of almost all film journalism became love. Some attempts were made later to perceive it as work (Rauf Ahmed's version of *Filmfare* and *Super*, for example). However, film journalism was, and still is, largely restricted to heterosexual love affairs between stars; or stars and star directors. Change is central to this kind of journalism. A couple of stars may be allowed monogamous images but only as a counterpoint to the hectic shifts and stratagems of the large majority. Copy is far more easily generated when something happens, as opposed to nothing happening or things remaining the same. This constancy—and with a visually uninteresting has-been like P.N. Arora—meant that the new gossip-soaked magazines had little time for Helen.

By 1975, things were beginning to look a little bleak. In *Sanyasi*, the ultimate male fantasy film in which a willing Champa (Hema Malini) pursues a reluctant celibate, Ram (Manoj Kumar), Helen gets half a song with *Tu mera din hai, main teri raat, aajaa* (You are my day, I your night, come to me) before everyone from Nazima to Hema Malini takes over. In *Zakhmee*, a tired tale of revenge and double-crossing, she plays Sheela, the villain's moll, and turns up in a red negligee over dark underwear in one scene and in black leather in another. By now it would seem that the director and producer felt that audiences would be more interested in the rising star Reena Roy's flesh than Helen's. Reena Roy appears regularly in shorts, minis and other western clothes. She keeps a scorpion in a matchbox to test the bravery of the men who claim her hand. Her songs are provocative and sensual (*Jalta hai jeeya mera bheegi-bheegi raaton mein*—'My heart burns in these drenched nights'). By contrast Helen has no songs at all in *Zakhmee*. In the biryani western *Kaala Sona*, she is paired with Keshto Mukherji. This in itself is not a problem, as we have seen that there is a history of pairing the vamp with a comic actor. However, as resident sexpot in a drug-smuggling gang, Chameli (Helen) only gets half a dance (*Koi aaya aane bhi de/ Koi gaya jaane bhi de*—'Let he who arrives, arrive; Let he who departs, depart') which she shares with Durga (Parveen Babi), whose apple farm is being used as a cover for the opium smugglers. Durga, on the other hand, gets a dance to herself: And we see more male skin (Danny and Feroze Khan) than anything else.

From 1975 onwards, it is possible to show Helen's growing irrelevance almost chronologically:

1975: *Dharmatma*

The son of the head of a crime syndicate, Ranvir (Feroze Khan) has left his home and his property to work as the manager of an estate in Afghanistan. There he meets Reshma (Hema Malini), falls in love and wins her hand. His father

(Premnath) has enemies who rig his jeep but kill Reshma instead. In the course of getting his revenge, Ranvir has an assignation at a nightclub. African drums shoot into the screen along with an owl and a man painted in tiger stripes. The man-tiger has a snake over his shoulders with which he torments/tantalizes Helen who is prone on the floor. With Hema Malini playing a tribal and therefore allowed a great deal of mobility and Rekha playing second string, Helen doesn't even get to sing. All she gets is to laugh—'ha ha ha'—at the beginning of the sequence.

1976: *Sharafat Chhod Di Maine*

Raju (Feroze Khan) abandons decency when he is jilted by Preeta (Hema Malini), who has, in fact, been forced to marry someone else. She dies in childbirth, and the infant is brought up by her younger sister. The infant grows up to be Radha (Neetu Singh), and somehow her path crosses that of an older, still-handsome Raju. He begins to fall in love with her, and shows signs of becoming less bitter, less cynical. Aware of what it will do to the older man if she rejects him, Radha agrees to marry him and sacrifice her own love. It is at the celebration attendant upon this marriage that Helen sings: *Aaj ki mehfil, aaj ki shaam/ Aap ki khaatir, aap ke naam* (This celebration, this evening,/ All of it is for you, all in your name). She has as little as 20 per cent of the screen time since the song is intercut with shots of Raju on the balcony above, Radha being dressed as a bride and mourning her lost love, various lovers holding hands, and Raju's Parsi friend Jehangir (Jagdeep) drinking.

1978: *Parmatma*

If a temple treasure needs to be looted, surely Johnny (Ranjit) will send in his most faithful agent?

'Who is the agent, boss?' asks a sidekick. 'The agent is... (significant pause)... Lily.'

Cut to a red feathery boa covering a shapely thigh. The boa parts to reveal the name 'Lily' embroidered in sequins on dark pink hot pants. We see only a pair of legs, while the owner has her back to us. All this might lead you to think Helen is going to burst on to the scene. Only, this time it is Aruna Irani, playing at being Helen.

They're not the only ones after the temple treasure. There's Zorawar Singh and his gang of dacoits and an escaped criminal pretending to be good in Bhairon Singh (Shatrughan Sinha). Lily is actually very good. She manages to get the treasure and whisks it off to Bombay. A reformed Bhairon Singh and Deepa (Rekha) come to the city to find the treasure. Here Rekha gets her chance at a dance too, with *Suraangani Suraangani/ Kamaal karegi* (Suraangani, Suraangani/ She'll perform miracles). She is in a pink and black flamenco outfit. If that sounds familiar, you got it. She'd doing a Helen too.

When Bhairon Singh finally meets Zorawar Singh in the latter's hideout, we find the original in a red pant suit and halter top tied beneath her breasts, table dancing after drinking alcohol from a glass with hands tied behind her back. *Aankh ladti hai lad jaane de/ Baat badhti hai badh jaane de* (If our eyes meet, let them/ And if this affair rages, well, let it.) She is watched by a greasy bunch of men, dwarfs and serving girls. The song, remarkable for its lack of shot coherence and the absence of any choreography, ends in a catfight between Helen and a young mute woman, which ends with Helen pinned between the mute's legs, pulling the blouse off her shoulder.

1979: *The Great Gambler*

This should have been Helen's film since it has more than its fair share of casinos, hotels, airports and underworld dens. However, she makes a small appearance as a woman dancing in a film reel. There is something sad and dreadful about this figure, without its normal accoutrements of men, musicians, audience, dancing alone in a little room. Vijay (Amitabh Bachchan), the CID Inspector, guesses that her gestures are a code; this is how the smugglers are passing their message. But, asks his boss (Iftikhar), the other cop in the room, what do the gestures stand for?

Amitabh Bachchan goes in search of the dancer, who is all kitted up to die in a bouffant and a red-and-gold gown. When he frog-marches her off, one of the goons sees them and kills her. She dies in his arms, leaving him with a name as a clue.

The gang needs another dancer. Shabnam (Zeenat Aman) steps in. She has two sensuous numbers: a standard disco number in *Oh deewanon dil sambhalo, dil churaane aayi hoon main* (Hey you crazed men, watch out, I've come to steal your hearts) and a 'belly dance' in *Rakkaaza mera naam* (My name is Rakkaaza). This is because Zeenat Aman is heroine and heroines get such songs now that they are willing to show leg and cleavage and wiggle.

~

Which leads us to another current explanation for the decline of Helen's career. Her downfall, and of vamps in general, has been assigned easily enough to the rise of another kind of heroine. When the new, westernized female lead was willing to show a little skin and to dance with erotic energy (without needing the perpetual excuse of a charity show), what need of a vamp? So, while the tribe of Helen grew through the seventies, they also began to look like also-rans. A mere handful of people, or even less, can tell Faryal from Komilla Wirk or the difference between the sisters Meena and Jayshree T. Only Bindu and Aruna Irani managed to stand out. As for the rest, they were interchangeable pretty faces with pretty bodies attached.

Yet it was not a heroine who rang in the change. It was a sister. And a super hero.

Zeenat Aman had won the Miss India title at a time when contestants still went backstage and raised their saris for the judges to examine their legs. In 1971, she made her debut in *Hulchul*, where she and Kabir Bedi went unnoticed. The same year, she also appeared as Dev Anand's kid sister in *Hare Rama Hare Krishna*, a young woman led astray by the hippies of the West in search of the wisdom of the East. The film, set in Montreal and Kathmandu, was an instant hit.

The seminal song from the film—*Dum maaro dum, mit jaaye gham* (Take a puff, drown your sorrows)—which can still bring reluctant dancers onto the floor at most discos, would, even five years prior to that, have been classic Helen, one of her songs of forgetfulness. The good women in the hero's life—and most communication in songs is directed at him—would urge him to live for others, to consider the future or the good of his immortal soul. But now, here was the hero's sister singing a song of alienation and disenchantment, asking: *Duniya ne humko diya kya/ Duniya se humne liya kya/ Hum uski parwaah karen kyun/ Kisne hamaara kiya kya?* (What has the world given us/ What have we got from it?/ Why should it bother us?/ What has anyone done for us?). Here was the anthem of doomed youth. Not only was the woman in a public space, she was also in a disco, she was wearing pants and she was smoking pot. The eyes of the world were upon her and she only shrugged.

Although it was clear from the moralistic tone of the film that this was not really something that a good girl should be singing (or doing), it was indicative of the sea change that Indian cinema would be going through in the seventies.

One of the most elemental changes would be in the nature of the hero. Until then, heroes were generally men in love. The trials and tribulations they faced were associated with that emotion or due to the machinations of family members who wanted to disinherit them, generally because they were in love. There were a couple of exceptions—Sunil Dutt as

Birju in *Mother India* (1957) and Dilip Kumar as Ganga in *Ganga Jamuna* (1961)—but even here, *ugra* rasa, or anger, was not the central force in their lives. The first ugra hero was Amitabh Bachchan, who, it is said, brought his four years out in the cold backwaters of Hindi cinema to the raging, tormented Vijay of *Zanjeer* (1973). Alternative explanations for his stunning performance have implicated the revolutionary poetics of his father, Harivanshrai Bachchan; the powerful script by Salim Khan and Javed Akhtar; the clarity of the focus on the hero's rage (he sings no songs in the film, which, legend maintains, is why Dev Anand turned down the role); and the loss of Independent India's innocence that had left audiences hungry for something other than pallid heroes singing pretty duets and touching their elders' feet.

Amitabh Bachchan wasn't just an angry young man. He was a man in a towering rage. He would flout society's laws if they stood in his way, even if he was supposed to uphold them as a policeman in *Zanjeer*. He would refuse the solace of God and even of his mother, preferring money and sex in *Deewar* (1975). He would attack his father in a titanic Oedipal battle in *Trishul* (1978) and he would win. In these three films, now seen as the archetypal Bachchan films, he did not simply beat up villains, he reorganized society. And he dealt a bodyblow to the weeping lovers and chocolate-box heroes who had preceeded him.

This volcanic rage would also have repercussions for the female figures in the films. Mothers would gain some ground, since the Oedipal conflict between the Bachchan figure and his father became increasingly central from *Deewar* onwards. Heroines, however, would get less and less screen time, until they were reduced to a few scenes and a couple of dances. Helen was safe as long as it was a heroine uncomfortable with the idea of dancing, but now for some heroines dancing was the only thing they were good at or were allowed to do. Along with the heroine's new willingness to show skin, this meant less need for Helen.

Next, the second lead began to go through a

transformation. Instead of a comic presence, it began to be increasingly another dominant male figure, subordinate only to the first lead. *Sholay*, that path-breaking film in so many respects, proved to be the turning point here as well, establishing clearly that two men can be better than one. The dominant relationships within the film are those between the friends Jai (Amitabh Bachchan) and Veeru (Dharmendra) and between the sworn enemies Thakur (Sanjeev Kumar) and Gabbar Singh (Amjad Khan). The two heroines, Basanti (Hema Malini) and Radha (Jaya Bhaduri), get very little screen time. Jai seems to be intent on sabotaging Veeru's wooing of Basanti and it is only his death that allows enough space in his friend's life for Basanti. In such a universe, where even the heroine was not strictly required—she was, in fact, the temporary diversion—what hope could there be for the vamp?

Not surprising, then, that Helen's is a non-speaking, non-singing role in *Sholay*. She is not even a signifier because we already know how evil Gabbar Singh is. She is an anonymous fantasy gypsy here, the kind that we do not see in India. We

know this because it is a campfire song and because Jalal Agha wears a European gypsy costume and plays a mandolin while lip-synching the now-famous *Mehbooba, mehbooba/ Oooh-oooh-ooh/ Gulshan mein gul khilte hain/ Jab sehra mein milte hain/ Mein aur tu-uu-uu* (My love, flowers blossom in the gardens when we meet in the desert).

In the background, Jai and Veeru are wiring up the place for an explosion, and for us, *that* is the matter of interest.

Of course, there is only one *Sholay*. The Amitabh-Dharmendra pairing would wait a long time, nearly five years, before it was repeated in *Ram Balram* and even then it would fail. Meanwhile, other, lesser male figures took over: Vinod Khanna (*Hera Pheri, Khoon Pasina, Muqaddar ka Sikandar*), Shashi Kapoor (*Suhaag, Do Aur Do Paanch*), Randhir Kapoor (*Kasme Vaade, Pukar*) Shatrughan Sinha (*Dostaana, Naseeb*) and Rishi Kapoor (*Coolie, Naseeb, Ajooba*). None of them would be paired with Helen because the producers would be eager to bring in the heroines with whom these actors had been paired in smaller successful films, or the heroines with whom they were rumoured to be having off-screen liaisons.

Helen had no off-screen liaisons with actors. She seems to have gone from the shadowy P.N. Arora straight to Salim Khan. While both these men had repercussions on her career, they were certainly not screen material. And it would have to be a very big hero whose reputation would be large enough to place an imprimatur on Helen's image as a fallen woman. Bachchan was later to be that hero in the unsuccessful *Imaan Dharam*, but in the early seventies, he was in no position to take chances either.

After Manmohan Desai's *Amar Akbar Anthony* (1977), Bachchan also showed that a hero could offer himself up to ridicule without losing his machismo or his star status. When Desai dressed all three of his leads up in ridiculous costumes (Vinod Khanna was a one-man band, Rishi Kapoor was a tailor and Amitabh, a priest), he was reinventing the climax, introducing into its histrionics both cathartic violence and a note of laughter. In the process, he also reinvented the Hindi film hero. (Later, in *Naseeb*, also starring Bachchan, Desai would reprise this climax with a matador, a Cossack and Charlie Chaplin, throwing in three women as a flamenco dancer, an Arabian dancer and Heidi for good measure.) You now got two for the price of one: a hero and a comedian rolled into a single powerhouse package.

The comic as second lead was redundant. His desperation about his sex life, too, was unnecessary. It was valid only so long as the hero's sex life was the central motif of the film. Now that the hero wanted revenge, not victory in love, he would need another pair of eyes to watch his back—hence the the second hero. And this second hero was also, often, the staid, upright foil to the hero's rage. Dependable, responsible, loyal, he had no space in his life for a pair of hot lips. He had no use for the vamp.

The comic would only return in the eighties when the non-actors were beginning to take over the smaller films and needed the likes of Kadar Khan and Shakti Kapoor to shore up their acts. Again, this extremely successful pairing did not need women for their variety of risqué and misogynistic comedy.

And so it is only natural that Helen's role in *Amar Akbar Anthony*, a film with three heroes, three heroines, and no comic, should take barely a moment of screen time. When Pran needs an impersonator for his adoptive daughter in order to foil a kidnap attempt, he gets Helen. She is duly kidnapped, leaving the world safe for the real daughter, Jennifer (Parveen Babi), so we can get on with this rollick of a film.

In the changing cinema of the seventies, the old, familiar claustrophobic spaces were getting smaller and smaller for Helen—paradoxically, because they were growing larger inside the film. Earlier, the hero wandered into the underworld; he did not belong there. Helen's presence was a marker that he was now out of his natural territory and was going to have to find his way back. But the Bachchan figure did not wander into the underworld; it was his natural environment. In many of his films (*Suhaag*, *Do Aur Do Paanch*, *Muqaddar ka Sikandar*, *Don*) he seemed to be a product of the underworld. And if he turned his violence against it, he did it outside the purview of the law. Either way, he owned/possessed it.

This should have been Helen's big chance since it was her space, this dark world of evil deeds and criminal gangs. Instead it was her undoing.

There are two options for the antisocial element. S/he must die or be tamed. Bachchan was good at dying, because he usually refused to be tamed. In *Shakti* and *Deewar*, he went too far from the family. Neither Raakhee nor Nirupa Roy could sanitize his rage. And so he died. In *Muqaddar Ka Sikandar* and *Sholay*, he was in free fall, with no family and almost no religion. In both films, he transgressed social barriers, loving above his status—the daughter and the daughter-in-law of his employers. And so he died again.

Each time he died, he went a little further in establishing the rule that if Bachchan died, the film lived. The other kind of death, the death in which he was reincarnated (*Aakhri Raasta*, *Kasme Vaade*, *Don*) would also be successful.

When Bachchan was dying so potently, who needed Helen to die? When the threat of the lover who did not need a family for context had been codified into the leading character, how much could the vamp do? It is odd to think of Helen's hips and Bachchan's fists as acting out the same fantasy-cum-moral fable, but they do. Sex and violence damage the status quo when they are unchained. She was love, even if it was outlawed love; he was death.

And as in all patriarchal societies, death triumphed over love.

Luckily for Helen, fate intervened. In 1981, she married Salim Khan and retired, although she would still dance in a few films. She told Shashi Baliga in the magazine *Savvy*

(February 1989), 'Something about Salim set him apart from the rest of the industry men. I respected him tremendously because he helped me out without trying to exploit me.' She had not expected Salim to marry her, for he was already married, and had grown-up children. Salma, his first wife, admits, in the same interview, to being 'depressed and disturbed at first'. It took her a year to accept another woman in Salim's life. It was she who made the move to reconcile the three of them.

And so, finally, Helen had the happy ending she had never had in her film career. 'When I married Salim, I found a security I had always missed before,' she says in *The Britannica Encyclopaedia of Hindi Cinema*. She found a ready-made family.

But there was still enough in the old trooper for a new phase in her career, still some get up and go in the workhorse. She would return to the screen from time to time but these were rare appearances in unremarkable films. From 1981 to 1989, I can only find twenty-three films in which Helen acted. There may be more in which she was not credited but I don't think the number would rise above fifty. She had all but retired.

But, like a good Hindi film, the happy ending was at hand. By the nineties, she was playing maternal roles and had turned into a legend, an icon. She won her *Filmfare* Lifetime Achievement Award in 1998, sharing it with Manoj Kumar. While that isn't precisely the Dadasaheb Phalke Award, it is still an achievement, if you combine it with the Best Supporting Actress Awards for *Gumnaam* (1965) and *Lahu Ke Do Rang* (1979). Now her name would only grace the marquee when big names were involved: Salman Khan, Karan Johar, Amitabh Bachchan. When her name turns up in the credits of a television serial like *Do Lafzon ki Kahani*, it makes news in the manner of the stars.

Helen was finally a star. No, more than a star. She was an icon, a legend in her own lifetime.

Eleven

The Making of a Legend

Tumhe sunkar taajjub hoga ki is dancing hall *mein poore teen saal ke baad maine aaj kadam rakha hai. Is* hotel *ki maalkin hone ke alaawa main yahaan ki* cabaret dancer *bhi thi. Door door se log is* hotel *mein aate the, mera* cabaret *dekhne. Mujhe bachpan se hi* dance *karne ka shauq tha. Jab main* stage *pe aati, to saara* hall *taaliyon se goonj utthta. Aur mujhe aise lagta...ki saari duniya taaliyon ki goonj se mera swaagat kar rahi hai. Aur main...maare khushi ke be-ikhtiyaar jhoom jaati.* (You will be surprised to hear this, but I have stepped into this dancing hall after three whole years. Besides being the owner of this hotel, I was also the cabaret dancer here. People would come from far away to watch my cabaret. I loved dancing even as a child. When I made my entry on the stage, the hall would resound with applause. And I felt...I felt that the whole world was welcoming me. And my...my joy would be uncontrollable.)

—Helen, leaning on a cane, in *Raakhi aur Hathkadi* (1972).
(But of course, immediately afterwards, she bursts into a dance, to indicate that the past is not another country; it is only a flashback away.)

In 2003, when I was halfway into the writing of this book, a VCD of seduction songs was released: *Haseenon ka Hungama*, priced at Rs 60, produced by Indus Video Private Limited. I was glad to have got hold of it. It joined my collection of VCDs of this kind—among them, *Piya Tu Ab To Aa Ja* (Indus, 1997) and *Golden Girl Helen* (UltraIndia.com; date not stated)—with which I reminded myself why I was doing this book whenever the grunt work got me down. There was something peculiar about *Haseenon Ka Hungama*, though. It had well-known contemporary heroines like Kaajol, Urmila Matondkar, Raveena Tandon et al strutting their stuff, but there was not a single Helen song. And yet Helen features twice on the cover of that VCD, in her signature flamenco outfit and in her Paris chorine leotards from *Caravan*. The same thing happened a year later when I found a copy of *Hungama Ho Gaya* (Indus, 1999). Inside, heroines like Kimi Katkar, Sridevi and Madhuri Dixit were to be found dancing. Need I say that none had the vivacity and sensual presence of Helen? Need I say that some of them seemed to be consciously or unconsciously offering versions of Helen? (For confirmation, check out Pooja Bhatt dancing *Roza Roza* in *Naraaz*.) Need I tell you that on the cover there were three images of Helen?

Helen is now shorthand, an indicator for a certain kind of dance. She's still a presence enough to make producers want to stick her on the cover of a VCD even at the risk of being accused of misleading advertising.

~

When the whistling dies, it is difficult to say how a film legend is made. For instance, common wisdom might hold that first you need to be a star. But Helen was not a star in the way Hindi cinema defines stardom. Her name in the cast was not enough to pull in the punters, never mind ensuring a repeat audience. Few people, if any, would go to see a film only because Helen was in it. But were she in a film that you did want to see, your anticipation would be heightened by her presence.

As a heroine, she had no major hits, with the sole exception of *Cha Cha Cha*. Since film-making is about entire teams working together to a purpose, we know that it wasn't Helen's failure alone. Most of the films in which she was heroine were bad films. The special effects were lousy, the scripts were cobbled together from old themes, the music was pedestrian. But as we know, in public opinion both the success and failure of a film is unfairly apportioned to the lead actors.

That takes care of the notion that it's stardom that does it.

Nor does media attention. If you go through the *Filmfare* files of 1958, you find double spreads on milksop heroines like Nalini Chonkar and Peace Kanwal. You read about Dilip Kumar's reading habits. You even find an article on Czechoslovakian cinema. But there is not a single line on Helen, though this was the year she finally managed to break through into the public consciousness, the year she danced *Mera naam Chin-Chin-Choo*.

The neglect was only marginally less in later years. Journalists don't get paid much; nor are they rewarded for research. Almost every film journalist who has ever interviewed Helen has got the same set of replies. The same questions were avoided, the same topics came up. Few would prepare by going to see what Helen actually did, perhaps because they all felt they knew what she did. She danced for the men in the cheap seats, didn't she? That was all they needed to know. As for her off-screen life, as we have seen, it wasn't interesting enough for them.

Even recent profiles of Helen merely describe her best songs, a list that will now live forever and will be circulated endlessly, thanks to the Internet. The rest of her career is whitewashed, perhaps out of respect, perhaps out of ignorance.

Common wisdom also holds that you have to stick around a long time to make it to the hall of fame, or you have to die young. Helen did manage to stick around for quite a while. But then so did Jeetendra, who romanced four generations of heroines, starting with Rajshree and ending with Anita Raj, and *he* hasn't made it. The same could be said of any number of actors of varying levels of success.

Then there is the competency argument. You have to be exceptional at what you do; it is not enough to be good at it. There is no doubt that Helen was a brilliant dancer, even when the choreography demanded the fancy footwork of Kathak. But again, Johnny Walker was an exceptional comedian and Sulochana was brilliant at what she did (suffering maternity), yet they aren't counted as icons, legends, whatever. Helen was their equivalent, cinematically. Like their characters, she was rarely central to the plot. Her roles were generally incidental, sometimes irrelevant, often divertissements. Despite this, the same industry began to turn her into an icon.

It is possible to trace a cinematic origin for this process.

It began as early as 1978, when in *Chor Ke Ghar Chor* director Vijay Sadanah gave the dance sequence with the seductive movements, tribal outfit and suggestive words (*Nathaniya kaaga lekar bhaagaa*—'A crow robbed me of my nose-ring/virginity')—to his heroine Meena (Zeenat Aman). And Helen he turned into a mnemonic of her earlier glamour.

The film revolves dizzily around the theft of an idol from a temple. The many twists and turns in it are impossible to summarize, so assume whatever train of events you desire to arrive at two middle-aged men, Ranjit and Mangal (played by two stars from the past, Ashok Kumar and Pran), one keen to restore the idol and the other to get hold of it; one driven mad by circumstances and the other pretending insanity. This means that they are both in funny wigs and rags when they turn up at a kotha where Helen is dancing in a purple and white mujra costume. She continues singing to the two ragged madmen: *Har cheez jaanti hoon, har raaz jaanti hoon/ par jaao saiyyan main na kahoongi* (I know all there is to know, I know every secret/ But go away, love, for I'm not about to tell).

The comic and the nostalgic collide to ugly effect in the sequence. Here is the woman who sang *Mera naam Chin-Chin-Choo* to a younger Ashok Kumar, in what was the highlight of that film. She is still portrayed as appealing, she is still a dancer, but her appeal is not directed at the hero. It is directed at a couple of old misfits. Unable to handle a woman who would not age, the film lets her down by placing her in a situation where her dancing is no longer the central motif but part of an array of asinine exploits by two ageing men in what might have been, under more skilful direction, a good-natured romp. Consider the sharp contrast to Waheeda Rehman's mujra in *Namkeen* (1982), central to the cinematic moment, brilliantly shot, respectful of the dancer and her memory, especially since she was playing an old woman in the rest of the film.

This is not to suggest that Sadanah was actually making a cinematically self-conscious reference to an earlier Helen so as to invoke an earlier Ashok Kumar. It is equally dangerous to suggest that the response he wanted of us was the memory of an earlier affection, an earlier lust. But the song is clearly part of a pattern.

In less than two years time, Helen would be an old woman. She would play a mother in *Lahu Ke Do Rang* (1979) and win a *Filmfare* award for Best Supporting Actress. Odd, because she was not the hero's mother, and even the mothers of heroes don't get supporting actress awards, unless they are Nirupa Roy. Odd also because there was nothing in the role that a hundred other senior actors had not done, and done better. The film stars Vinod Khanna as Shamsher, an Indian freedom fighter on the run from the British colonial forces in Hong Kong. He takes shelter in Suzie's (Helen) house. There he has an affair with her, and marries her in a Buddhist temple. She is half-Indian, she tells him, so she knows Hindi and even remembers a song her mother used to sing to her: *Maathe ki bindiya bole, kaahe ko gori dole, saajna gaye re pardes* (The bindi on my forehead asks: why are you so happy; your lover has gone away).

Shamsher returns to India where we discover that he is already married and has a son. He is betrayed and is killed. Back in Hong Kong, Suzie gives birth to Suraj (Danny) who turns into a small-time hood. He seems to feel only contempt for his mother who fasts for a husband who has abandoned her. The two sons meet when Suraj is hired as a diver to retrieve sunken treasure and Raj (Vinod Khanna again) is a policeman on the trail. Suzie follows her son to India, and, by a series of coincidences, finds her husband's other family. But she hates no one, condemns no one and weeps and forgives a lot.

Helen's face was beginning to show signs of age now—the softening chin, the early jowls, the crow's feet—even if her body was holding up perfectly. And towards the end of the film, there are quite a few close-up shots of her face.

Perhaps it was the industry's way of encouraging her to take up her 'proper' role in the world of cinema. Perhaps the patriarchy, uncomfortable with this agelessness, was willing her to turn into a mother.

They wouldn't have their way yet.

In 1979, other than *Lahu Ke Do Rang*, she appeared in eight films: *Duniya Meri Jeb Mein*, *Guru Ho Ja Shuru*, *Jhootha Kahin Ka*, *Kanoon Ka Shikaar*, *Magroor*, *Raakhi ki Saugandh*, *Teen Ikke* and *The Great Gambler*. In almost all these films, she has a single song to sing, but in *Jhootha Kahin Ka* Miss Helen is still 'the most sensational show in town'. At the end of her performance (the *Khade khade loot gaye* song), we have a flashback to an earlier Helen. For while she has a wealth of beefcake on display through the song, in the form of literally panting bodybuilders, it is old Dara Singh who walks in, clad in a dressing gown. He strips it off to reveal a body far less-developed than the boys but since he is a bigger star (in these lower reaches) he gets to whip her up in his arms, whirl her round and then drop her on the floor.

In 1980, she was still dancing in *Abdullah*, *Angaar*, *Bereham*, *Dostaana*, *Garam Khoon*, *Hum Kadam*, *Jaayen To Jaayen Kahaan*, *Karwa Chouth*, *The Great Gambler* and turning up for a special appearance in *Shaan*. In that year's release *Raakhi ki Saugandh*, she plays Sweety, another famous cabaret dancer, another member of another gang. Seth Chamanlal (Ajit) heads this one and organizes a bank robbery. Inspector Shankar (Vinod Mehra) finds that the car used for the heist belongs to Sweety and comes calling at her nightclub. A golden cage drops over him and a bunch of caricature tribal Africans surround him, poking at him with spears. This is obviously a replay of the seminal *Intequam* song—*Aaa Jaane jaan*—again a harking back. The only difference is that this is no inarticulate savage in the cage; this is the hero. Helen can mock him, singing, *Khud hi phas gaya pinjre mein/ Tu shikaari bada anaari hai* (You fell into your own trap/What a hunter you are!), but eventually he'll kick his way out in style.

Although she again played a mother in *Ram Balram* in 1981, Helen was *still* dancing in *Bhula Na Dena*, *Bulundi*, *Chhuppa Chhuppi*, *Josh*, *Paanch Qaidi*, *Raaz*, *Sannaata*, and *Shaaka*. In *Bulundi* (1981), the story of a charismatic professor—Raj Kumar—and his attempt to change the lives of four rich boys whose parents are the elite of the criminal underworld, she has a quick number when the boys are chasing a killer. Our first view of her is a rump shot. She is at the top of a staircase and begins descending after she has wiggled her rear to the percussion. She sings: *Tera dil oh re babu/ Tere kheeshe mein rakho/ Na baba, na re baba/ Mereko nako-nako* (Put your heart back in your pocket, good sir/ I want nothing to do with it). Once again, the inclusion of the character actor and comic Bhagwan as the bartender implicates an earlier era, seeks to establish nostalgia for the past.

But because nothing in Hindi cinema will ever follow any graph, however retrospective, in 1981, Helen also danced in Sanjay Khan's *Abdullah*. The song forms part of the celebration of the wedding of the hero Mohammad (Sanjay Khan) and the heroine Zarina (Zeenat Aman). Helen in an Arabian fantasy costume proves that she has the moves in *Jashn-e-bahaara, mehfil-e-yaara aabaad rah* (May the festivities of spring and this meeting of friends be favoured by fortune).

In 1982, there were *Alladdin and His Wonderful Lamp*, *Ayyash*, *Chorni*, *Eent Ka Jawaab Paththar*, *Heeron Ka Chor*, *Kachche Heere*, *Sawaal*, *Teesri Aankh* and *Waqt Waqt Ki Baat*. In *Ayyash*, a ham-handed update of Guru Dutt's classic *Saahib, Bibi Aur Ghulaam*, four mujras are performed as indicators of the *ayyashi* (decadence) of Thakur Jaswant Singh (Sanjeev Kumar). Helen dances in the last of these, sung to celebrate the birth of a child (*Topiwaale ne kar ke salaam mujhe badnaam kiya*—'The policeman greeted me and ruined my reputation'), and it works almost as a tribute to her memory.

It was only after 1983 that she finally began to slow down, with a single film, *Haadsa*. The other production from that year which has her in the credits is not really a film at all, despite its title, *Film Hi Film*. It has a depressingly thin storyline about a director who resurrects his career with a bunch of young actors. As they make the film, he tells them about cinema, using clips of movies that never got made. Helen appears in one of these clips.

The following few years would be the years of retirement. She made just a couple of appearances, in *Pakhandee* and *Bond 303*. Her next big release would be a film Salim Khan wrote, *Akayla* (1991), standard issue late-Bachchan. Vijay Verma (Bachchan) is a good cop—even if one with an alcohol problem—who turns vigilante. In a flashback we are told that his best buddies were Seema (Meenakshi Sheshadri) and Shekhar (Jackie Shroff). Vijay and Seema loved each other but on the day that he wanted to offer for her hand, Shekhar confessed his love for Seema and asked him to present his case to her mother (Helen). The bigger star is always allowed the sacrifice and Vijay has his first drink that evening.

There are two Helen moments in the film, two references to her past, although one is allusive. This allusion is in the moment in which Vijay, or Akayla, the loner, meets his new love interest, Sapna (Amrita Singh), a nightclub dancer. Success casts a long shadow and here it is particularly clear:

Sapna is wearing a flamenco outfit in red and black. The other Helen moment is when Vijay comes to her grandson Bobby's birthday party. The three of them together sing a song: *Jeenewaalon jeevan chhuk chhuk gaadi* (The train of life runs on). And then, suddenly, in an act of obeisance, the band plays a riff from *Mera naam Chin-Chin-Choo* and Helen takes off, kicking away and whirling the skirts of her sari, until she recollects her age and her status and flounces off happily.

In a post-modern moment, the figure of Seema's mother, Bobby's grandmother, suddenly dissolves and the actress playing her surfaces with all her screen history.

This would be repeated again in *Mohabbatein* (2000). Helen has one of those minor add-on roles that you might miss if you sneezed and then blew your nose. Narayan Shankar (Amitabh Bachchan) is the principal of a school who believes in rules, not love. Raj (Shah Rukh Khan), who was once in love with Narayan's daughter Megha (Aishwarya Rai) but lost her to her father's intransigence, comes to the school to teach the principal the value of love. In charge of the boy's hostel, Raj plays cupid. Helen as Miss Monica is in charge of the girl's hostel, a role hitherto assigned to the mad-eyed character artiste Manorama. At the annual get-together, Raj plays a riff from *Ai haseena zulfonwaali jaan-e-jahaan* on his violin, and Helen lets down her hair and dances for a few moments.

This is how iconization works. The assumption is that you would know why she is called Miss Monica, a reference to her all-time hit from *Caravan*. The assumption is also that you would know the *Ai haseena* song. This means that the song is familiar, has lost none of its potency and can be referred to without explanation and certainly without disrupting the story. It is a self-reflexive moment in a cinema not given to self-reflexivity. Very few Hindi films have been made on the making of cinema, for example, and those have not been commercial successes, not even Guru Dutt's spectacularly beautiful *Kaagaz ke Phool* (1959).

While Hindi cinema has never been commercially or critically successful in treating itself as subject, it does know how to make a playful bow to its own icons. The longest of such sequences is in Manmohan Desai's *Naseeb*, in which John Jaani Janardhan (Amitabh Bachchan) plays a waiter at a ritzy hotel. Desai thought up a novel way to expand his already diverse star cast. By having a song set in a party to celebrate the 50th week of a Manmohan Desai film (*Dharam Veer*, which was released in 1977), he managed to refer to his own successes, pay homage to Raj Kapoor *and* have a procession of big-name actors adding value to his new film.

The stars come in as Bachchan (who is, of course, the biggest star) sings: *Har picture dekh-ke socha/ Main bhi actor ban jaaoon/ Kismat ne ghoomaaya/ Hotel mein pahunchaaya* (After every film I saw, I thought/ I too should be an actor/ But fate set me to wander/ And brought me to this hotel). At one point, Raj Kapoor is given an accordion and asked to play it, bringing back memories of other films, other tunes.

Of course, Raj Kapoor was playing himself, in a way that Helen would never be asked to play Helen. She could only remind us of the persona she had created over thirty years of acting, and eventually she did what almost all ageing actresses do. She turned into a mother figure.

In *Khamoshi—The Musical* (1996), she plays Mariamma without any traces of Helen, the dancer. It is true that she executes a vigorous skirt-waving, petticoat-displaying number, but she is an old lady and there are no traces of the coquette, no references to Lilly or Jenny or Kitty. Mariamma is the quintessential old lady: warm, reassuring, mothering, optimistic, straight-talking. Her granddaughter Annie Joseph Braganza's (Manisha Koirala) world is split into the silence of her deaf-mute parents (Nana Patekar and Seema Biswas) and the music that Mariamma (an odd South Indian name for a Goan lady, although the cross on her grave reads 'Mary') plays on the piano. The first song is the song in which we are introduced to the family's happiness. As raindrops begin falling on their heads, the young Annie and Mariamma whisk a piece of plastic over the piano and over their heads and begin to sing: *Mausam ki sargam ko sun/ Kya gaa raha hai samaa/ Tu bhi gaa, tere sangh/ Gaye saara jahaan* (Listen to the season's song/ Listen to what the land sings/ Sing with it, and the world will sing with you).

Later, when Annie steals some fish for their dinner and her father throws her out of the house, Mariamma gives him a piece of her mind—and deals some very low blows: his freedom fighter father had hanged himself because of his deaf-mute son. It is one of the few instances in Indian cinema when a matriarch is allowed a moment in which she lets down her guard and attacks with whatever comes to hand. Helen seems strangely right for this. It is difficult to see the usual character artists who have played Indian mothers being trusted with such an outburst.

Her second song is when the piano is sold and the family is desolate. Like Pollyanna, she sees the good in evil and claims, *Gaate the pehle akele/ Aaj gaata hai saara jahaan* (Before, we sang alone/ Now the world sings with us). It is here that she dances.

Afterwards, the piano is covered with a white cloth, a shroud. Just as it is about to be loaded on to the ferry, she runs to it and plays one last time. Then she pulls the shroud off it and runs away into the dusk, one of the most effective cinematic metaphors for death.

Not all of Helen's recent films have been quite so big budget, nor were all of them successes. In the B-Grade *Saazish—The Conspiracy* (1998), she is a social worker, a lay nun, an aunt, a mother figure, all rolled into a black dress, with concerned and tearful eyes as accessories. David Braganza (Mithun Chakraborty) plays a grave-digger who has sacrificed everything to keep his brother Tony (Vikas Bhalla) in medical school. David is an alcoholic who is torn between the competing love of Mrs D'Costa (Aruna Irani), who runs a bar, and Mary Aunty (Helen), who is intent on closing down that bar as part of her social development endeavours. What was obviously meant to be a funny subplot gets lost because neither the dialogue nor the direction explores any of the possibilities of the situation. Both women come off poorly. Their feud ends when David is faced with the problem of paying for the last year of Tony's degree. He needs a lakh. Mary Aunty writes to the missionaries and gets a loan. Mrs D'Costa sells her bar and the two sworn enemies make up. Unfortunately, Tony discovers a drug scam and gets bumped off by a bunch of goons.

The next year, however, she was back in a blockbuster, *Hum Dil De Chuke Sanam*. Half Italian and half Indian, Sameer (Salman Khan) comes to a picturesque haveli in the desert regions of Gujarat to learn music and to find his roots. He falls in love with Nandini, the daughter of the house. The marriage is forbidden by her father, who, as guru dakshina, asks Sameer to forget Nandini. Sameer returns, heartbroken, to Italy (played by Poland) to be comforted by his Italian mother (played by Helen). There is an added frisson in this casting: Helen being Salman's (step)mother in real life. She really does not have much to do in the film. She gets a single punchline—'I love you, Jesus'—delivered when she hears that Nandini may be within Sameer's reach after all. She isn't.

In *Shararat* (2001), Anuradha Mathur (Helen) is one of the inmates of an old-age home to which Rahul Khanna (Abhishek Bachchan) has been sent to do social service in expiation of his crime of turning off the traffic lights and causing the mother of all accidents. She is a new arrival whose son is going to Canada—'for training', he says, but she knows that she has been abandoned, as she tells Prajapati (Amrish Puri), the inmate whose benevolent tyranny has been accepted by all the others. The central battle of the film is between Rahul and Prajapati. Anuradha is peacemaker, the voice of Rahul's conscience. The only Helen moment is when she dances with Rahul at the birthday party that the residents of the home organize for him.

Other than the regrettable *Saazish*, it is interesting to note that Helen returned to the big banners with a vengeance. She is now not just another name, she is a value-add to the cast. A new generation of young people queues up to see her, even in such a tiresome film as *Dil Ne Jise Apna Kahaa* (2004), where she plays the adoptive mother of Dhaani (Bhumika Chawla), who has a heart problem. When the heroine Dr Parineeta (Preity Zinta) dies, Dhaani receives her heart and her emotions and therefore immediately falls in love with the good doctor's widower, Rishabh (Salman Khan). The failure of *Dil Ne Jise Apna Kahaa* proves that Helen still cannot make a film a success any more than her presence can guarantee that a television serial starring her will at least get a headstart on the competition.

But an appreciation of her now seems synonymous with an appreciation of what Hindi cinema really is.

Bad girls sometimes make good.

How?

~

In some ways, 1981 was the turning point. Helen married Salim Khan, and settled down to the life of a second wife. In time, she was integrated into the original family. As far as I can remember there were no scandalized whispers, no public outrage. This may have been because the principals in the drama were not stars; or it may have been because none of them spoke to the media, except for that one exclusive interview to *Savvy*. But I like to think it is because of the goodwill Helen had earned over the thirty years she had been in the film industry.

The year 1982 was her last fully 'active' year. After that Helen, the dancer, turned into a scarce commodity. At the height of her career, you couldn't see a film without seeing those famous legs. She was everywhere and she was all things to all men. And while everyone enjoyed her dancing, even in her silliest, most idiotic moments, it may have been that this was too much of a good thing. In the last twenty odd years, however, she has appeared in just a handful of films.

Now when the next Helen film comes out, someone, perhaps Shah Rukh Khan, is going to say that he is waiting to see the film because of her. When the reviews come out, they will all bemoan the shortness of her role. This never happened when she was at the peak of her fame, it certainly didn't happen when she was still dancing in the late seventies.

Next, Helen acquired a new respectability with age. Rehabilitation is important and it comes when the scandal loses its teeth, when the shock has turned into a fond memory of being shocked. The tearaway has now been revealed to be one of us, all along. This means a certain amount of ironing out and a collective amnesia. It is important to point out here that Helen was almost never scandalous. She saved that for the screen. In the course of her long career, even the gossip magazines had nothing to say about her. Now, of course, she is a good woman even on-screen.

Now that the exotic and the dangerous have been coopted, we remember only that Helen was a great dancer. We do not choose to remember that she was surrounded by second-rate dance directors, colour-blind art directors, and dress designers with some pretty wild notions about what a dancer should wear. We choose not to remember the bad and the ugly moments, of which there were plenty. But then, our own notions of ugliness have changed, now that the middle class has decided that it has the confidence to appreciate the tinsel attractions of kitsch. While the over-the-top outfits in her better numbers are now subjected to an interested and faux-bemused scrutiny, we really have no memory of Helen as Rubaba in *Mujhe dekhiye main koi dastaan hoon* (Look at me, I am a story) from the film *Lootera* (1965), dancing in a mauve blouse with the breasts picked out in gold, a multicoloured skirt of knotted scarves, pink leggings, and her hair in russet rat-tails.

It won't surprise me at all if Helen has no memory of this either.

~

But there is something else at work here. When I once asked an editor if I could review Hindi cinema for his newspaper, he asked me why.

'Because I like it,' I said.

'That's the problem,' he said. 'My readers don't like Hindi cinema. *I* don't like it.'

We were not supposed to like Hindi cinema then, we the educated middle class. I remember meeting my physics teacher coming out of the first day, first show of *Mr Natwarlal* (for which my sister and I had braved an eight-hour queue for tickets) and I remember her embarrassment at being caught at a theatre.

We don't have that problem today. Thanks to our new-found confidence (we are the second-largest consumer market, are we not?) or to western appreciation and critical discourse on Hindi cinema, we're allowed to like it. This latitude has also been extended to Hindi film music, which is now ubiquitous. Television countdowns have multiplied and promos, also song-based, seem to dominate television time. FM radio now competes with All India Radio (which once handed over all its audience to Radio Ceylon by refusing to play Hindi film music in the fifties) to keep playing a judicious mix of old and new songs.

And of course, the remix artists have found a treasure

trove of danceable tunes. They already carry an enviable freight of goodwill and recognition value, only a couple of percussion instruments need to be added to create a new song entirely. Helen's songs fit in naturally. Most of them are dance tunes.

Added to all this is a new ironic appreciation of kitsch and those costumes—Helen's, especially—which were sneered at for their bad taste and are now displayed in specially curated upmarket exhibitions.

Whether it is Canadian drag queens or bhangra babes in Bradford or simply a bunch of young people in Mumbai finding their second wind at a disco, the queen has been re-enthroned.

Helen has returned. As a cult classic.

Of course, when music channels play Helen numbers, they stick to the old favourites, the numbers we all carry around with us in our heads, the ones that come to mind when her name pops up. But there are more opportunities to see her now than there ever were when she was at her peak. Through the writing of this book, friends would ring up to tell me that a Helen song was playing on Channel So-and-So or that a new compilation of her songs was available on the streets of the city.

Many of these songs are ludicrous. But that, in an odd way, helps maintain the legend. Now that we are all comfortable with kitsch, we can celebrate the worst aesthetic excesses of Hindi cinema. The hybrid costumes which came from a variety of sources—from Heidi to the kothas of Lucknow—the exaggerated make-up which included sequins to outline eyebrows and spiky eyelashes that looked like they might tear the skin of anyone who came close enough to kiss, the improbable sets with their bottles of Vat 69 and weedy white people as props, even the irrelevance of the songs, everything was validated because it wasn't just kitsch, it was High Kitsch and we were all allowed to enjoy it.

Kitsch is the key.

Four films have been made on or about Helen, and all four have been made by Western film-makers or film-makers settled in the West. Nasreen Munni Kabir's *Helen: Always In Step* has been discussed earlier. It is built around an interview and is clearly affectionate in its treatment of Hindi films and Helen.

The first film on Helen was made by a British film-maker in the age before Orientalism became a catchphrase. He called it *Helen, Queen of the Nautch Girls.* It is obvious that it was James Ivory's response to the sheer Otherness of the cinema he experienced in India. The Merchant-Ivory film now is something of a cliché; it is tasteful to the point of lacking any flavour; it has some beautiful performances, finely tuned, perfectly poised, as artificial as a Bloomsbury conversation; it has, in short, a very clear aesthetic defining it all. It is the aesthetic of the cosmopolite, and it travels easily. In 1973, the year that *Queen of the Nautch Girls* was made, this aesthetic might have been in its formative stages but it was already becoming clear.

Ivory came to India quite often, and he would still have been thinking in water colours while all around him, commercial Hindi cinema was daubing colour extravagantly in the bright shades of a box of crayons. Every time Ivory came to India, then, he must have been inundated with the glossy lavishness of it all, by the complete lack of any thought of the market in Cannes or the statuettes of the Academy, by the way in which a medium was being redefined in total ignorance of what an international market might want. His films travelled; in 1973, Indian films didn't. There were no Saturday night shows at the multiplex at Piccadilly; no reviews in *The New York Times*; no self-aware love of kitsch.

And while Helen was, by 1973, no longer central to this circus of the East, the idea of a Franco-Burmese woman as the reigning Love Goddess of it all, dressed in feathery creations that would not have raised an eyebrow in Las Vegas, appearing in the narrative breaks that songs meant to the Westerner, must have been delicious. I am sure James Ivory may have had many more and far subtler reasons to make *Helen, Queen of the Nautch Girls*. I am sure that he would not have named it that today. I am sure I have wronged him and if I have, I'm quite prepared to apologize. But if you watch it today, it becomes clear that Ivory sees Hindi cinema as an opiate of the masses ('mindless escapist fantasies'). His tone is condescending: 'Sleek plumpness seems a virtue in a land of undernourishment.' And yes, he wrote the script. He brutalizes the films he picks, never naming them, even turning the *Aa jaan-e-jaan* number from *Inteqam* from colour to black and white.

Nearly thirty years later, and cinematically that is a very long time, another film-maker, a Canadian of Indian origin, Eisha Marjara, made *Desperately Seeking Helen*, a documentary that is as much about Eisha Marjara's perception of Helen as it is about Helen. Like me, she did not get to meet Helen, and uses the iconic image as a way of interrogating the construction of femininity—for herself, as a Canadian of Indian origin, and for the subcontinent.

Marjara said in an interview: 'Helen was a larger-than-life figure, the icon of Indian cinema which is the world's largest dream factory. More than a movie star, she was a glittering figure of desire and playfulness, the mistress of a thousand disguises, yet always herself.'

In 2004, US-based Anuj Vaidya offered us *Bad Girl with a Heart of Gold*, a film in which he explores the reasons why Helen had to die on-screen. He himself plays four Helen roles, another exploration of what Helen meant for a marginalized community. Inhabiting these roles allows Vaidya to comment upon the marginalization of homosexuals while ostensibly talking about Helen's cinema. It is apparent that while Vaidya enjoys the sheer exuberance of the dance sequences he incorporates, they are his tools for an analysis of quite another situation.

Whatever the mechanics of it, Helen is now a legend in her lifetime. A legend reminds us about the way we were when they were big. We must have an earlier, less-conditional emotional response to call up when the legend shows up in a later avatar. This older response is the one against which we test all the new information we have about her; the Helen who goes to church on Sundays, practices reiki and praanic healing is only delicious because she may be placed against Monica ripping her clothes off in a fever of sensual impatience or Kitty lisping warnings from a swathe of fur. But there must be an emotional response that was once shared and which has now been accepted as a common mythology.

We have a Helen mythology today. It is one that has been reshaped and refashioned so that its appeal can cut across communities. Men, women, the trans-gendered, the old, the young, Hindi cinema buffs, the new constituencies which view cinema through irony-tinted roseate lenses, the old constituencies which have followed every move, all these are now part of the Helen cult.

Twelve

The Cult of Helen

Main bhi ek raaz hoon
(I, too, am a mystery)

—Lyrics from Helen's song in *Raaz* (1981)

Miss Kitty herself is there, shaking her groove thing and further cementing her position as the character we'd least like to lose. She's a heck of a looker, a charming actress, and...a terrific dancer.

—From the review of *Gumnaam* by Scott Hamilton and Chris Holland on stomptokyo.com

The ancient cab driver was fascinated.

'Helen?'

Yes, I said, Helen, preparing to defend my territory.

'I pray for her.'

I looked up.

'She made me very happy when I was a young man.'

His eyes were shining in the rear view mirror.

~

In a way, this book has tried to explain what Helen meant to Hindi cinema and the ways in which three generations of film directors chose to employ what she represented: the multivalent figure of the white woman. It has also been, thus far, my viewing.

But it hasn't been a solitary experience. Every time I said I was writing a book on Helen, eyes would light up. It was as if her name alone was enough to conjure up all the jouissance of the subcontinental experience of viewing Hindi cinema; as if she were simultaneously a catalyst for memory and a way back into a less politicized, perhaps more innocent, way of experiencing cinema. The standard conversation then ran on these lines:

'...a book on Helen.'

'Helen? The dancer?'

'That Helen.'

'Oh great. Have you seen...'

Like Abhay Sardesai, poet, translator and editor of the monthly *Art India Magazine,* many remembered 'the erotic charge' that Helen's name in the film-credits carried. '*Picchharan Helen aasa. Mhantakuch tasle scenes aastale* (The film has Helen in it, so it's bound to have "that kind" of scene), I recall my elder cousins whispering,' Abhay told me. I have heard variations of this coming from people of very different backgrounds, and always said with the same hint of nostalgic wonder.

For Hindi cinema is a near-universal memory, a collective encounter in most of India. And since Helen has danced in films across linguistic barriers, lip-synching lines of love and desire and seduction and mockery in Hindi, Tamil, Bhojpuri, Malayalam, Rajasthani, to name a few, there are memories of her across the country.

In most cases, the memory of Helen is the memory of a dance. The 'Helen song' became, and still is, a signifier. It could often be divorced from its surroundings, remembered in isolation from the rest of the film. Vikram Kapadia, actor, director and playwright, suggests that even the lyrics were not the point in a Helen number; only she was: 'I can't really remember my favourite Helen song. The lyrics or melody did not matter as much as watching her dance...Besides, her kind of numbers were not the sentimental or emotional ballads that I would sing while driving a car or having a shower.'

To Kapadia, Helen was 'a pretty Indian [film] dancer who looked like a foreigner' and thus represented 'a relief from the Indianness of the rest of the film. She looked Caucasian, spoke with an accent, wore enticing costumes and showed her stuff, which was far more exciting than watching a sati savitri attempt amateurish Bharatanatyam in a mangalsutra and a sari. And yet there was no loss of dignity in Helen's act...She was never, never vulgar. She was graceful.'

But she was a lot more than just that to most men, including Kapadia. 'I now realize that Helen was an integral part of my life, of growing up,' he says. 'She was there, no questions asked. She was immortal because heroines came and went but Helen went on for ever. I now look back and feel that she was literally a masala in the dish of Hindi cinema. And more often than not hers was a complete act in itself and not a link in the plot. We don't question why this particular masala is required, but we lap it up. It is a custom, a tradition.'

'A thousand films?'

Ritu is surprised but pleased. As one of the assistants in Video Plaza, Lamington Road, he expects to make a killing.

A week later, when I return, he is a bit disconsolate.

'Those &*%*s haven't put *Alif Laila* on VCD. Can I get you a video cassette?'

He finds that he can't.

'Look at those %&^@#s. Don't they have any respect? Such a great artiste and her films are not available.'

I agree that I also find it shocking.

'This is Bombay. One day you're on top and the next day you can't find a place to take a dump.'

Fahad Samaar, independent producer, film-maker and director, who was behind the televised 'Golden Girl Tribute' in 2001, agrees. 'She remains an indelible part of the whole experience of cinema because she was part of your rites of passage. She represented the first wet dream for two, perhaps three generations of Indian men.' As a pioneer of television's Hindi film countdowns, Samaar would often escape the tedium of number-crunching and dealing with teenyboppers with huge egos by putting together Specials. 'The Helen Special was always a big hit; you couldn't go wrong with her. There was such a body of work, of such extraordinary variety and range, that you could pick almost at random and come up with a brilliant segment.'

He remembers his first encounter with Helen. 'It was at the Mehboob Khan Studios, where she was dancing. There may have been other stars present, more important in a commercial sense, but I couldn't take my eyes off her. And then a spot boy made a lewd remark, the kind that every man was thinking as Helen shook her booty. She got to hear of it and the spot boy was fired. On the spot. I remember him weeping and asking for his job back, to no avail. But I guess, when you're doing the kind of dances she did, in a set filled with Indian men, almost all of whom see women as objects, you have to have some defences. It was well known that she wore a body suit, so that the flesh she showed was not flesh at all but simulated flesh.'

In a way, this helped support that ubiquitous remark about Helen, that she was never vulgar. Kapadia has already said it above. Here's Shah Rukh Khan, repeating pretty much the same sentiment to the now missin'-in-action website pyara.com: 'She [Helen] was a cabaret artiste who did not look cheap. Just like Cuckoo. My father was a great fan of hers. I am not taking away anything from Nana, Manisha or Salman but I want to go and see the on-the-floors *Khamoshi* for Helen and I know a lot of people like me who feel the same way.'

For her male viewers then, the relationship seems to have been a complex one, carrying with it the impersonal charge of public sexuality, which seems to be necessarily demeaning, and a personalized affection which works against any sexual objectification. Hence, perhaps, the need to continually reassert the lack of vulgarity in Helen's dances.

~

I have just returned to my hotel from trying to track down *Alif Laila* at the National Film Archive and have been told that it isn't available. I am hot and tired and angry. I believe *Alif Laila* is there, I have just been stonewalled. And the bag in which I am carrying my material breaks, spilling Helen pictures all over the floor. The ancient receptionist helps me pick them up and looks at one.

'Helen?'

I explain.

'I would see all her films. If there was a film with no other actor of note I would still see the film for her. I would wait for the song and once it was finished, I would still wait, hoping she would come back again for another song.'

Did he whistle, shout, throw money?

'I was an officer in the railways before retirement,' he says haughtily. 'Officers do not behave like that.'

I smile apologetically. He relents.

'But I wanted to whistle.'

~

That Helen should have a legion of male fans seems obvious. But such is the power of her persona, the complexity of her position, that I also met almost as many female fans, many of whom would call themselves feminists, although they would perhaps nuance the word differently in each case.

'Helen,' says Rachel Dwyer, Reader in Indian Studies and Cinema, SOAS, UK, 'does not threaten women, because she is always naughty but never evil.' In fact, for film-maker and writer Paromita Vohra, Helen did exactly the opposite of unsettling or threatening her. 'Helen was one way in which I could access the pleasure principle. When you watch a film, you attach yourself to certain moments and these can have some role in defining who you are. To me, Helen was one of those moments. She seemed to be about pleasure, but about the kind of pleasure that was a good thing.

'The pleasures into which Helen could release you were the ideas of dressing up, dancing, being in your body, making a display of yourself in a manner that is both sexual and socially sanctioned. In my family, I was the brainy girl and my sister was the pretty girl. That meant I had no way to construct myself as a sexual being. There seemed to be few non-typical spaces that I could occupy. In some way, and I can only say this in retrospect, Helen offered a concept of femaleness that I would not have found myself able to accept. Helen had a lack of agency in most of her roles as a vamp; her love was a masochistic surrender to the notion of love. These are seductive notions in themselves and they are ways of accessing mainstream discourses of romance.'

To Arshia Sattar, writer, translator and teacher, Helen represented 'the first shock of recognition of ourselves as sexual beings'. To her, Helen was unmatched. 'As a "cabaret artist", she was far superior to Jayshree T. and Bindu and even Prema Narayan. I think I understood that she really was sexier than all the rest. I knew she was "Burmese". She was slinky and exotic—her slanted eyes, her permanent pout, her fair skin, all made her stand out. And she seemed to be enjoying herself as she danced.

'Maybe I was able to like her better because she was so clearly different. She didn't look like us and she had an Anglo name—all mechanisms of distance and separation—so nothing she did—act sexy, deliver come-on lines—impinged on me and my desire to be a good girl. Sometimes, the other vamps made me cringe and embarrassed me with all that they stood for, but Helen never did.

'When I saw her in *Sholay*, dancing to *Mehbooba*, all the love and admiration I had for Helen came flooding back. It is still my most favourite song-picturization in Hindi films. When I think of her, it is this song that comes into my head. Those scenes capture everything about Helen that I loved the most—her sensuality, her physical grace, her freedom, her exoticness, her exuberance.

'Much later, after being schooled in Orientalism, I...was sure that she was being cruelly exploited. She seemed to be the perfect subaltern, an Anglo-Indian woman being forced to demean herself by a classist and racist system. It was as if she was carrying the burden of all our prejudices about Anglo-Indians, and about Anglo-Indian women in particular, in her role as the illicit woman, the vamp, the moll, the slut. And I could not decide whether to pity her for being a victim or be mad at her for being complicit. But this was the po-co-po-mo-po-fem consciousness of the 1980s that I now realize needs far more nuances and shades.'

For Sumati Nagrath, a Ph.D student working on Hindi cinema as popular culture, Helen has transcended time. Sumati grew up in the late 1980s and early 1990s, by which time Helen had long retired. The typical Bollywood film, too, had changed and the new heroines had usurped the vamp's territory. And yet Sumati is a serious fan. 'She occupies so much of my mind space when I think about Hindi movies. My mother loved Helen as much as my dad did, or perhaps more. Maybe that is where my love for her stems from. They would sit together and hum her songs and tell me about how gorgeous she looked in this film, that song. Their favourite was *Mera naam Chin-Chin-Choo*. I first saw it on *Chitrahaar*, I think. There she was, dancing, full of life, and with a smile that touched your heart instantly. Helen did the impossible, she managed to win your heart when you were meant to despise her. She was almost always objectified and portrayed either as the highly sexualized temptress or as a threat to the moral fabric of society. But, as an actor, she rose above all that. I loved her because she danced with such abandon, like she didn't care about the people looking at her, the hero's disapproval, the heroine's moral high ground.

'Her every movement seemed to mock the morality of those around her, right down to *Khamoshi* and *Mohabbatein*. Helen has been replaced by item numbers and that makes me ill. Where is the *fun*? Yes—that, I think, was what appealed to me the most about Helen: she always seemed to be enjoying herself. And that enthusiasm was infectious, especially if you see the heroines of that time who stood there shaking their pallu or prancing around trees. At least when Helen pranced she did it with panache.'

In Vohra's opinion, Helen transcended not just time but also categories. 'To me, Helen was always a sexualized figure. Which is why she seems to transcend categories like white-black-brown, Catholic-Hindu-Muslim. The story into which I would put Helen is a story in which she would not be trapped by these. She would be like the character Maggie Gyllenhaal played in *Secretary*, a self-destructive social misfit who takes a job as a secretary and finds that her sadomasochistic relationship with her boss releases her.'

To say that Helen was a sexualized figure might also be a way of saying that she was routinely the object of the male gaze. 'You can't get away from that,' agrees Ruchi Narain, a film-maker. 'There is no denying that she was objectified in her most famous avatar, that of a dancer. But reality is not so simple. Objectification may also be a choice, especially in a country like ours, where the prescribed good girl is clad from head to toe, practically in a burqa. In this context,

Helen is empowered by the very act of choosing to be seen. We could, of course, extend this to the Miss India contest and beauty pageants of the kind. It may be politically incorrect to judge a woman on the length of her legs or the smoothness of the upper slopes of her bosom, but once again, these women *choose* to be so seen. There is something encouraging about Miss Bhatinda or Miss Bhubaneshwar, especially encouraging that their mothers support them. It is in this respect that Helen becomes empowering. She emboldened a generation of women—the adult women of today grew up watching her shake her booty.

'I'm not arguing that she was the feminist movement here or that she was the cause of the new freedom women have with their bodies. Helen simply had a greater reach because Hindi films have that kind of reach. Yes, she could have been used better, cast as a sassy woman who knew her mind and her sexuality, because that is what she had: she had sexuality while the other screen women had hearts and ghunghats and wombs.'

~

It is not surprising that Helen the outsider would also find a following in the gay community that has always been Othered and held up to scorn by Indian cinema. Although there has been a tradition of homoerosis in many classical Indian art forms, the gay man and the lesbian woman have yet to be represented fairly in Hindi films. A tentative attempt at understanding had been made as early as 1971 in *Badnaam Basti*, but the homosexual community was otherwise served by transvestites, transsexuals or simply limp-wristed catamites who would bed anyone. At the time of writing, Hindi cinema may have discovered the use of lesbian fantasies (played out with a barely disguised misogyny) for heterosexual men in films like *Girlfriend* (2004), and *My Brother Nikhil* (2005) has dealt with homosexuals fairly, but otherwise gays and lesbians have been kept out of the frame.

Stars matter because they act out aspects of life that matter to us; for the homosexual man the very fact of Helen's *existence* and her defiant declaration of it is important. On her supple form and her heightened projection of the feminine, audiences could play out a variety of fantasies—most of them sexual, many of them aspirational, some of them identificatory.

'I always wanted to be Helen,' says Anil K. (name changed to protect identity), an insurance salesman. 'Not that I wanted to dress up like that and dance, but because I have spent my life slinking around, looking for love, while she pursued it openly. My sex life has been spent in toilets, in maidans or on the beaches at night. Helen always had the lights turned on to her. And the characters she played could speak about love and desire openly. I wanted that.'

'I always admired the way she dressed, or was dressed,' he adds. 'She seemed to be saying, "Look at me, look at me." She was saying, "I am here and I won't go away." I'm afraid that I will never get to the point when I can say that. I am afraid that I *will* get to the point when I will have to say it.'

In her hyper-femininity, Helen was almost as much of an 'ambulatory archive of womanhood' as a drag queen, synthesizing all that was defined as feminine—as opposed to what actually constitutes the feminine—into three minutes of dancing.

Her standard costume was built only to play revelation against concealment. The big hair, rainbow make-up and costume jewellery were so outrageous and outlandish that it became clear that they were more than just accessories. They were as much part of the persona as the over-large mouth (painted to caricature) or the bump and grind routines. Her power over men was also mythologized, both in the lyrics of her songs as well as in the choreography. We can begin at *Baarish* (1957), where she claims, *Jo bhi dekhe mera jalwa ho jaaye qurbaan* (One glimpse of me is all it takes to fell any man) and knocks the male dancers over so that they lie helpless on their backs, and go on to *Raaz* (1981), where she's still crooning, *Main bhi ek raaz hoon* (I, too, am a mystery).

There was nothing small or even life-sized about Helen. This was the original over-the-top girl. This extravagance, this reckless pursuit and seduction, matters to the marginal because of its in-your-face nature.

It is this sense of the unreal that also makes it possible for heterosexual men to 'play Helen'. All over Hindi-movie-watching India, young men will wriggle their hips and make play with their eyelashes and even go lap-leaping. At one level, they are simply caricaturing the object of their desire, distancing themselves from what they want and reducing it to what they can handle. At another level, Helen liberates the sense of rhythm, or the innate desire to slip and slide over a continuum of sexual roles. It is also possible, dressed up safely as Helen and 'only performing', to experience the nature of *being desirable*, as opposed to desiring which, especially in the Indian moral context, is invariably the male lot.

Perhaps this is why Anuj Vaidya chooses Helen as his way of interrogating issues like sex, death and marginality in *Bad Girl with a Heart of Gold*. Says Viraf H., advertising executive, 'I see Anuj's film as a way of looking at what it means to be silenced. Helen died in many of her films; those of us with alternative persuasions are killed by degrees. Our families don't want to recognize us. They may love us but they don't want to love what they see as our "abnormal tendencies". Society wants us to conform. Even we want us to conform. Check out the gay listings. "Straight-acting" is highly prized because no one wants to meet someone who may be advertising his sexuality. And then there is Helen, always advertising her sexuality, emphasizing it, playing it up, rubbing the noses of the bourgeoisie in it. How could she not be our heroine? When she dies, we know why she dies. We know because we die a little every day.'

The one regret that I have is that I did not meet Helen.

It's not just my regret:

'I'm doing a book on Helen.'

'Are you going to meet her?'

Three years ago, when I started writing this book, I began by saying, 'Yes.' Two years ago, I made that a 'Maybe'. A year ago, I made it 'I hope so'. Then I stopped calling her and began to make excuses.

'I don't need to meet her. This is not a biography.'

'Awwww.'

'It just didn't happen.'

'Awwww.'

I know. I feel it too.

~

And I miss Helen. It's nice to watch her as an old woman in *Dil Ne Jisse Apna Kahaa*, but I miss that electric presence. I miss the enthusiastic dancing. I miss the thrill of affection I always felt when she began to lisp her lines. I miss the films of the seventies—perhaps because I grew up on them but also perhaps because I could sense that they were treading a careful line, deliberately playing with expectation and hope, calibrating the degrees to which they could play with the sexual. When I watch an item number now, so much more glossy, so much better choreographed, the women with bodies honed to reptilian perfection and dressed in much better clothes, the men all gloss and muscle, I miss the old dances in which Helen performed. I miss the way in which colours clashed, bordello red against sunset orange. I miss the extras standing around in their stale clothes and the frumpy supporting dancers in their odd outfits. I miss the laboured camera movements and the unremarkable editing. I miss the ability to feel superior, to laugh a little at and with the cinema of my childhood.

The item numbers of the 00s take themselves very seriously. In the moue that is the standard sexualized challenge on every female dancer's face, I do not find the laughing invitation to naughtiness that I remember in Helen's. You would not dare laugh at—no, not even *with*—these women. In their catlike sinuousness and their perfection, I find a lack of specificity and an erasure of nuance. None of these women would ever be able to carry off crescent moon earrings in bright orange, sequins over the eyebrows, blue eyeshadow, a russet-gold bouffant and figured stockings and then claim, as Helen did to James Ivory, that she designed those outfits and did her own make-up. None of these women would be able to wield a raincoat or a slipper or a handkerchief with the right degree of coquettishness and sensuality. They're never out of step but they're not having fun.

I miss Helen.

The industry does too.

And there can be no greater tribute than that.

Acknowledgements

Thanks must go out to the following people:

To Andrea, my sister, who slept through the crash-bang-wail of thousands of minutes of Hindi film, and listened while I agonized, theorized and complained;

To Lalitha Luke, who typed my handwritten notes;

To Harish Raghuwanshi who helped build the filmography;

To Paromita Vohra, who lent me her copy of *Desperately Seeking Helen*, pointed out other films and trashed the first draft;

To the staff of Video Plaza, Lamington Road, Mumbai, Mukhtarbhai and Ritu Kumar, for digging out Helen films with a great deal of enthusiasm;

To Angela Nagraj, who checked the facts and suffered through endless lists;

To Rahul Srivastava, Arundhathi Subramaniam, Naresh Fernandes, Rachel Dwyer and Sumati Nagrath who read the manuscript at different stages and offered critical comments and suggestions;

To all those who contributed their thoughts and opinions in the last chapter;

To the staff of *Man's World*, who gasped at the right moments when I described Helen films, listened bemused as I hummed Helen songs off-key, and laughed obligingly when I laughed;

And to its editor and publisher, Radhakrishnan Nair, whose quiet support and empathy have helped this book in ways that cannot be explained adequately;

To Manoj Menon and Priya Nair and Dia and Kian who opened their doors so I could work on the third draft of the first few chapters;

To Niloufer Venkatraman and Andre Morris for *brun pao* and butter and the fresh Lonavla air of Writer's Bloc, where I retreated to get past the third draft of the last few chapters;

To Mehlli Gobhai, at whose house I worked on draft four;

To Nasreen Munni Kabir who promised me her film on Helen and then came through with breathtaking efficiency;

To Shashi Baliga, editor, *Filmfare*, for permission to quote from the magazine, and from her own interview with Helen that appeared in *Savvy*;

To Ravi Singh, who is to blame.

List of Photographs

Long before it became fashionable to use Hindi-film posters as living-room decoration, or the kitsch value of stills was turned into commerce, I would walk the streets of Mumbai looking for pictures of the film stars who often seemed more real than many of the people in my life. I bought several of the pictures in this book from the streets around Lamington Road, from the iron railing of a park, from little stalls like the one owned by Husseinibhai (who called me, for his own reasons, 'pehelwan' and my sister, who sometimes accompanied me, 'Mala Sinha'). Those were the days when it was possible to get a lovely still of Helen for twenty rupees. (It must be remembered that since a complete vegetarian meal cost Rs 4.50, I spent the equivalent of many meals on each picture.) Thus, some of these pictures are from films that I have not been able to identify. But Helen is so pretty in all of them, so special, I wanted them in here.

Here's the list of those that I could identify, a task made a little easier, for this revised edition, by the Internet (the number on the left, in each case, is the page on which the picture appears):

Filmography

This is not a definitive filmography. It represents what I have been able to find in Rajendra Ojha's *80 Glorious Years of Indian Cinema* and from material sent to me by Harish Raghuwanshi. Need I say that I would be delighted if this did become the definitive filmography? Meanwhile, the ones in boldface type are the films I have seen.

1951

KHAZAANA, 35mm, B/W
Producer: Bakshi Brothers; Director: M. Sadiq; Music Director: C. Ramachandra
Main Cast: Madhubala, Nasir Khan, Gope, Om Prakash, Cuckoo, Helen

SHABISTAN, 35mm, B/W
P: Filmistan; D: B Mitra; M: C. Ramachandra and Madan Mohan
C: Naseem, Shyam, Sapru, Murad, Cuckoo, Helen

1952

AMBAR, 35mm, B/W
P: Jagat Pictures; D: Jayant Desai; M: Gulam Mohammed
C: Nargis, Raj Kapoor, Agha, Baby Tanuja, Cuckoo, Helen

BADNAAM, 35mm, B/W
P: Filmistan; D: D.D. Kashyap; M: Basant Prakash
C: Shyama, Balraj Sahni, Ulhas, Murad, Sheila, Jankidas, Helen

NAZARIYA, 35mm, B/W
P: M & T Films; D: Murtaza Changezi; M: Bhola Shreshta
C: Geeta Bali, Begum Para, David, Madan Puri, Helen

RANGEELA, 35mm, B/W
P: Bhagwan Art Productions; D: Bhagwan; M: Jamal Sen
C: Bhagwan, Purnima, Badri Prasad, Indira Kale, Helen

1953

ALIF LAILA, 35mm, B/W
P: K. Amarnath Productions; D: K. Amarnath; M: Shyam Sunder
C: Nimmi, Asha Mathur, Vijay Kumar, Pran, Helen

KHOJ, 35mm, B/W
P: Durga Films; D: Balwant Bhatt; M: Nissar
C: Shammi Kapoor, Shammi, Mahipal, Helen

MALIKA SALOMI, 35 m, B/W
P: Comedy Pics; D: Mohd. Hussein; M: Iqbal & K. Dayal
C: Roopa Verman, Kamran, Krishna Kumari, Helen, Dara

RAIL KA DIBBA, 35mm, B/W
P: All India Pictures; D: P.N. Arora; M: Gulam Mohammed
C: Madhubala, Shammi Kapoor, Helen, Om Prakash

1954

ALIBABA AND 40 THIEVES, 35mm, B/W
P: Basant; D: Homi Wadia; M: S.N. Tripathi & Chandragupta

C: Shakila, Mahipal, Helen, S.N. Tripathi, Maruti, Sharda

KASTURI, 35mm, B/W
P: Sargam; D: Vrajendra Gaur;
M: Pankaj Mullick & Jamal Sen
C: Nimmi, Sajjan, Bipin Gupta, Helen, Anand Prasad, Samson

LALPARI, 35mm, B/W
P: N.C. Films D: Kedar Kapoor
M: Hansraj Behl
C: Shakila, Mahipal, Kuldip Kaur, Helen, Johnny Walker

MAYURPANKH, 35 mm, Colour
P: Sahu Films; D: Kishore Sahu;
M: Shankar-Jaikishen
C: Kishore Sahu, Sumitra Devi, Odette Fergusson, Jankidas, Reginald Jackson, Cuckoo, Asha Mathur, Helen

PEHLI JHALAK, 35mm, B/W
P: Jagat Pictures; D: M.V. Raman;
M: C. Ramachandra
C: Vyjayathimala, Kishore Kumar, Pran, Om Prakash, Dara Singh, Shammi, Helen

PILIPILI SAAHEB, 35mm, B/W
P: Kwatra Films; D: H.S. Kwatra;
M: Sardul Kwatra
C: Shyama, Agha, Pran, Sunder, Helen, Mumtaz, Mehmood

SHARTH, 35mm, B/W
P: Filmistan; D: B Mitra;
M: Hemant Kumar
C: Shyama, Deepak, Shashikala, I.S. Johar, Sulochana, Chaman Puri, Helen

1955

AB-E-HAYAT, 35mm, B/W
P: Filmistan; D: Ramanlal Dessai;
M: Sardar Malik
C: Premnath, Shashikala, Smriti Biswas, Pran, Helen

HATIMTAI KI BETI, 35mm, B/W
P: N. Vakil; D: N. Vakil;
M: A.R. Qureshi
C: Chitra, Mahipal, Daljit, Krishna Kumari, Kumkum, Helen, Naaz

HOOR-E-ARAB, 35mm, B/W
P: All India Pics; D: P.N. Arora;
M: Gulam Mohammed
C: Pradeep Kumar, Chitra, Om Prakash, Helen, Shashikala

JAGADGURU SHANKARACHARYA, 35mm, B/W
P: Celestial Pics; D: S. Fatehlal;
M: Avinash Vyas
C: Abhi Bhattacharya, Sulochana Chatterji, Durga Khote, Sapru, Helen

MAST QALANDAR, 35mm, B/W
P: N.C. Films; D: Kedar Kapoor;
M: Hansraj Behl
C: Shakila, Mahipal, Kuldip Kaur, Tiwari, Johnny Walker, Helen

MISS COCA COLA, 35mm, B/W
P: Danny Films; D: Kedar Kapoor;
M: O.P. Nayyar
C: Geeta Bali, Shammi Kapoor, Kuldip Kaur, Johnny Walker, Om Prakash, Lalita Pawar, Helen

SHAH BEHRAM, 35mm, B/W
P: Baharistan Productions; D: N. Vakil; M: Hansraj Behl
C: Asha Mathur, Mahipal, Hiralal, Sunder, Tiwari, Helen

SITARA, 35mm, B/W
P: All India Pics; D: S.K. Ojha;
M: Gulam Mohammed
C: Vyjayantimala, Pradeep Kumar, Gope, Om Prakash, Shashikala, Jayant, Begum Para, Helen

TEERANDAZ, 35mm, B/W
P: Roshni Films; D: H.S. Rawail;
M: C. Ramchandra
C: Madhubala, Ajit, Gope, Kuldip Kaur, Chandrashekhar, Helen

VEER RAJPUTANI, 35mm, B/W
P: Basant; D: J.B.H. Wadia;
M: Bulo C. Rani
C: Shakila, Manhar Desai, Meenakshi, Bipin Gupta, Helen

1956

AANKH KA NASHA, 35mm, B/W
P: Natraj Prod.; D: Ved-Mohan;
M: Dhaniram
C: Anita Guha, M Rajan, Shammi, Helen, Gope, Raj Mehra

AAWAAZ, 35mm, B/W
P: Mehboob Productions; D: Zia Sarhady; M: Salil Choudhuri
C: Nalini Jaywant, Usha Kiran, Rajendra Kumar, Achla Sachdev, Manorama, Raj Kumar, Helen

ANJAAN, 35mm, B/W
P: All India Pics; D: M. Sadiq;
M: Hemant Kumar
C: Vyjayantimala, Pradeep Kumar, Johnny Walker, Jeevan, Mubarak, Helen, Minoo Mumtaz

BAGHI SARDAR, 35mm, B/W
P: Baroda Theatres; D: Majnu;
M: B.N. Bali
C: Daljit, Chitra, Ameeta, Amarnath, Majnu, Helen, Kammo

CHAR MINAR, 35mm, B/W
P: Nagina Films; D: Ravindra Dave; M: Sardul Kwatra
C: Jabeen Jalil, Nasir Khan, Helen, Altaf, Bhagwan

DELHI DURBAR, 35mm, B/W
P: Gandhi & Chokshi; D: Chandrakant; M: S.N. Tripathi
C: Sumitra Devi, Rehana, Veena, Prem Adeeb, Ullhas, Helen

FIFTY-FIFTY, 35mm, B/W
P: Roop Nagar; D: R.L. Malhotra;
M: Madan Mohan
C: Nalini Jaywant, M Rajan, Manmohan Krishna, Om Prakash, Helen, Tun Tun, David

HALAKU, 35mm, B/W
P: All India Pics; D: D.D. Kashyap; M: Shanker-Jaikishen
C: Meena Kumari, Ajit, Pran, Veena, Niranjan Sharma, Minoo Mumtaz, Sunder, Helen

HATIMTAI, 35mm, B/W
P: Basant; D: Homi Wadia;
M: S.N. Tripathi
C: Jairaj, Shakila, B.M. Vyas, Meenaxi, Krishna Kumari, Helen

INQUILAB, 35mm, B/W
P: W.S. Films; D: Kedar Kapoor;
M: Hansraj Behl
C: Ranjan, Shyama, Tiwari, Kuldip Kaur, Sunder, Helen

INSAAF, 35mm, B/W
P: Bhagyoday Pics; D: Kedar Kapoor; M: Hansraj Behl
C: Nalini Jaywant, Durga Khote, Johnny Walker, Helen

KAARWAN, 35mm, B/W
P: Shahkar Productions; D: Rafiq Rizvi; M: S. Mohinder
C: Shakila, Mahipal, Hiralal, Yashodhara Katju, Helen

KHUL JA SIM SIM, 35mm, B/W
P: Golden Movies; D: Nanubhai Vakil; M: Hansraj Behl
C: Shakila, Mahipal, Hiralal, Helen

KISMET, B/W
P: Starland Prod; D: Nanabhai Bhatt; M: Chitragupta
C: Ranjan, Peace Kanwal, Tiwari, Nishi, Gope, Helen

LAL-E-YAMAN, 35mm, B/W
P: Vakil Productions; D: Nanubhai Vakil; M: A.R. Qureishi
C: Chitra, Daljit, Mahipal, Hiralal, Sunder, Helen

MR LAMBU, 35mm, B/W
P: Sheikh Mukhtar; D: N.A. Ansari; M: O.P. Nayyar
C: Sheikh Mukhtar, Suraiya, Bhagwan, Kamaljeet, Helen

NAYA AADMI, 35 mm, B/W
P: Jupiter Pics; D: C.P. Dixit; M: Vishwanathan & Rammoorthy
C: Anjali Devi, N T Rama Rao, Anwar, Gope, Jamuna, Ragini, Helen, R. Nagendra Rao

PATRANI, 35mm, B/W
P: Prakash; D: Vijay Bhatt; M: Shankar Jaikishen
C: Vyjayantimala, Pradeep Kumar, Om Prakash, Shashikala, Durga Khote, David, Jeevan, Helen

RAJ HATH, 35mm, B/W
P: Minerva; D: Sohrab Modi; M: Shanker-Jaikishen
C: Madhubala, Pradeep Kumar, Sohrab Modi, Ulhas, Helen

SAILAAB, 35mm, B/W
P: Emar Films; D: Guru Dutt; M: Mukul Roy
C: Abhi Bhattacharya, Geeta Bali, Smriti Biswas, Bipin Gupta, Ram Singh, Helen

SHATRANJ, 35mm, B/W
P: Revati Productions; D: Gyan Mukherjee; M: C. Ramachandra
C: Ashok Kumar, Meena Kumari, Jagdish Sethi, Vijayalakshmi, Yakub, Nana Palsikar, Helen

SIPAHSALAR, 35mm, B/W
P: Eagle Films; D: Mohd Hussein; M: Iqbal
C: Shammi Kapoor, Nadira, S. Nazir, Kumkum, Helen, Samson, Cuckoo

SHRIMATI 420, 35mm, B/W
P: Sippy Films; D: G.P. Sippy; M: N. Dutta
C: Meena, Om Prakash, Johnny Walker, Helen

TAJ, 35mm, B/W
P: Dossi Films; D: Nandlal Jaswantlal; M: Hemant Kumar
C: Vyjayantimala, Pradeep Kumar, Bipin Gupta, Jeevan, Helen

TAKSAAL, 35mm, B/W
P: Hemen Gupta Prod; D: Hemen Gupta; M: Roshan
C: Balraj Sahni, Nirupa Roy, Smriti Biswas, Helen

YAHUDI KI BETI, 35mm, B/W
P: Desai Films; D: Nanubhai Vakil; M: Kamal Mitra
C: Anita Guha, Daljeet, Tiwari, Tabassum, Helen

1957

AMARSINGH RATHOD, 35mm, B/W
P: Dinesh Films; D: Jaswant Jhaveri; M: Sanmukh Babu
C: Jairaj, Nirupa Roy, Al-Nasir, Ram Singh, Veena, Helen

BAARISH, 35mm, B/W
P: Alankar Chitra; D: Shanker Mukherji; M: C. Ramachandra
C: Dev Anand, Nutan, Jagdish Sethi, Lalita Pawar, Mehmood, Madan Puri, Helen

BEGUNAH, 35mm, B/W
P: Roop Kamal Chitra; D: Narendra Suri; M: Shanker-Jaikishen
C: Shakila, Kishore Kumar, Raja Nene, Krishnakant, Helen

CHAMAK CHANDNI, 35mm, B/W
P: Chitra Bharati; D: Manibhai Vyas; M: Sardar Mallick
C: Shakila, Mahipal, Tiwari, Maruti, Chandrashekhar, Helen

CHANGEZ KHAN, 35mm, B/W
P: N.C. Films; D: Kedar Kapoor; M: Hansraj Behl

C: Bina Rai, Premnath, Shaikh Mukhtar, Johnny Walker, Helen

CHHOTE BABU, 35mm, B/W
P: Movie Stars; D: Harsukh Bhatt; M: Madan Mohan
C: Nimmi, Shekhar, Abhi Bhattacharya, Kanhaiyalal, Helen

COFFEE HOUSE, 35mm, B/W
P: Nitie Art Prod; D: Hari Walia; M: Roshan
C: Geeta Bali, Shammi Kapoor, Chanchal, Bhagwan, Helen

DUNIYA RANG RANGILI, 35mm, B/W
P: Sadiq Productions; D: M. Sadiq; M: O.P. Nayyar
C: Rajendra Kumar, Johnny Walker, Shyama, Chand Usmani, Helen, Amar

MR X, 35mm, B/W
P: Sippy Films; D: Nanabhai Bhatt; M: N. Dutt
C: Ashok Kumar, Nalini Jaywant, Pran, Johnny Walker, Amirbai Karnatki, Helen

NAAG MANI, 35mm, B/W
P: Bombay M; D: Raman B. Desai; M: Avinash Vyas
C: Nirupa Roy, Trilok Kapoor, Manhar Desai, Helen

NAU DO GYAARAH, 35mm, B/W
P: Navketan; D: Vijay Anand; M: S.D. Burman
C: Dev Anand, Kalpana Kartik, Jeevan, Shashikala, Rashid Khan, Lalita Pawar, Helen

NEELOFAR, 35mm, B/W
P: All India Pics; D: P.N. Arora; M: Basant Prakash
C: Chitra, Suresh, Nishi, Sunder, Amar, Shyam Kumar, Helen

PAVANPUTRA HANUMAN, 35mm, B/W
P: Basant; D: Babubhai Mistry; M: Chitragupta
C: S N Tripathi, Mahipal, Anita Guha, Amirbai Karnataki, Helen

QAIDI, 35mm, B/W
P: Eagle Films; D: Mohd. Hussein; M: O.P. Nayyar
C: Padmini, Suresh, Agha, Anwar, Helen, Johnny Walker, Ragini

SHAHI BAZAR, 35 mm, B/W
P: Chandni Ch; D: Balwant Dave, Padmakant Pathak; M: Dhaniram
C: Chitra, Mahipal, Sapru, Sheikh, Naazi, Raj Kumar, Helen

SHER-E-BAGHDAD, 35mm, B/W
P: Hind Pics; D: Om Sonik; M: Jimmy
C: Nigar Sultana, Mahipal, Hiralal, Helen

YAHOODI KI LADKI, 35mm, B/W
P: New Oriental Pics; D: S.D. Narang; M: Hemant Kumar
C: Madhubala, Pradeep Kumar, Jagirdar, Hiralal, Helen

1958

CHALTI KA NAAM GAADI, 35mm, B/W
P: K.S. Pics; D: Satyen Bose; M: S.D. Burman
C: Ashok Kumar, Madhubala, Anoop Kumar, Kishore Kumar, Helen, K.N. Singh, Cuckoo

HOWRAH BRIDGE, 35mm, B/W
P: Shri Shakti Films; D: Shakti Samanta; M: O.P. Nayyar
C: Ashok Kumar, Madhubala, K.N. Singh, Dhumal, Om Prakash, Helen, Kammo, Madan Puri

KABHI ANDHERA KABHI UJAALA, 35mm, B/W
P: Mehtab Films; D: C.P. Dixit;

M: O.P. Nayyar
C: Nutan, Kishore Kumar, Chitra, Lalita Pawar, K.N. Singh, Yakub, Madan Puri, Helen

KARIGAR, 35mm, B/W
P: Panchdeep Chitra; D: Vasant Joglekar; M: C. Ramchandran
C: Ashok Kumar, Nirupa Roy, Agha, Lalita Pawar, Om Prakash, Sumati Gupte, Helen, Minoo Mumtaz

KHAZANCHI, 35mm, B/W
P: All India Pics; D: P.N. Arora; M: Madan Mohan
C: Balraj Sahni, Shyama, Rajendra Kumar, Chitra, Manorama, Helen

MILAN, 35mm, B/W
P: N.C. Films; D: Kedar Kapoor; M: Hansraj Behl
C: Nalini Jaywant, Daisy Irani, Ajit, Nishi, Tiwari, Maruti, Helen

NIGHT CLUB, 35mm, B/W
P: Varma Pics; D: Naresh Saigal; M: Madan Mohan
C: Ashok Kumar, Kamini Kaushal, Mubarak, Nishi, Helen, Iftekhar

PIYA MILAN, 35mm, B/W
P: R.R. Prod; D: Raghunath; M: Ramesh
C: Vyjayantimala, Raja Sulochana, Helen, Reeta

SIM SIM MARJINA, 35mm, B/W
P: Golden Movies; D: Narindra Dave; M: A.R. Qureshi
C: Shakila, Mahipal, Hiralal, Helen, Roopmala

SITAMGAR, 35mm, B/W
P: Venus Pics; D: T. Prakash Rao; M: G. Ramnathan
C: Padmini, Ragini, Shivaji Ganesan, Helen, Tanga Velini

TAQDEER, 35mm, B/W
P: Neela Prod; D: Lekhraj Bhakri; M: Dhaniram
C: Shyama, Karan Dewan, Asha Mathur, Madan Puri, Helen

TWELVE O'CLOCK, 35mm, B/W
P: Sippy Films; D: Pramod Chakraborty; M: O.P. Nayyar
C: Guru Dutt, Waheeda Rehman, Shashikala, Johnny Walker, Tun Tun, Helen

YAHUDI, 35mm, B/W
P: Bombay Films; D: Bimal Roy; M: Shanker-Jaikishen
C: Sohrab Modi, Meena Kumari, Nigar Sultana, Nazir Hussain, Baby Naaz, Helen, Cuckoo

1959

ANARI, 35mm, B/W
P: L.B. Films; D: Hrishikesh Mukherjee; M: Shanker-Jaikishen
C: Raj Kapoor, Nutan, Lalita Pawar, Motilal, Shobha Khote, Mukhri, Nazir, Helen

BAAZIGAR, 35mm, B/W
P: Mukul Pics; D: Nanabhai Bhatt; M: Chitragupta
C: Nirupa Roy, Jairaj, Romi, Tiwari, Helen, Sunder

BEDARD ZAMAANA KYA JAANE, 35mm, B/W
P: Subhash Films; D: Babubhai Mistry; M: Kalyanji-Anandji
C: Ashok Kumar, Nirupa Roy, Jabeen Jalil, Pran, Helen

CHACHA ZINDABAD, 35mm, B/W
P: Light & Shade; D: Om Prakash; M: Madan Mohan
C: Kishore Kumar, Anita Guha, Om Prakash, Bhagwan, Anoop Kumar, Manorama, Tun Tun

CHAND, 35mm, B/W
P: Tasveeristan; D: Lekhraj Bhakri; M: Hemant Kumar
C: Meena Kumari, Balraj Sahni,

Pandari Bai, Helen, Manoj Kumar, Achla Sachdev, Kuldip Kaur

CID GIRL, 35mm, B/W
P: Shanti Niketan Films;
D: Ravindra Dave; M: Roshan
C: Geeta Bali, Balraj Sahni, Kanhaiyalal, Helen, Nadira

COMMANDER, 35 mm, B/W
P: Mehar Movies; D: Kedar Kapoor; M: Chitragupta
C: Ranjan, Nigar Sultana, Kumkum, Helen, Tiwari

DOCTOR Z, 35mm, B/W
P: Baliwala Films D: Jal
M: Manohar
C: Mahipal, Nirupa Roy, Mirza Mushraff

GUEST HOUSE, 35mm, B/W
P: Golden Movies; D: Ravindra Dave; M: Chitragupta
C: Shakila, Ajit, Pran, Tiwari, Helen, Lalita Pawar, Maruti

KANGAN, 35mm, B/W
P: Uma Shankar Productions;
D: Nanabhai Bhatt;
M: Chitragupta
C: Ashok Kumar, Nirupa Roy, Manhar Desai, Helen

KEECHAK VAADA, 35mm, B/W
P: Janta Chitra; D: Tara Harish;
M: Chitragupta
C: Shakila, Chandrashekhar, Sumati Gupte, Agha, K.N. Singh, Mukhri, Helen

MAIN NASHE MEIN HOON, 35mm, B/W
P: Verma Pics; D: Naresh Saigal;
M: Shanker-Jaikishen
C: Raj Kapoor, Mala Sinha, Mubarak, Helen, Dhumal

HEERA MOTI, 35 mm, B/W
P: Rupalaya; D: Krishan Chopra;
M: Roshan
C: Nirupa Roy, Balraj Sahni, Shubha Khote, Ashim Kumar, Baby Naaz, Helen, Cuckoo

JAALSAAZ, 35mm, B/W
P: Lalit Kala Mandir; D: Arvind Sen; M: N. Dutta
C: Kishore Kumar, Mala Sinha, Pran, Nazir Hussain, Achla Sachdeva, Asit Sen, Helen

JAWANI KI HAWA, 35mm, B/W
P: All India Pics; D: M. Sadiq;
M: Ravi
C: Vyjayantimala, Pradeep Kumar, Purnima, Johnny Walker, Badri Prasad, Helen

LOVE MARRIAGE, 35mm, B/W
P: Subodh Mukherji Prod.;
D: Subodh Mukherji;
M: Shanker-Jaikishen
C: Dev Anand, Mala Sinha, Abhi Bhattacharya, Helen

MR JOHN, 35mm, B/W
P: N.K. Prod; D: Inder; M: N. Dutta
C: Johnny Walker, Shyama, Lalita Pawar, Helen, Tun Tun

NAACH GHAR, 35mm, B/W
P: Kwality Pics; D: R.S. Tara;
M: N. Dutta
C: Ashok Kumar, Anoop Kumar, Shubha Khote, Gopi Krishna, Helen

O TERA KYA KEHENA, 35mm, B/W
P: Young Technicians; D: K. Parvez; M: Kalyanji Veerji
C: Chitra, Mehmood, Helen, Bhagwan, Kammo, Sheikh, Fazlu

PYAR KI RAAHEN, 35mm, B/W
P: Thakur Pics; D: Lekhraj Bhakri;
M: Kanu Ghose
C: Pradeep Kuamr, Anita Guha, Pran, Helen, Jeevan, Kuldip Kaur

SAAWAN, 35mm, B/W
P: N.C. Films; D: R. Tiwari;

M: Hansraj Behl
C: Ameeta, Bharat Bhushan, Leela Mishra, Achla Sachdev, Helen

ZARA BACH KE, 35mm, B/W
P: Rafiq Arabi; D: N.A. Ansari; M: Naushad
C: Johnny Walker, Nanda, Suresh, Helen, Anwar, Shammi, Murad

1960

ABDULLA, 35mm, B/W
P: Amrit Singh; D: Akkoo; M: Bulo C. Rani
C: Shakila, Mahipal, Hiralal, Helen, Maruti

ANGULIMALA, 35mm, B/W
P: Thai Information Service; D: Vijay Bhatt; M: Anil Biswas
C: Nimmi, Bharat Bhushan, Anita Guha, Ullhas, Chandrashekhar, Achla Sachdev, Helen

BAHAANA, 35mm, B/W
P: Silver Films; D: Kumar; M: Madan Mohan
C: Meena Kumari, Sajjan, Anwar, Krishna Kumari, Azurie, Helen

BEWAQOOF, 35mm, B/W
P: I.S. Johar; D: I.S. Johar; M: S.D. Burman
C: Kishore Kumar, Mala Sinha, Pran, Leela Chitnis, Helen

BHAKTI MAHIMA, 35mm, B/W
P: M.R.M Productions; D: K. Shankar; M: Dilip Roy
C: Jamuna, B. Saroja Devi, N.T. Rama Rao, Helen, A. Nageshwar Rao, Kamla Laxman

BUS CONDUCTOR, 35 mm, B/W
P: Ashok Bhambri; D: Dwarka Khosla; M: Bipin and Babul
C: Shyama, Prem Nath, Sadhana, Helen, Cuckoo

CHHABILI, 35mm, B/W
P: Shobhana Pics; D: Shobhana Samarth; M: Snehal Bhatkar
C: Nutan, Tanuja, Kaysi Mehra, K.N. Singh, Agha, Helen

DIL APNA AUR PREET PARAI, 35mm, B/W
P: Mohal Pics; D: Kishore Sahu; M: Shanker-Jaikishen
C: Meena Kumari, Raj Kumar, Nadira, Om Prakash, Naaz, Helen, Shammi, Sulochana

DO DOST, 35mm, B/W
P: Deep Ch; D: K. Anand; M: Chandrakant
C: Chitra, Kamran, Helen, Mehmood

DR SHAITAN, 35 mm, B/W
P: Shreeram; D: Ram Kumar; M: N. Dutta
C: Prem Nath, Shakila, Iftekhar, Helen, Nasreen, Indira

GHUNGHAT, 35mm, B/W
P: Gemini; D: Ramanand Sagar; M: Ravi
C: Bina Rai, Asha Parekh, Pradeep Kumar, Bharat Bhushan, Rehman, Leela Chitnis, Rajendranath, Helen

HUM HINDUSTANI, 35mm, B/W
P: Filmalaya; D: Ram Mukerji; M: Usha Khanna
C: Sunil Dutt, Asha Parekh, Joy Mukerji, Helen, Leela Chitnis

JAALI NOTE, 35mm, B/W
P: S.P. Pics; D: Shakti Samanta; M: O.P. Nayyar
C: Dev Anand, Madhubala, Om Prakash, Helen, Madan Puri

KAALA BAAZAAR, 35mm, B/W
P: Navketan; D: Vijay Anand; M: S.D. Burman
C: Dev Anand, Waheeda Rehman, Nanda, Vijay Anand, Leela Chitnis, Kishore Sahu

MUDH MUDH KE NA DEKH, 35mm, B/W
P: N.C. Films; D: R. Tiwari; M: Hansraj Behl
C: Bharat Bhushan, Anita Guha, Jeevan, Tiwari, Krishna Kumari

LAL QILLA, 35mm, B/W
P: H.L.K Productions; D: Nanabhai Bhatt; M: S.N. Tripathi
C: Jairaj, Nirupa Roy, Tiwari, Helen, B.M. Vyas

NACHE NAGIN BAJE BEEN, 35mm, B/W
P: Janta Ch; D: Tara Harish; M: Chitragupta
C: Kumkum, Chandrashekhar, K.N. Singh, Agha, Helen, Sunder

POLICE DETECTIVE, 35mm, B/W
P: Neo Life Films; D: Nanabhai Bhatt; M: Chitragupta
C: Sudesh Kumar, Shyama, David, Jayshree Gadkar, Helen

RETURN OF SUPERMAN, 35mm, B/W
P: Manmohan Films; D: Manmohan Sabir; M: Anil Biswas
C: Jairaj, Sheila Ramani, Helen, David, Shammi

ROAD NO. 303, 35mm, B/W
P: Mahesh Pics; D: Dharam Kumar; M: C. Arjun
C: Mehmood, Shubha Khote, Bhagwan, K.N. Singh, Helen

SINGAPORE, 35mm, B/W
P: Eagle Films; D: Shakti Samanta; M: Shanker-Jaikishen
C: Shammi Kapoor, Padmini, Maria Merado, Agha, Shashikala, K.N. Singh, Madan Puri, Helen

SUPERMAN, 35mm, B/W
P: Mukul Pics; D: Mohd. Hussein, Anant Thakur; M: Sardar Malik
C: Jairaj, Nirupa Roy, Neeta, Tiwari, Mridula, Majnu, Helen

TRUNK CALL, 35mm, B/W
P: May Fair Films; D: Balraj Mehta; M: Ravi
C: Shyama, Abhi Bhattacharya, Pran, Helen, Shammi, Randhir

TU NAHIN AUR SAHI, 35mm, B/W
P: Radhika Ch; D: Brij; M: Ravi
C: Pradeep Kumar, Kumkum, Nishi, Minoo Mumtaz, Helen, Murad, Kundan, Tun Tun

1961

BAGHDAD, 35mm, B/W
P: Southern Movies; D: T.R. Sundaram; M: Roshan
C: Vyjayantimala, M.G. Ramchandran, Helen, Gopal Krishna, Sandhya

CHHOTE NAWAB, 35mm, B/W
P: Mumtaz Films; D: S.A. Akbar; M: R.D. Burman
C: Ameeta, Mehmood, Johnny Walker, Helen, Minoo Mumtaz

DO BHAI, 35mm, B/W
P: All India Pics; D: Vishram Bedekar; M: N. Dutta
C: Shakila, Abhi Bhattacharya, Anil Kumar, Sulochana, Durga Khote, Manorama, Helen

ELEPHANT QUEEN, 35mm, B/W
P: Rajani Chitra; D: Rajendra; M: Suresh & Talwar
C: Helen, Azad, Sunder, Sherry, Shakila Banu Bhopali, Tun Tun

FLAT NO. 9, 35mm, B/W
P: W.S. Films; D: Ramesh Sharma; M: Usha Khanna
C: Ashok Kumar, Sayeeda Khan, Dinesh Kumar, Helen, Jagdish

GANGA JAMUNA, 35mm, Colour
P: Citizen Films; D: Nitin Bose;

M: Naushad
C: Dilip Kumar, Vyjayanthimala, Nasir Khan, Azra, Kanhaiyalal, Leela Chitnis, Helen

JADOO NAGRI, 35mm, B/W
P: Mukul Pics; D: Radhakant; M: S.N. Tripati
C: Rajan, Vijaya Choudhary, Tiwari, Helen, Majnu

JUNGLEE, 35mm, Colour
P: Subodh Mukerji; D: Subodh Mukerji; M: Shanker-Jaikishen
C: Shammi Kapoor, Saira Banu, Shashikala, Lalita Pawar, Helen

LUCKY NUMBER, 35mm, B/W
P: Manmohan Films;
D: Manmohan; M: Anil Biswas
C: Ameeta, David, Heeralal, Helen, Bhagwan, Tun Tun

MAIN AUR MERA BHAI, 35mm, B/W
P: Mahesh Pics; D: Dharam Kumar; M: C. Arjun
C: Ameeta, Ajit, Mehmood, Nadira, Lalita Pawar, Mukhri, Helen, Tun Tun

MAYA, 35mm, B/W
P: Light of Asia Films; D: D.D. Kashyap; M: Salil Choudhry
C: Dev Anand, Mala Sinha, Lalita Pawar, Agha, Helen

MISS CHAALBAAZ, 35mm, B/W
P: Hind Pics; D: Pyarelal;
M: Jimmy
C: Helen, Shah Agha, K.N. Singh

MODERN GIRL, 35mm, B/W
P: Rainbow Movies; D: R. Bhattacharya; M: Ravi
C: Pradeep Kumar, Sayeeda Khan, Smriti Biswas, Johnny Walker, Madan Puri, Nalini Chonkar, Tun Tun, Bhagwan, Helen

MR INDIA, 35mm, B/W
P: Sippy Films; D: G.P. Sippy;
M: G.S. Kohli
C: I.S. Johar, Geeta Bali, Kamaljeet, Helen

PASSPORT, 35 mm, B/W
P: Nutan Films; D: Pramod Chakravorty; M: Kalyanji-Anandji
C: Madhubala, Helen, Naseer Hussain, K.N. Singh

PYAR KI DASTAAN, 35mm, B/W
P: Pushpa Pics; D: P.L. Santoshi;
M: Naushad
C: Ameeta, Sudesh Kumar, Shubha Khote, Helen

RESHMI ROOMAL, 35mm, B/W
P: Zar Prod; D: Harsukh Bhatt;
M: Babul
C: Shakila, Manoj Kumar, K.N. Singh, Shivraj, Shammi, Helen, Sulochana Chatterji

SAAYA, 35mm, B/W
P: B.N.T. Films; D: Shreeram;
M: Ram Ganguly
C: Nigar Sultana, Nasir Khan, Chitra, Helen, Madan Puri

SAMPOORNA RAMAYANA, 35mm, Colour
P: Basant; D: Babubhai Mistry;
M: Vasant Desai
C: Anita Guha, Mahipal, Sulochana, Lalita Pawar, Gopi Krishna, Achla Sachdev, Raj Kumar, Helen

SAPNE SUHAANE, 35mm, B/W
P: K.R. Films; D: Kedar Kapoor;
M: Salil Choudhry
C: Balraj Sahni, Geeta Bali, Bhagwan, Chandrashekhar, K.N. Singh, Helen

SHOLA JO BHADKE, 35mm, B/W
P: Bhagwan Bros; D: Bhagwan;
M: Nissar
C: Radhika, Kumkum, Purnima, Suresh, Anwar, Helen, Bhagwan

UMAR QAID, 35mm, B/W
P: Super Pics; D: Aspi; M: Iqbal Qureshi
C: Sheikh Mukhtar, Sudhir, Nazima, Mukhri, Hiralal, Helen, Sulochana, Mohan Choti

WANTED, 35mm, B/W
P: Golden Films; D: N.A. Ansari; M: Ravi
C: Sayeeda Khan, Vijay Kumar, Helen, N.A. Ansari, Johnny Walker, Manorama

WARRANT, 35mm, B/W
P: Shanti Niketan Films; D: Kedar Kapoor; M: Roshan
C: Ashok Kumar, Shakila, Raj Mehra, Helen, Cuckoo

ZAMAANA BADAL GAYA, 35mm, B/W
P: Hemlata Pics; D: Jayant Desai; M: Iqbal Qureshi
C: Chand Usmani, Charlie, Iftekhar, Bhagwan, Helen

1962

BEZUBAAN, 35mm, B/W
P: Gope Prod; D: Ram Kamlani; M: Chitragupta
C: Ashok Kumar, Nirupa Roy, Anoop Kumar, David, Pritibala, Shammi, Bablu, Helen

BOMBAY KA CHOR, 35mm, B/W
P: New Oriental Pics; D: S.D. Narang; M: Ravi
C: Mala Sinha, Kishore Kumar, Honey Irani, Helen, Amar

CHINA TOWN, 35mm, B/W
P: Shakti Films; D: Shakti Samanta; M: Ravi
C: Shammi Kapoor, Shakila, Helen, Madan Puri, Shetty

DR VIDYA, 35mm, B/W
P: Deluxe Films; D: Rajendra Bhatia; M: S.D. Burman
C: Vyjayantimala, Manoj Kumar, Helen, Prem Chopra

GYARA HAZAR LADKIYAN, 35mm, B/W
P: Film Friends; D: K.A. Abbas; M: N. Dutta
C: Mala Sinha, Bharat Bhushan, Murad, Madhvi, Imtiaz, Helen

HALF TICKET, 35mm, B/W
P: Cine Technicians; D: Kalidas; M: Salil Choudhry
C: Madhubala, Kishore Kumar, Om Prakash, Helen, Pran

HARIYALI AUR RAASTA, 35mm, B/W
P: Shri Prakash Prod; D: Vijay Bhatt; M: Shanker-Jaikishen
C: Mala Sinha, Manoj Kumar, Shashikala, Om Prakash, Helen

HAWA MAHAL, 35mm, B/W
P: Nav Kala Niketan; D: B.J. Patel; M: Avinash Vyas
C: Ranjan, Helen, Tiwari, Ram Avtar, Babloo Raje, Bela Bose

HONG KONG, 35mm, Colour
P: Pachhi Prod ; D: Pachhi; M: O.P. Nayyar
C: Ashok Kumar, B Saroja Devi, Lilly, Leo, K.N. Singh, Helen, Om Prakash, King Kong

ISI KA NAAM DUNIYA HAI, 35mm, B/W
P: J P Prod; D: Shakti Samanta; M: Ravi
C: Ashok Kumar, Shyama, Sahira, Mehmood, K.N. Singh, Nazir Hussain, Helen, Om Prakash

JADOO MAHAL, 35mm, B/W
P: Akoo Prod; D: Akoo; M: Bulo C Rani
C: Azad, Helen, Hiralal, Krishna Kumari, Ram Kumar, Ajit

JADUGAR DAKU, 35mm, B/W
P: Joy Films; D: Chandrakant;
M: S.N. Tripathi
C: Jairaj, Jabeen Jalil, Madhumati, Helen, Bela Bose, Ajit

MADAM ZORRO, 35mm, B/W
P: A.D. Prod; D: Akoo; M: Bulo C Rani
C: Nadira, Azad, Helen, Bhagwan

MAIN CHUP RAHUNGI, 35mm, B/W
P: AVM; D: A. Bhimsingh;
M: Chtiragupta
C: Meena Kumar, Sunil Dutt, Nana Palsikar, Mohan Choti, Helen

NEELI AANKHEN, 35mm, B/W
P: Society Pics; D: Ved Mohan;
M: Dattaram
C: Ajit, Shakila, Helen, Johnny Walker, Shetty, Tun Tun

SACHCHE MOTI, 35mm, B/W
P: Shri Dilip Chitra; D: Omi;
M: N. Dutta
C: Jabeen Jalil, Suresh, Johnny Walker, Sulochana, Helen

1963

AWARA ABDULLA, 35mm, B/W
P: Hanna Films; D: Tara Harish;
M: N. Dutta
C: Dara Singh, Chandrashekhar, Praveen Choudhry, Helen

BEEN KA JAADOO, 35mm, B/W
P: S.A. Films; D: N. Rajesh;
M: S.N. Tripathi
C: Mahipal, Helen, Kammo, Tiwari, Mohan Choti, Ullhas

CAPTAIN SHEROO, 35mm, B/W
P: Bina Chtira; D: Dharam Kumar;
M: S. Mohinder
C: Jairaj, Helen, Niranjan Sharma, Lajwanti, Tun Tun

DEKHA PYAR TUMHARA, 35mm, B/W
P: Teharbhai Akbar Ali; D: K. Parvez; M: Raj Ratan
C: Naaz, Subiraj, Bhagwan, Helen, Madan Puri

EK THA ALIBABA, 35mm, B/W
P: Shankar Movies; D: Harbans;
M: Hansraj Bhel
C: Dara Singh, Nishi, Tiwari, Hiralal, Helen

GANGA MAIYA TOHE PIYARI CHADAIBO
P: B.P. Shahabadi; D: Kundan Kumar; M: Chitragupt
C: Kum Kum, Asim Kumar, Nazir Hussain, Helen, Tun Tun

HARISHCHANDRA TARAMATI, 35mm, B/W
P: Adarshlok; D: Adarsh;
M: Laxmikant Pyerelal
C: Prithviraj Kapoor, Jaymala, B.M. Vyas, Ullhas, Helen

KABLI KHAN, 35 mm, Colour
P: Amarnath Prod; D: K. Amarnath; M: Chitragupta
C: Ajit, Helen, Samson, Mukhri, Jayant, Salim, W.M. Khan

MAYA MAHAL, 35mm, B/W
P: Mona Films; D: Chandrakant;
M: Naushad
C: Mahipal, Helen, Indira, Tiwari

MULZIM, 35mm, B/W
P: Bundel Khand Films; D: N.A. Ansari; M: Ravi
C: Pradeep Kumar, Shakila, Johnny Walker, N.A. Ansari, Nilofer, Nasreen, Helen

PARASMANI, 35mm, B/W
P: Movieland; D: Babubhai Mistry;
M: Laxmikant Pyarelal
C: Mahipal, Geetanjali, Manhar Desai, Nalini Chonkar, Helen

PATAL NAGRI, 35 mm B/W
P: Madan Chitra; D: Ram Kumar;

M: B.N. Bali
C: Chitra, Azad, Ram Kumar, Kesari, Helen, King Kong

PYAR KA BANDHAN, 35mm, B/W
P: N.S. Films; D: Naresh Saigal; M: Ravi
C: Raj Kumar, Nishi, Naaz, Johnny Walker, Helen

PYAR KIYA TO DARNA KYA, 35mm, B/W
P: Vikram prod; D: B.S. Ranga; M: Ravi
C: Shammi Kapoor, B. Saroja Devi, Prithviraj Kapoor, Om Prakash, Pran, Helen

RAJA, 35mm, B/W
P: Mukul Pics; D: Radhakant; M: S.N. Tripathi
C: Jagdeep, Vijaya Choudhry, Ullhas, Jeevan, Helen, Sunder

SHIKARI, 35 mm, Colour
P: Eagle Films; D: Mohammed Hussain; M: G.G. Kohli
C: Ragini, Ajit, Helen, K.N. Singh, Madan Puri, Kamal Mehra

SUNEHRI NAAGIN, 35mm, Partly in Colour
P: Everest Pics; D: Babubhai Mistry; M: Kalyanji-Anandji
C: Mahipal, Helen, Anwar, Pritibala, Ullhas

TAJ MAHAL, 35mm, Colour
P: Pushpa Pics; D: M. Sadiq; M: Roshan
C: Bina Rai, Pradeep Kumar, Veena, Jeevan, Rehman, Helen, Minoo Mumtaz, Mohan Choti

USTADON KE USTAD, 35mm, B/W
P: Films & Television; D: Brij; M: Ravi
C: Ashok Kumar, Pradeep Kumar, Shakila, Johnny Walker, Helen

1964

AAYA TOOFAN, 35mm, B/W
P: R.M. Art Prod.; D: Mohd. Hussain M: Laxmikant Payrelal
C: Dara Singh, Helen, Anwar

AWARA BADAL, 35mm, B/W
P: Amar Jyoti; D: Kedar Kapoor; M: Usha Khanna
C: Ajit, Ragini, Jagdish Sethi, Dhumal, Helen

BAGHI, 35mm, Colour
P: Mukul Movies; D: Ram Dayal; M: Chitragupta
C: Pradeep Kumar, Leela Naidu, Jagdeep, Mumtaz, Jeevan, Helen

BALMA BADA NADAAN, 35mm, B/W
P: Rajkumar Kohli; D: Baldeo Jhinjan; M: Hemanta Kumar
C: Ashim Kumar, Nishi, Helen

HAMEER HATH, 35mm, B/W
P: Jagdish Films; D: Jaswant Jhaveri; M: Sanmukh Babu
C: Nirupa Roy, Jairaj, Anita Guha, Sapru, Manhar Desai, Helen

HERCULES, 35mm, Colour
P: Bohra Bros; D: Shriram; M: N. Dutta
C: Dara Singh, Nishi, Mumtaz, Indira, Randhawa, Helen

HIS HIGHNESS, 35mm, B/W
P: Nitie Films; D: A. Joshi; M: Bhanu Thaker
C: Jairaj, Helen, Maruti, Ratnamala, Chand Usmani

MAHARANI PADMINI, 35mm, B/W
P: Delite Movies; D: Jaswant Jhaveri; M: Sardar Mallick
C: Anita Guha, Jairaj, Sajjan, Indira, Helen, Shyama

SHABNAM, 35mm, B/W

P: Super Pics; D: Aspi Irani;
M: Usha Khanna
C: Mehmood, L. Vijayalaxmi, Sheikh Mukhtar, Helen, Jeevan

WOH KAUN THI, 35mm, B/W
P: Prithvi Pics; D: Raj Khosla;
M: Madan Mohan
C: Manoj Kumar, Sadhana, Helen, K.N. Singh, Ratnamala, Mohan Choti, Prem Chopra

ZINDAGI, 35mm, B/W
P: Gemini; D: Ramanand Sagar;
M: Shanker-Jaikishen
C: Vyjayanthimala, Rajendra Kumar, Raj Kumar, Mehmood, Jayant, Helen, Leela Chitnis

1965

BAGHI HASEENA, 35mm, B/W
P: Award Films; D: Ram; M: P.D. Sharma
C: Jairaj, Chitra, Sherry, Helen

BHAKTA PRAHLAD, 35 mm, B/W
P: Madan Movies; D: Mamal Sharma; M: B.N. Bali
C: Anjali Devi, Babloo, Malika, Sheikh, Helen

CHA CHA CHA, 35 mm, B/W
P: Bhavdeep Films;
D: Chandrashekhar; M: Iqbal Qureishi
C: Chandrashekhar, Helen, O.P. Ralhan, Om Prakash, Bela Bose, Tun Tun, Polson, Iftekhar

CHOR DARWAZA, 35mm, B/W
P: R.S. Movies; D: Pradeep Nayyar; M: Frankie
C: Mahipal, Helen, Bhagwan, Dulari, Tun Tun, Samson

EK SAAL PAHALE, 35mm, B/W
P: S.B. Films; D: Dharam Kumar;
M: Arjun
C: Sayeeda Khan, Sujit Kumar, K.N. Singh, Jagirdar, Asit Sen, Mohan Choti, Helen

FAISLA, 35mm, B/W
P: Jugal Prod.; D: Jugal Kishore;
M: Usha Khanna
C: Sheikh Mukhtar, L. Vijayalaxmi, Jugal Kishore, Jagdeep, Helen, Jeevan

FARAAR, 35mm, B/W
P: Geetanjali Pics; D: Pinaki Mukherjee; M: Hemant Kumar
C: Anil Chatterjee, Shabnam, Balraj Sahni, Leela Chitnis, Helen, K.N. Singh, Anwar

FLYING MAN, 35mm, B/W
P: Aar Tee Films; D: Pratap Nayyar; M: Naushad
C: Ranjan, Helen, Bhagwan, Hiralal, Iftekhar, Padma Chavan

GUMNAAM, 35mm, Colour
P: Prithvi Pics; D: Raja Nawathe;
M: Shanker-Jaikishen
C: Nanda, Manoj Kumar, Mehmood, Helen, Madan Puri, Pran, Dhumal

HUM DIWANE, 35mm, B/W
P: Young India Entertainers;
D: Bhagwan; M: C. Ramchandra
C: Mumtaz, Chandrashekhar, Bhagwan, Helen, Iftekhar, Anwar

KAAJAL, 35mm, Colour
P: Kalpanalok; D: Ram Maheshwari; M: Ravi
C: Meena Kumari, Raj Kumar, Dharmendra, Padmini, Mumtaz, Mehmood, Helen, Durga Khote

KHAANDAAN, 35mm, Colour
P: Vasu Films; D: Bhim Singh;
M: Ravi
C: Sunil Dutt, Nutan, Pran, Mumtaz, Sudesh Kumar, Helen, Lalita Pawar, Om Prakash

LOOTERA, 35mm, Colour
P: Shankar Movies; D: Harbans;
M: Laxmikant Pyarelal

C: Prithviraj Kapoor, Dara Singh, Nishi, Kammo, Jeevan, Helen

MOHABBAT ISKO KAHETE HAIN, 35mm, Colour
P: United Technicians; D: Akhtar Mirza; M: Khayyam
C: Nanda, Shashi Kapoor, Leela Chitnis, Ramesh Deo, Helen, Madan Puri, Tabassum

NAMASTEJI, 35 mm, B/W
P: D.M. Movies; D: Daljit Krishan; M: G.S. Kohli
C: Ameeta, Mehmood, I.S. Johar, Nalini Chonkar, Ulhas, Manorama, Helen, Ajit

NISHAN, 35mm, Colour
P: Basant; D: Aspi; M: Usha Khanna
C: Sheikh Mukhtar, Nazima, Sanjeev Kumar, Helen, Prem Chopra, Mukhri, Shammi

RUSTOM-E-HIND, 35mm, B/W
P: K.R. Films; D: Kedar Kapoor; M: Hansraj Bhel
C: Dara Singh, Mumtaz, K.N. Singh, Mohan Choti, Helen

SANGRAM, 35mm, B/W
P: Film India; D: Babubhai Mistry; M: Lala Asar Sattar
C: Dara Singh, Geetanjali, Randhawa, Helen, King Kong

SANT TUKARAM, 35 mm, B/W
P: Ashok Films; D: Rajesh Nanda; M: Vedpal
C: Anita Guha, Shahu Modak, B.M. Vyas, Helen, Rohit Kumar

SHANKAR SEETA ANSUYA, 35mm, B/W
P: Madhuar Films; D: Manibhai Vyas; M: Shivram
C: Mahipal, Shahu Modak, Nirupa Roy, Sulochana, Anita Guha, Manhar Desai, Helen, Dev Kumar

SINDBAD, ALIBABA & ALLADIN, 35mm, Colour
P: All India Pics; D: P.N. Arora; M: Ravi
C: Pradeep Kumar, Sayeda Khan, Agha, Bhagwan, Helen, Ullhas

SIKANDAR-E-AZAM, 35mm, Colour
P: N.C. Films; D: Kedar Kapoor; M: Hansraj Behl
C: Mumtaz, Dara Singh, Prithviraj Kapoor, Helen, Jeevan, Premnath

TARZAN COMES TO DELHI, 35mm, B/W
P: Amar Chhaya; D: Kedar Kapoor; M: Dattaram
C: Dara Singh, Mumtaz, Siddhu, Bhagwan, Helen, Vishwa Mehra

1966

AFSANA, 35mm, Colour
P: Devi Movies; D: Brij; M: Chitragupta
C: Ashok Kumar, Pradeep Kumar, Padmini, Helen, Anwar Hussain, Jagdeep, Amar, Tun Tun

BAADAL, 35mm, B/W
P: Super Pic; D: Aspi; M: Usha Khanna
C: Sanjeev Kumar, K. Vijayalaxmi, Sheikh Mukhtar, Helen

BIRAADARI, 35mm, B/W
P: Gope Prod.; D: Ram Kamlani; M: Chitragupta
C: Shashi Kapoor, Faryal, Pran, Mehmood, Lalita Pawar, David, Helen, Nana Palsikar

CHALE HAIN SASURAL, 35mm, B/W
P: Krishnadeep Prod.; D: Dharam Kumar; M: C. Arjun
C: Chandrashekhar, Bhagwan, Helen, Meenaxi, Madhumati, Sherry, Sunder, Aruna Irani

CHADDIAN DI DOLI, 35 mm, B/W

D: Lal Singh Kalsi
C: I.S. Johar, Helen, Majnu

DADA, 35mm, B/W
P: Amarjyot Films; D: Kedar Kapoor; M: Usha Khanna
C: Dara Singh, Jayanti, Savita, Sudhir, Helen, Mohan Choti

DO MATWALE, 35mm, B/W
P: Rainbow Films; D: Kamran; M: G.S. Kohli
C: Randhawa, Malika, Kamran, Helen, Madan Puri, Madhumati

DULHAN EK RAAT KI, 35mm B/W
P: Taxila; D: D.D. Kashyap; M: Madan Mohan
C: Nutan, Dharmendra, Rahman, Johnny Walker, Leela Chitnis, Kanhaiyalal, Helen, Tabassum

DUS LAKH, 35mm, Colour
P: Goel Cine Corp.; D: D.C. Goel; M: Ravi
C: Sanjay Khan, Babita, Pran, Helen, Manorama, Om Prakash

INSAAF, 35mm, B/W
P: Sargam Chitra; D: Radhakant; M: Usha Khanna
C: Prithviraj Kapoor, Dara Singh, Praveen Choudhary, Lalita Pawar, Azad, Indira, Helen, Sunder

JADOO, 35mm, B/W
P: Fine Art Pics; D: B. Gupta; M: Bulo C. Rani
C: Ranjan, Chitra, Sunder, Helen

KUNWARI, 35mm, B/W
P: Ravi Kala Chitra; D: S.N. Tripathi; M: S.N. Tripathi
C: Indrani Mukherji, Ravindra Kapur, Prem Chopra, Leela Mishra, Murad, Helen, Jeevan

LOVE & MURDER, 35mm, B/W
P: Adarshlok; D: Raja Paranjpe; M: O.P. Nayyar
C: Prithviraj Kapoor, Ramesh Deo, Jaymala, Hiralal, Helen

NAUJAWAN, 35mm, Colour
P: S.S. Films; D: Chand; M: G.S. Kohli
C: Dara Singh, Ajit, Nishi, Helen, Randhawa, Veena, Madan Puri

SAGAAI, 35mm, Colour
P: Narang Films; D: S.D. Narang; M: Ravi
C: Rajshree, Biswajeet, Rehman, Jayant, Rajendranath, Prem Chopra, Durga Khote, Helen

SARHADI LOOTERA, 35mm, B/W
P: S.M.S. Prod.; D: S.M. Sagar; M: Iqbal
C: Sheikh Mukhtar, Salim, Sunita, Jagdeep, Shyam Kumar, Helen

SMUGGLER, 35mm, B/W
P: R.M. Art Prod; D: Aspi; M: Ganesh
C: Sheikh Muktar, Kumkum, Sanjeev Kumar, Helen, Mukhri

SPY IN GOA, 35 mm, B/W
P: Suresh Pics; D: Dharam Kumar; M: Robin Banerji
C: Sheikh Mukhtar, Randhawa, Malika, Hercules, Helen

TASVEER, 35mm, Colour
P: Wadia Movietone; D: J.B.H. Wadia; M: C. Ramchandran
C: Kalpana, Feroz Khan, Helen, Rajendranath

TEESRI MANZIL, 35mm, Colour
P: Nasir Hussain Films; D: Vijay Anand; M: R.D. Burman
C: Shammi Kapoor, Asha Parekh, Premnath, Helen, Prem Chopra

THAKUR JARNAIL SINGH, 35mm, B/W
P: R.M. Art Prod.; D: Mohd. Hussasin; M: Ganesh

C: Dara Singh, Sheikh Mukhtar, Helen, Jayant, Sunder, Tun Tun

VIDYARTHI, 35mm, B/W
P: S.M. Pics; D: Talib Hussaini; M: Babu Singh
C: Surekha, Trideep, Sulochana, Madhukar Bihari, Helen

YEH RAAT PHIR NA AAYEGI, 35mm, Colour
P: Sri Krishna Films; D: Brij; M: O.P. Nayyar
C: Prithviraj Kapoor, Biswajeet, Sharmila Tagore, Sailesh Kumar, Mumtaz, Asit Sen, Helen

1967

BAHU BEGUM, 35mm, Colour
P: Sanamkada; D: M. Sadiq; M: Roshan
C: Meena Kumari, Ashok Kumar, Pradeep Kumar, Johnny Walker, Lalita Pawar, Helen

CID 909, 35mm, B/W
P: Bindu Kala Mandir; D: Mohd. Hussain; M: O.P. Nayyar
C: Feroz Khan, Mumtaz, Helen, Brahm Bharadwaj, Ram Mohan

DIL NE PUKAARA, 35mm, Colour
P: Mohan Films; D: Mohan; M: Kalyanji-Anandji
C: Shashi Kapoor, Rajashree, Sanjay, Mehmood, Helen

DILRUBA, 35mm, B/W
P: Festival Films; D: Mohd Hussain; M: Usha Khanna
C: Ajit, Kumkum, Madan Puri, Madhumati, Helen

HARE KAANCH KI CHOORIYAN, 35mm, Colour
P: Kishore Sahu Prod.; D: Kishore Sahu; M: Shanker-Jaikishen
C: Biswajeet, Naina Sahu, Shiv Kumar, Lalita Pawar, Rajendranath, Helen

JAAL, 35mm, Colour
P: New World Pics; D: Moni Bhattacharya; M: Laxmikant Payrelal
C: Mala Sinha, Biswajeet, Nirupa Roy, Johnny Walker, Sujit Kumar, Tarun Bose, Helen, Asit Sen

JEWEL THIEF, 35mm, Colour
P: Navketan; D: Vijay Anand; M: S.D. Burman
C: Ashok Kuamr, Dev Anand, Vyjanthimala, Tanuja, Helen, Faryal, Anju Mahendru

LAMBOO IN HONGKONG, 35mm, B/W
P: S.B. Films; D: Harsukh Bhatt; M: C. Arjun
C: Sheikh Mukhtar, Kumkum, Sujit Kumar, Jayant, Helen

MILAN KI RAAT, 35mm, B/W
P: Musical Movies; D: R. Bhattacharya; M: Laxmikant Pyarelal
C: Sharmila Tagore, Sanjay Khan, Helen, Johnny Walker, Abhi Bhattacharya, Sulochana

MOHABBAT AUR JUNG, 35mm, B/W
P: Uppal Productions; M: Iqbal

NASIHAT, 35mm, Colour
P: Deedar Movies; D: Om Patwar; M: O.P. Nayyar
C: Dara Singh, L Vijayalaxmi, Savita, Randhawa, Helen

NIGHT IN LONDON, 35mm, Colour
P: Kapoor Films; D: Brij; M: Laxmikant Pyarelal
C: Mala Sinha, Biswajeet, Johnny Walker, Helen, Anwar, Shetty

NOOR JEHAN, 35mm, Colour
P: Zenith Prod.; D: M. Sadiq; M: Roshan

C: Meena Kumari, Pradeep Kumar, Sheikh Mukhtar, Johnny Walker, Helen, Rehman

RAAT ANDHERI THI, 35mm, B/W
P: Sargam Chitra; D: Shiv Kumar; M: Usha Khanna
C: Feroz Khan, Sheikh Mukhtar, Lolita Chatterji, Helen

RAJOO, 35mm, B/W
P: Shri Dilip Chitra; D: Omi Bedi; M: N. Dutta
C: Sushil Kumar, Jabeen Jalil, Sulochana, Jeevan, Johnny Walker, Helen, Tun Tun

SAB KA USTAD, 35mm, B/W
P: R.M. Art Prod.; D: R. Thakker; M: Ganesh
C: Sheikh Mukhtar, Kumkum, Sujit Kumar, Maruti, Helen

SARDAR, 35mm, B/W
P: M.U.N. Prod.; D: Babubhai Mistry; M: Usha Khanna
C: Sheikh Mukhtar, Dara Singh, Ajit, Nishi, Helen, Jayant

SHAMSHEER, 35mm, B/W
P: Sangram Pics; D: Babubhai Mistry; M: Lala Sattar
C: Prithviraj Kapoor, Sheikh Mukhtar, Ajit Singh, Helen

TRIP TO MOON, 35mm, B/W
P: Cauvery Prod.; D: T.P. Sundaram; M: Usha Khanna
C: Dara Singh, C. Ratna, Bhagwan, Anwar, Helen

1968

ANJAM, 35mm, B/W
P: Sargam Chitra; D: Shiv Kumar; M: Ganesh
C: Feroz Khan, Shahida, N A Ansari, Helen, Azad, Sherry

AULAD, 35mm, Colour
P: Kundan Films; D: Kundan Kumar; M: Chitragupta
C: Jeetendra, Babita, Sujit Kumar, Mehmood, Aruna Irani, Helen

BAAZI, 35mm, Colour
P: Golden Films; D: Moni Bhattacharya; M: Kalyanji-Anandji
C: Waheeda Rehman, Dharmendra, Johnny Walker, Chand Usmani, Amar, Helen

EK PHOOL EK BHOOL, 35mm, B/W
P: Kalayug; D: Kedar Kapoor; M: Usha Khanna
C: Dev Kumar, Jayanthi, Sudhir, Madan Puri, Helen

GOLDEN EYE SECRET AGENT 077, 35mm, Colour
P: Madan Chitra; D: Kamal Sharmaq; M: Baldev Nath
C: Mumtaz, Shailesh Kumar, Helen, Ram Kumar

HAR HAR GANGE, 35mm, B/W
P: Nitin Chitra ; D: Babubhai Mistry; M: S.N. Tripathi
C: Jayashree Gadkar, Abhi Bhattacharya, Mahesh Desai, Bharti, Jeevan, Sulochana, Helen

KAHIN DIN KAHIN RAAT, 35mm, B/W
P: Shree Krishna Films; D: Darshan; M: O.P. Nayyar
C: Biswajeet, Sapna, Helen, Pran, Nadira, Malika, Johnny Walker

KISMET, 35mm, Colour
P: Pride of Asia Films; D: Manmohan Desai; M: O.P. Nayyar
C: Biswajeet, Babita, Helen, Kamal Mehra, Hiralal, Ullhas

LADY KILLER, 35mm, Colour
P: People Pics; D: B.J. Patel; M: Ajit Merchant
C: Helen, Arun Sarnaik, Shabnam, David, Nilofer

SHIKAR, 35mm, Colour
P: Guru Dutt Films; D: Atmaram; M: Shanker-Jaikishen
C: Asha Parekh, Dharmendra, Sanjeev Kumar, Johnny Walker, Rehman, Helen, Bela Bose

THIEF OF BAGHDAD, 35mm, Colour
P: Bohra Bros; D: Shreeram; M: Baldev Nath
C: Dara Singh, Nishim, Helen, Ram Kumar, P. Kailash

VAASNA, 35mm, Colour
P: Anurita Arts; D: T. Prakash Rao; M: Chitragupta
C: Raj Kumar, Padmini, Biswajeet, Kumud, Sayeeda Khan, Rajendranath, David, Helen

1969

ANJAN HAI KOI, 35mm, B/W
P: Anand Films; D: Babubhai Mistry; M: Usha Khanna
C: Feroz Khan, Nalini, Aruna Irani, Helen, Mohan Choti

AANSOO BAN GAYE PHOOL, 35mm, Colour
P: Anoop Kumar Prod.; D: Satyen Bose; M: Laxmikant Pyarelal
C: Ashok Kumar, Deb Mukherji, Alka, Pran, Nirupa Roy, Helen

BADMASH, 35mm, B/W
P: Saras Chitra; D: B J Patel; M: Avinash Vyas
C: Sheikh Mukhtar, Helen, Chandrashekhar, Padma, Ansari

BHAI BEHEN, 35mm, Colour
P: Vikram Prod; D: A Bhim Singh; M: Shanker-Jaikishen
C: Ashok Kumar, Sunil Dutt, Nutan, Pran, Padmini, Sulochana, Helen, Divakar, Mukhri

EK MASOOM, 35mm, B/W
P: G.N.S. Films; D: Akhtar Khalid; M: N. Dutta
C: Tanuja, S. Durrani, Uma, Abhi Bhattacharya, Prem Chopra, Azra, Sulochana, Helen, Jagdeep

EK SHRIMAN EK SHRIMATI, 35mm, Colour
P: Amar Chhaya; D: Bhappi Sonie; M: Kalyanji-Anandji
C: Shashi Kapoor, Babita, Rajendranath, Prem Chopra, Om Prakash, Kamini Kaushal, Helen

GUNDA, 35mm, B/W
P: Smart Films; D: Mohd. Hussain; M: G.S. Kohli
C: Sheikh Mukhtar, Jayanthi, Sujit Kumar, Helen, Bhagwan

HUM EK HAIN, 35mm, B/W
P: R.B. Films; D: Daljeeet; M: Usha Khanna
C: Dara Singh, Balraj Sahni, Nirupa Roy, Deepali, Lalita Pawar, Naina Rajbans, Helen

INTEQUAM, 35mm, Colour
P: Shaktiman Enterprises; D: R.K. Nayyar; M: Laxmikant Pyarelal
C: Ashok Kumar, Sadhana, Sanjay Khan, Rehman, Helen, Anju Mahendru, Jeevan, Rajendranath

JAHAN PYAR MILEY, 35mm, Colour
P: L.R.T. Films; D: Lekh Tandon; M: Shanker-Jaikishen
C: Shashi Kapoor, Hema Malini, Naaz, Anjali Kadam, Zeb Rehman, Helen, Nazir Hussain, Nadira, Jeevan, Badri Prasad

JIYO AUR JEENE DO, 35mm, B/W
P: Apsara Arts; D: B. Mastan; M: Jaidev
C: Tanuja, Sailesh Kumar, Jeevan, Helen, Mohan Choti

KILLERS, 35mm, B/W
P: Sangam Films; D: Maruti; M: O.P. Nayyar

C: Dara Singh, Sheikh Mukhtar, Ajit, Helen, Leela Chitnis

PRINCE, 35mm, Colour
P: Eagle Films; D: Lekh Tandon; M: Shanker-Jaikishen
C: Shammi Kapoor, Vyjayantimala, Rajendranath, Ajit, Leela Chitnis, Helen

PYAAR HI PYAAR, 35mm, Colour
P: R.S. Prod.; D: Bhappi Sonie; M: Shanker-Jaikishen
C: Vyjayantimala, Dharmendra, Pran, Helen, Mehmood

PYAR KA SAPNA, 35mm, Colour
P: Modern Pics; D: Hrishikesh Mukherjee; M: Chitragupta
C: Ashok Kumar, Mala Sinha, Biswajeet, Johnny Walker, Helen

PYAASI SHYAM, 35mm, Colour
P: Kewaljit Productions; D: Amar Kumar; M: Laxmikant-Pyarelal
C: Sunil Dutt, Sharmila Tagore, Feroz Khan, Om Prakash, Helen

ROAD TO SIKKIM, 35mm, B/W
P: Kirti Films; D: Ravindra Dave; M: Vijai Shinghji
C: Dev Kumar, Anju Mahendru, Helen, Lalita Pawar, Jayant

SACHAAI, 35mm, Colour
P: Em Ce R Films; D: K. Shankar; M: Shanker-Jaikishen
C: Shammi Kapoor, Sadhana, Sanjeev Kumar, Pran, Johnny Walker, Helen, Sulochana

SHATRANJ, 35 mm, Colour
P: Gemini; D: S.S. Vasan; M: Shanker-Jaikishen
C: Rajendra Kumar, Waheeda Rehman, Mehmood, Shashikala, Helen, Achla Sachdev, Agha

TALASH, 35mm, Colour
P: Ralhan Prod.; D: O.P. Ralhan; M: S.D. Burman
C: Rajendra Kumar, Sharmila Tagore, Balraj Sahni, Helen, O.P. Ralhan, Sulochana, Madan Puri

TOOFAN, 35mm, B/W
P: Sargam Chitra; D: Radhakant; M: Daansingh
C: Dara Singh, Anita, Helen, Ansari, Johnny Walker

YAKEEN, 35mm, Colour
P: Navratna Films; D: Brij; M: Shanker-Jaikishen
C: Dharmendra, Sharmila Tagore, David, Kamini Kaushal, Anwar Hussain, Asit Sen, Helen, Shetty

1970

AAG AUR DAAG, 35mm, Colour
P: Swaran Singh; D: A. Salaam; M: N. Dutta
C: Joy Mukherji, Komal, Jayant, Madan Puri, I.S. Johar, Helen

BHAGWAN PARSHURAM, 35mm, Colour
P: Mewar Films; D: Baboobhai Mistry; M: Jaikumar
C: Abhi Bhattacharya, Jayshree Gadkar, Niranjan Sharma, Helen

BEGUNAH, 35mm, B/W
P: Amrit Kala Mandir; D: Shiv Kumar; M: Usha Khanna
C: Sheikh Mukhtar, Dev Dutt, Shahida, Helen

DAGABAJ, 35mm, Colour
P: Nitin Pictures; D: Shiv Kumar; M: Dilip Rai
C: Dev Kumar, Jayshree Gadkhar, Chandrashekhar, Helen

EHSAN, 35mm, Colour
P: S.J. Rajdeo; D: Shiv Kumar; M: R.D. Burman
C: Joy Mukherji, Anjana, Rajendranath, Bobby, Helen, Aruna Irani, K.N. Singh

EK NANHI MUNNI LADKI THI, 35mm, Colour
P: F.U. Ramsay; D: Vishram, Bedekar; M: Ganesh
C: Mumtaz, Prithviraj Kapoor, Surendra Kumar, Shatrughan Sinha, Jayant, Helen

HARISHCHANDRA TARAMATI, 35mm, Colour
P: Jaymala; D: B.K. Adarsh; M: Hridaynath Mangeshkar
C: Pradeep Kumar, Jaymala, Shyama, Madan Puri, Bela Bose, Jayshree T., Helen, Tun Tun

INSPECTOR, 35mm, Colour
P: Kapoor Films; D: Chand; M: N. Dutta
C: Joy Mukherji, Alka, Helen, Jayant, Kiran Kumar

KAB? KYON? AUR KAHAN?, 35mm, Colour
P: Arjun Hingorani; D: Arjun Hingorani; M: Kalyanji-Anandji
C: Dharmendra, Babita, Pran, Helen, Ashoo, Dhumal, Asit Sen

MAHARAAJA, 35mm, Colour
P: N.S. Films; D: Naresh Saigal; M: Madan Mohan
C: Nutan, Sanjay Khan, Rajendranath, Rajan Haksar, Murad, Helen, Nirupa Roy

PAGLA KAHIN KA, 35mm, Colour
P: Ajit Chakraborty; D: Shakti Samanta; M: Shanker-Jaikishen
C: Shammi Kapoor, Asha Parekh, Prem Chopra, Helen

PURASKAR, 35mm, Colour
P: Ram Kumar ; D: Ram Kumar; M: R.D. Burman
C: Joy Mukherji, Sapna, Helen, Faryal, I.S. Johar, Abhi Bhattacharya, Farida Jalal

TAAQAT AUR TALWAR, 35mm, Colour
P: Kanchangunga Films; M: Avinash Vyas

THE TRAIN, 35mm, Colour
P: Ramesh Behl; D: Ravee Nagaich; M: R.D. Burman
C: Nanda, Rajesh Khanna, Helen, Rajendranath, Madan Puri

TRUCK DRIVER, 35mm, Colour
P: R.K. Multani & Shyam Goyal; D: Dharam; M: Sonik Omi
C: Dev Kumar, Indrani Mukherji, Surekha, Rohit Kumar, Helen

TUM HASEEN MAIN JAWAN, 35mm, Colour
P: Bhappie Sonie; D: Bhappie Sonie; M: Shanker-Jaikishen
C: Dharmendra, Hema Malini, Pran, Rajendranath, Helen

YEH KHOON RANG LAYEGA, 35mm, Colour
P: Sanjay Films; D: Roshan Bhardwaj; M: Robin Banerjee
C: Helen, Randhawa, Mukhri

1971

ADHIKAR, 35mm, Colour
P: Noor; D: S.M. Sagar; M: R.D. Burman
C: Ashok Kumar, Nanda, Deb Mukerji, Pran, Raj Mehra, Shammi, Tabassum, Helen

BEHROOPIYA, 35mm, Colour
P: Ram Kumar; D: Rajesh Nanda; M: Usha Khanna
C: Dheeraj Kumar, Snehlata, Ram Kumar, Helen, Mehmood (Jr)

BIKHRE MOTI, 35mm, Colour
P: Omee Arora; D: Chanakya; M: Laxmikant Pyarelal
C: Jeetendra, Babita, Helen, Kamini Kaushal, Sujit Kumar

BOMBAY TALKIES, 35mm, Colour
P: Merchant Ivory Production;
D: James Ivory;
M: Shankar Jaikishen
C: Shashi Kapoor, Jennifer Kapoor, Aparna Sen, Utpal Dutt, Nadira, Sulochana, Helen

CARAVAN, 35mm, Colour
P: Tahir Hussain; D: Nasir Hussain;
M: R.D. Burman
C: Asha Parekh, Jeetendra, Aruna Irani, Helen, Madan Puri, Manorama, Murad

ELAAN, 35mm, Colour
P: F.C. Mehra; D: K. Ramanlal;
M: Shanker-Jaikishen
C: Vinod Mehra, Rekha, Vinod Khanna, Rajendranath, Helen

HASEENON KA DEVTA, 35mm, Colour
P: Ram Dayal; D: Ravee Nagaich;
M: Laxmikant Pyarelal
C: Sanjay Khan, Rekha, Sujit Kumar, Bela Bose, Helen, Bindu

HULCHUL, 35mm, Colour
P: O.P. Ralhan; D: O.P. Ralhan;
M: R.D. Burman
C: O.P. Ralhan, Prem Chopra, Sonia Sahni, Helen, Anjali, Madan Puri

HUM TUM AUR WOH, 35mm, Colour
P: Shiv Kumar; D: Shiv Kumar;
M: Kalyanji-Anandji
C: Ashok Kumar, Vinod Khanna, Bharati, Helen, Chandrashekhar, Aruna Irani, K.N. Singh

HUNGAMA, 35mm, Colour
P: Mohanlal Chainrai & Babulal Chainrai; D: S.M. Abbas;
M: R.D. Burman
C: Kishore Kumar, Mehmood, Johnny Walker, Vinod Khanna, Zeenat Aman, Aruna Irani, Faryal, Helen, Dhumal

JAANE ANJAANE, 35mm, Colour
P: Shakti Samanta; D: Shakti Samanta; M: Shanker-Jaikishen
C: Shammi Kapoor, Leena Chandavarkar, Sandhya Roy, Vinod Khanna, Helen, Sulochana

KAHIN AAR KAHIN PAAR, 35mm, Colour
P: S. Srivastava; D: Maruti;
M: Ganesh
C: Joy Mukerji, Vimi, Helen, Shaikh Mukhtar, Nadira, Shetty

KATHPUTLI, 35mm, Colour
P: Brij; D: Brij ; M: Kalyanji-Anandji
C: Jeetendra, Mumtaz, Helen, Manmohan, Malika, Bhagwan

MAN MANDIR, 35mm, Colour
P: Soodesh Kuamr; D: Chanakya;
M: Laxmikant Pyarelal
C: Sanjeev Kumar, Waheeda Rehman, Helen, Rakesh Roshan, Aruna Irani, Mehmood

MARYAADA, 35mm, Colour
P: Arbind Sen; D: Arbind Sen;
M: Kalyanji-Anandji
C: Mala Sinha, Raj Kumar, Rajesh Khanna, Pran, Asit Sen, Helen, Jankidas, Rajendranath

NADAAN, 35mm, Colour
P: Deven Verma; D: Deven Verma; M: Shanker-Jaikishen
C: Asha Parekh, Navin Nischol, Nirupa Roy, Deven Verma, Madan Puri, Helen

PARWANA, 35mm, Colour
P: R L Suri & Jai Pawar; D: Jyoti Swaroop; M: Madan Mohan
C: Navin Nischol, Amitabh Bachchan, Yogita Bali, Shatrughan Sinha, Laita Pawar, Helen

PREETAM, 35mm, Colour
P: Bhappie Sonie; D: Bhappie Sonie; M: Shanker-Jaikishen
C: Shammi Kapoor, Leena Chandravarkar, Mehmood, Vinod Khanna, Helen, Sulochana

SRI KRISHNA ARJUN YUDDH, 35mm, Colour
P: Singhania Prod; D: Babubhai Mistry; M: Nandu Pyare
C: Abhi Bhattacharya, Mahipal, Jayshree Gadkar, Helen

UPAASNA, 35mm, Colour
P: Mohan; D: Mohan;
M: Kalyanji-Anandji
C: Sanjay Khan, Mumtaz, Feroz Khan, Helen, Sonia Sani

USTAD PEDRO, 35mm, Colour
P: Time Life Films; D: Chand;
M: C. Arjun
C: Shaikh Mukhtar, Meena Roy, Jeevan, Padma Khanna, Helen

1972

APRADH, 35mm, Colour
P: Feroz Khan; D: Feroz Khan;
M: Kalyanji-Anandji
C: Feroz Khan, Mumtaz, Prem Chopra, Faryal, Iftekhar, Kuljeet, Mukhri, Helen, Shetty

DHARKAN, 35mm, Colour
P: Devendra Goel; D: Devendra Goel; M: Ravi
C: Sanjay Khan, Mumtaz, David, Roopesh Kumar, Helen, Rajendranath, Bindu

DIL DAULAT DUNIYA, 35mm, Colour
P: P.N. Arora; D: P.N. Arora;
M: Shanker-Jaikishen
C: Ashok Kumar, Sadhana, Rajesh Khanna, Om Prakash, Helen

DOCTOR X, 35mm, Colour
P: Fine Art Pictures; D: B. Gupta;
M: Sonik Omi
C: Som Dutt, Farida Jalal, Sudhir, Helen, Randhir, Jagirdar, I.S. Johar, Rajendranath

DO GAZ ZAMEEN KE NEECHE, 35mm, Colour
P: F.U. Ramsay; D: Tulsi and Shyam Ramsay
C: Surendra Kapoor, Imtiaz Khan, Meena, Pooja, Helen, Jagdish Raj

GOMTI KE KINARE, 35mm, Colour
P: Sawan Kumar; D: Sawan Kumar;
M: R.D. Burman
C: Meena Kumari, Mumtaz, Sameer, I.S. Johar, Jalal Agha, Mukhri, Rehman, Agha, Helen

MERE JEEVAN SAATHI, 35mm, Colour
P: Vinod Shah & Harish;
D: Ravee Nagaich; M: R.D. Burman
C: Rajesh Khanna, Tanuja, Bindu, Sujit Kumar, Rajendranath, Helen, Utpal Dutt, Sulochana

MOME KI GUDIYA, 35mm, Colour
P: Mohan Kumar; D: Mohan Kumar; M: Laxmikant Pyarelal
C: Ratan Chopra, Jeevan, Brahmachari, Helen, Meena T., Rashid Khan, Premnath

RAJA JANI, 35mm, Colour
P: Madan Mohla; D: Mohan Segal; M: Laxmikant Pyarelal
C: Dharmendra, Hema Malini, Premnath, Prem Chopra, Johnny Walker, Durga Khote, Nadira, Bindu, Helen

RAKHI AUR HATHKADI, 35mm, Colour
P: S. Noor; D: S.M. Sagar;
M: R.D. Burman
C: Ashok Kumar, Asha Parekh, Vijay Arora, Helen, Kabir Bedi

SAVERA, 35mm, Colour
P: Gurman; D: V.K. Sharma;
M: R.D. Burman
C: Rehana Sultan, Kiran Kumar, Sajid Khan
Guests: Helen, Jayshree T.

SAZAA, 35mm, Colour
P: S.K. Kapur; D: Chand;
M: Sonik Omi
C: Ashok Kumar, Pran, Yogeeta Bali, Kabir Bedi, Helen, Rajendranath, Jeetendra, Rekha, Sonia Sahni

SULTANA DAKU, 35mm, Colour
P: A.V. Mohan; D: Mohd. Hussain;
M: Madan Mohan
C: Dara Singh, Ajit, Helen, Shaminder, Padma Khanna

YAAR MERA, 35mm, Colour
P: Raja Ram & Satish Wagle;
D: Atma Ram; M: Shanker-Jaikishen
C: Jeetendra, Raakhee, Nazima, Helen, Jayant, Manmohan

1973

AAJ KI TAAZA KHABAR, 35mm, Colour
P: Rajendra Bhatia; D: Rajendra Bhatia; M: Shanker-Jaikishen
C: Radha Saluja, Kiran Kumar, I.S. Johar, Asrani, Padma Khanna, Mehmood, Jayshree T., Helen

AGNI REKHA, 35mm, Colour
P: K.S. Melwani; D: Mahesh Kaul;
M: Kalyanji-Anandji
C: Sanjeev Kumar, Sahrda, Bindu, Durga Khote, Helen, Asrani

ANAMIKA, 35mm, Colour
P: Tahir Hussain; D: R. Jhalani;
M: R.D. Burman
C: Sanjeev Kumar, Jaya Bhaduri, Iftekhar, Asrani, A.K. Hangal, Helen, MacMohan

BADA KABOOTAR, 35mm, Colour
P: Deven Verma; D: Deven Verma; M: R.D. Burman
C: Ashok Kumar, Rehana Sultan, Nilkhilesh, Helen, Deven Verma

BARKHA BAHAAR, 35mm, Colour
P: Prahlad Kumar & Amar Kumar;
D: Amar Kumar; M: Laxmikant Pyarelal
C: Navin Nischol, Rekha, Kamran, Radhakrishan, Helen

CHHALIA, 35mm, Colour
P: Sudheshraj Gupta; D: Mukul Dutt; M: R.D. Burman
C: Nanda, Navin Nischol, Rajendranath, Helen, Asrani, Shatrughan Sinha

CHIMNI KA DHUAN, 35mm, Colour
P: Kamyani Pics; D: Prabhat Mukherji; M: Robin Mukherji
C: Motilal, Balraj Sahni, Achla Sachdev, Helen, Dhumal

DHAMKEE, 35mm, Colour
P: T.H. Shah; D: Parvez;
M: Ganesh
C: Vinod Khanna, Kumkum, Bela Bose, Jayshree T., Meena T., Imtiaz, Subhash Ghai (G), Ranjeet, Helen

HEERA, 35mm, Colour
P: Sultan Ahmed; D: Sultan Ahmed; M: Kalyanji-Anandji
C: Sunil Dutt, Asha Parekh, Farida Jalal, Shatrughan Sinha, Kanhaiyalal, Sulochana, Helen

HELEN, QUEEN OF THE NAUTCH GIRLS, 35mm, Colour
P: Merchant-Ivory; D: Anthony Korner
C: Helen

KHOON KHOON, 35mm, Colour
P: F.C. Mehra; D: Mohd. Hussain;
M: Vijay Singh
C: Mahendra Sandhu, Danny,

Jagdeep, Murad, Faryal, Padma Khanna, Rekha (Guest), Helen

KUNWARA BADAN, 35mm, Colour
P: Tulsi Films; D: Vimal Tiwari; M: Ganshyam
C: Rakesh Pandey, Madhu Chanda, Suresh Chatwal, Helen, Paintal

MEHMAAN, 35 mm, Colour
P: Shatrujeet Pal; D: K.P. Atma; M: Ravi
C: Biswajeet, Rekha, Anwar Hussain, Tarun, Helen, Joginder

PAANCH DUSHMAN, 35mm, Colour
P: Manu Narang; D: Bimal S. Rawal; M: R.D. Burman
C: Manu Narang, Rajee, Pran, Prem Chopra, Vinod Khanna, Shatrughan Sinha, Mehmood, Helen, Aruna Irani

PYASI NADI, 35mm, Colour
P: M.N. Bakia; D: Shankar Kinagi; M: Ratan Deep & Hemraj
C: Vikram, Vani Ganpaty, Sabina, Gulshan Arora, Helen

SHAREEF BADMAASH, 35mm, Colour
P: Dev Anand; D: Raj Khosla; M: R.D. Burman
C: Dev Anand, Hema Malini, Ajit, Jeevan, Bhagwan, Helen

TAXI DRIVER, 35mm, Colour
P: Mohd. Hussain; D: Mohd. Hussain; M: O.P. Nayyar
C: Ashok Kumar, Anupama, Vishal Anand, Helen, Nirupa Roy

1974

AMIR GARIB, 35mm, Colour
P: Mohan Kumar; D: Mohan Kumar; M: Laxmikant Pyarelal
C: Dev Anand, Hema Malini, Premnath, Tanuja, Helen

BENAAM, 35mm, Colour
P: Ranjeet Virk; D: Narendra Bedi; M: R.D. Burman
C: Amitabh Bachchan, Moushmi Chatterji, Madan Puri, Prem Chopra, Helen, Tun Tun

CALL GIRL, 35mm, Colour
P: Mukesh Sharma; D: Vijay Kapoor; M: Sapan Jagmohan
C: Zahira, Vikram, Helen, Keshto Mukherji, Jalal Agha

CHHOTE SARKAR, 35mm, Colour
P: Boney Talwar; D: K. Shankar; M: Shankar Jaikishen
C: Shammi Kapoor, Sadhana, Shashikala, Helen, Sunder

GEETA MERA NAAM, 35mm, Colour
P: Atma Prakash; D: Sadhana Nayyar; M: Laxmikant Pyarelal
C: Sunil Dutt, Sadhana, Firoz Khan, Achla Sachdev, Rajendranath, Agha, Helen

JAB ANDHERA HOTA HAI, 35mm, Colour
P: Kailash Chopra; D: Deepak Bahry; M: Sapan Chakraborty
C: Vikram, Prema Narayan, Madan Puri, Helen, Jalal Agha, Prem Chopra

JURM AUR SAZAA, 35mm, Colour
P: N.A. Ansari; D: N.A. Ansari; M: Laxmikant Pyarelal
C: Nanda, Vinod Mehra, Johnny Walker, N.A. Ansari, Helen

KSHITIJ, 35mm, Colour
P: Prem Kapoor; D: Prem Kapoor; M: Sharda
C: Zahira, Bharat Kapoor, Manmaujee, Om Shivpuri, Helen

MADHOSH, 35mm, Colour
P: Tahir Hussain; D: Desh Gautam; M: R.D. Burman
C: Mahendra Sandhu, Reena Roy,

Jayshree T, Helen, Rakesh Roshan, Johnny Walker

MEHMAAN, 35mm, Colour

SACHA MERA ROOP HAI, 35mm, Colour (Punjabi)
C: Manmohan Krishna, Mehar Mittal, Helen, Jeevan, Rajendranath, Ranjeet, Tun Tun

UJALA HI UJALA, 35mm, Colour
P: S.M. Sagar; D: S.M. Sagar; M: R.D. Burman
C: Ashok Kumar, Vinod Mehra, Yogeeta Bali, Rakesh Pandey, Mehmood, Helen

1975

ANDHERA, 35mm, Colour
P: F.U. Ramsay; D: Tulsi Ramsay & Shyam Ramsay; M: Sonik Omi
C: Sameer, Vani Ganpathi, Surinder Kumar, Imtiaz, Helen

APNE RANG HAZAAR, 35mm, Colour
P: Ravi Tandon; D: Ravi Tandon; M: Laxmikant Pyarelal
C: Sanjeev Kumar, Leena Chandavarkar, Bindu, Kamini Kaushal, Asrani, Helen

DHARMATMA, 35mm, Colour
P: Feroz Khan; D: Feroz Khan; M: Kalyanji-Anandji
C: Feroz Khan, Hema Malini, Rekha, Danny, Farida Jalal, Ranjeet, Madan Puri, Premnath, Jeevan, Helen

DHOTI LOTA AUR CHOWPATTY, 35mm, Colour
P: Mohan Choti; D: Mohan Choti; M: Shyamji Ghanshaymji
C: Farida Jalal, Ramesh Arora, Mohan Choti, Johnny Walker, Helen, Ranjeet, Rehman, Premnath, Bindu, Rajendranath, Jagdeep, Om Prakash, Mehmood

JAI MAHALAXMI MAA, 35mm, Colour
P: Kanti Kanakia and S Roshan; D: Vijay Sharma; M: Chitragupta
C: Ashish Kumar, Kanan Kaushal, Anita Guha, Chand Usmani, Sapru, Helen, Mahipal

KAAGAZ KI NAO, 35mm, Colour
P: B.R. Ishara; D: B.R. Ishara; M: Sapan Jagmohan
C: Sarika, Raj Kiran, Pradeep Kumar, Aruna Irani, Helen, I.S. Johar, Johnny Walker

KAAM SHASTRA, 35mm, Colour
P: Asif K.; D: Prem Kapoor; M: Brij Bhooshan
C: Alka, Ramesh Arora, Bindu, Manisha, Helen

KAALA SONA, 35mm, Colour
P: Vinod Shah & Harish Shah; D: Ravi Nagaich; M: R.D. Burman
C: Feroz Khan, Praveen Babi, Prem Chopra, Farida Jalal, Danny, Durga Khote, K.N. Singh, Helen, Agha, Bhagwan

MERA SAJNA, 35mm, Colour
P: Kewal Kumar; D: Kewal Kumar; M: Laxmikant Pyarelal
C: Raakhee, Navin Nishchol, Helen, Ajit, Murad

MERE SARTAJ, 35mm, Colour
P: K. Usman Sharif; D: A.R. Kardar; M: Ravi
C: Zaheera, Satish Kaul, Jagdeep, Roopesh Kumar, Padma Khanna, Alka, Helen

SAAZISH, 35mm, Colour
P: Kalidas; D: Kalidas; M: Shanker-Jaikishen
C: Saira Banu, Dharmendra, Dev Kumar, Rajendranath, Helen, Madan Puri, David

SANYASI, 35mm, Colour

P: Sohanlal Kanwar; D: Sohanlal Kanwar; M: Shanker-Jaikishen
C: Manoj Kumar, Hema Malini, Premnath, Prem Chopra, Aruna Irani, Prema Narayan, Helen, Pran

SHOLAY, 35mm, Colour
P: G.P. Sippy; D: Ramesh Sippy; M: R.D. Burman
C: Dharmendra, Sanjeev Kumar, Amitabh Bachchan, Hema Malini, Jaya Bhaduri, Amjad Khan, A.K. Hangal, Helen, Sachin, Asrani, Jagdeep

ZAKHMEE, 35mm, Colour
P: Tahir Hussain; D: Raja Thakur; M: Bhappi Lahiri
C: Sunil Dutt, Asha Parekh, Reena Roy, Rakesh Roshan, Imitiaz, Johnny Walker, Helen

ZINDAGI AUR TOOFAN, 35mm Colour
P: Lalit Mohan & Charu Mitra; D: U.R. Ishara; M: Brij Bhushan
C: Sajid Khan, Yogeeta Bali, Rehana Sultan, Helen

1976

AAJ KA YE GHAR, 35mm, Colour
P: Adarsh Arts; D: Surinder Shailaj; M: Anil Arun
C: Shreeram Lagu, Laita Pawar, I.S. Johar, Joginder, Jaymala, Jalal Agha, Helen

AAP BEETI, 35mm, Colour
P: Mohan Kumar; D: Mohan Kumar; M: Laxmikant Pyarelal
C: Shashi Kapoor, Hema Malini, Premnath, Asrani, Nirupa Roy, Aruna Irani, Helen

ALIBABA, 35mm, Colour
P: P.L. Sharma; D: Mohd. Hussain; M: Hansraj Bhel
C: Dara Singh, Komila Wirk, Dev Kumar, Rajendranath, Radha Saluja, Jayshree T., Helen

BAIRAAG, 35mm, Colour
P: Mushir Alam & Mohammed Riaz; D: Asit Sen; M: Kalyanji-Anandji
C: Dilip Kumar, Saira Banu, Leena Chandavarkar, Prem Chopra, Helen, Madan Puri

DEEWANGEE, 35 mm, Colour
P: Subodh Mukerji; D: Samir Ganguli; M: S.D. Burman
C: Shashi Kapoor, Zeenat Aman, Helen, Mehmood (Jr)

EK SE BADHKAR EK, 35mm, Colour
P: Brij; D: Brij ; M: Kalyanji-Anandji
C: Ashok Kumar, Raj Kumar, Navin Nischol, Sharmila Tagore, Deven Verma, David, Helen, Agha, Padma Khanna, Bhagwan

FAASLA, 35mm, Colour
P: K.A. Abbas; D: K.A. Abbas; M: Jaidev
C: Shabana Azmi, Raman Khanna, Komilla Wirk, David, Paintal, Nadira, Helen

GINNY AUR JOHNNY, 35mm, Colour
P: Amarlal P. Chhabria; D: Mehmood ; M: Rajesh Roshan
C: Mehmood, Ginny, Helen, Preeti Ganguly

HARFAN MAULA, 35mm, Colour
P: S.M. Sagar; D: S.M. Sagar; M: Shyamji Ghanshyamji
C: Ashok Kumar, Kabir Bedi, Asha Sachdev, Satish Kaul, Bindu, Mehmood, Aruna Irani, Helen, K.N. Singh

KAALICHARAN, 35mm Colour
P: N.N. Sippy; D: Subhash Ghai; M: Kalyanji-Anandji
C: Shatrughan Sinha, Premnath, Reena Roy, Helen, Madan Puri, Danny

RAEES, 35mm, Colour
P: Camera Arts; D: Vishnu Raaje;

M: Sapan Jagmohan
C: Yogeeta Bali, Kiran Kumar, A.K. Hangal, Utpal Dutt, Sulochana, Helen, Aruna Irani

RAEESZADA, 35mm, Colour
P: V.L. Khare; D: Raja Thakur; M: Ravindra Jain
C: Vikram, Zarina Wahab, Raakesh Roshan, Shreeram Lagu, Helen

RAKHI AUR RIFLE, 35mm, Colour
P: Amar Millan Prod.; D: Radhakant Sharma; M: Sapan Jagmohan
C: Dara Singh, Leela Mishra, Raman Khanna, Randhawa, Keshto Mukherji, Helen

SHANKAR DADA, 35mm, Colour
P: S.K. Kapoor; D: Shibu Mitra; M: Sonik Omi
C: Ashok Kumar, Shashi Kapoor, Neetu Singh, Pran, Bindu, Helen

SHARAAFAT CHHOD DI MAINE, 35mm, Colour
P: Damodar Menon, J.B. & V.M. Shah; D: Jagdev Bhambri; M: Rajesh Roshan
C: Hema Malini, Feroz Khan, Neetu Singh, Abhi Bhattacharya, Jagdeep, Bindu, Helen

SIKKA, 35mm, Colour
P: Mona Movies; D: Dilip Bose; M: Chitragupta
C: Anil Dhawan, Ambika Johar, Satyen Kappu, Helen

YAMLA JATT, 35mm, Colour (Punjabi)
D: I.S. Johar
C: Helen, I.S. Johar, Meher Mittal

1977

AAP KI KHATIR, 35mm, Colour
P: Harsh Kohli; D: Sudhendu Roy; M: Bappi Lahiri
C: Vinod Khanna, Rekha, Nadira, Tarun Ghosh, Helen

AGENT VINOD, 35mm, Colour
P: Sargam Pictures; D: Deepak Bahry; M: Ram Laxman
C: Mahendra Sandhu, Asha Sachdev, K.N. Singh, Rehana Sultan, Helen, Jayshree T.

AMAR AKBAR ANTHONY, 35mm, Colour
P: Manmohan Desai; D: Manmohan Desai; M: Laxmikant Pyarelal
C: Vinod Khanna, Rishi Kapoor, Amitabh Bachchan, Neetu Singh, Shabana Azmi, Praveen Babi, Nirupa Roy, Jeevan, Pran, Ranjeet, Nadira, Helen

CHAALU MERA NAAM, 35mm, Colour
P: B.C. Devra; D: Krishna Naidu; M: Kalyanji-Anandji
C: Vinod Mehra, Vidya Sinha, Mahendra Sandhu, Deven Verma, Madan Puri, Helen

CHALA MURARI HERO BANNE, 35mm, Colour
P: Advent Movies; D: Asrani; M: R.D. Burman
C: A.K. Hangal, Keshto Mukherji, Satyen Kappu, Asrani, Bindu, Helen, Simi, Bindiya Goswami, Ashok Kumar

DARLING DARLING, 35mm, Colour
P: Fortune Films Unit; D: Gogi Anand; M: R.D. Burman
C: Dev Anand, Zeenat Aman, Mehmood, Nadira, Dheeraj Kumar, Durga Khote, Helen

DUNIYADARI, 35mm, Colour
P: Sohanlal Kanwar; D: Ram Kelkar; M: Shanker-Jaikishen
C: Nutun, Vinod Mehra, Parikshit Sahni, Om Prakash, Shreeram Lagu, Bindya Goswami, Asrani, Aruna Irani, Shashikala, Helen

IMAAN DHARAM, 35mm, Colour
P: Premji; D: Desh Mukherjee;

M: Laxmikant Pyarelal
C: Shashi Kapoor, Sanjeev Kumar, Amitabh Bachchan, Rekha, Aparna Sen, Shreeram Lagu, Utpal Dutt, A.K. Hangal, Amrish Puri, Helen, Shetty

INKAAR, 35mm, Colour
P: Romu N. Sippy; D: Raj N. Sippy; M: Rajesh Roshan
C: Vinod Khanna, Vidya Sinha, Amjad Khan, Helen

JAGRITI, 35mm, Colour
P: Vimal Bhatia & Naresh Malhotra; D: Rajendra Bhatia; M: Laxmikant Pyarelal
C: Nutan, Vinod Mehra, Reena Roy, I.S. Johar, Prem Chopra, Helen, Jayshree T.

KACHCHA CHOR, 35mm, Colour
P: Movie Mughals; D: Jambu; M: Lamikant Pyarelal
C: Randhir Kapoor, Rekha, Ranjeet, Helen, Som Dutt

KHEL KHILARI KA, 35mm, Colour
P: Arjun Hingorani; D: Arjun Hingorani; M: Kalyanji-Anandji
C: Dharmendra, Shabana Azmi, Danny, Dev Kumar, Johnny Walker, Shakti Kapoor, Helen

KHEL KISMAT KA, 35mm, Colour
P: S.K. Luthra; D: S.K. Luthra; M: Kalyanji-Anandji
C: Vinod Mehra, Parikshit Sahni, Sarika, Bindu, Shakti Kapoor, Bindiya Goswami, Helen

KHOON PASINA, 35mm, Colour
P: Babboo Mehra; D: Rakesh Kumar; M: Kalyanji-Anandji
C: Amitabh Bachchan, Rekha, Vinod Khanna, Asrani, Aruna Irani, Nirupa Roy, Ranjeet, Kader Khan, Helen

PANDIT AUR PATHAN, 35mm, Colour
P: Joginder; D: Joginder; M: Sonik Omi
C: Joginder, Mehmood, Kiran Kumar, Asha Sachdev, Helen

THIEF OF BAGHDAD, 35mm, Colour
P: Ram Kumar Bohra; D: Ravikant Nagaich; M: Laxmikant Pyarelal
C: Shatrughan Sinha, Sulakshana Pandit, Kabir Bedi, Helen, Mehmood, Bindu, Prem Chopra, Prema Narayan

YAARON KA YAAR, 35mm, Colour
P: K.B. Chopra; D: A. Bhim Singh; M: Kalyanji-Anandji
C: Shatrughan Sinha, Leena Chandavarkar, Premnath, Helen

1978

APNA KHOON, 35mm, Colour
P: S.K. Kapur; D: B. Subhash; M: Sonik Omi
C: Ashok Kumar, Shashi Kapoor, Hema Malini, Amjad Khan, Bindu, Pran, Helen

BANDHI, 35mm, Colour
P: F.C. Mehra; D: Alo Sircar; M: Shyamal Mitra
C: Uttam Kumar, Sulakshana Pandit, Utpal Dutt, Amjad Khan, Padma Khanna, Amrish Puri, Helen, Prema Narayan

BESHARAM, 35mm, Colour
P: Deven Verma; D: Deven Verma; M: Kalyanji-Anandji
C: Sharmila Tagore, Amitabh Bachchan, Amjad Khan, Nirupa Roy, Deven Verma, Bindu, Helen, Jayshree T.

CHOR KE GHAR CHOR, 35mm, Colour
P: Chander Sadanah; D: Vijay Sadanah; M: Kalyanji-Anandji
C: Ashok Kumar, Pran, Randhir Kapoor, Zeenat Aman, Deven Verma, Helen

DON, 35mm, Colour
P: Nariman Irani; D: Chandra Barot; M: Kalyanji-Anandji
C: Amitabh Bachchan, Zeenat Aman, Pran, Om Shivpuri, Iftekhar, Helen

HUNTERWALI 77, 35mm, Colour
P: Mohan Choti; D: Mohan Choti; M: Annu Mallick
C: Bindu, Jateen, Asrani, Mohan Choti, Kanhaiyalal, Helen, Imtiaz, Aruna Irani, Kader Khan

JALAN, 35mm, Colour
P: Singh Cine Arts; D: H.A. Rahi; M: Madan Mohan
C: I.S. Johar, Ambika Johar, Bindu, Mehmood, Helen

KAALA AADMI, 35mm, Colour
P: G.S. Poddar & K.M. Poddar; D: Ramesh Lakhanpal; M: Laxmikant Pyarelal
C: Sunil Dutt, Saira Bhanu, Pran, Ranjeet, Sonia Sahni, Tom Alter, Satyen Kappu, Helen

PARMATMA, 35mm, Colour
P: Kuljit Pal; D: Chand; M: K. Babuji
C: Shatrughan Sinha, Rekha, Aruna Irani, Pradeep Kumar, Ranjeet, Helen

PHANDEBAAZ, 35mm, Colour
P: Surjit Aujla; D: Samir Ganguly; M: R.D. Burman
C: Dharmendra, Moushumi Chatterjee, Prem Chopra, Bindu, Ranjeet, Bhagwan, Helen

PHOOL KHILE HAIN GULSHAN GULSHAN, 35mm, Colour
P: Surinder Kapoor; D: Sikander Khanna; M: Laxmikant Pyarelal
C: Ashok Kumar, Rishi Kapoor, Moushmi Chatterjee, Amjad Khan, Asrani, Mithun Chakraborty, Helen

PREM BANDHAN, 35mm, Colour
P: Gauri Films Pvt. Ltd;
D: Ramanand Sagar;
M: Laxmikant Pyarelal
C: Rajesh Khanna, Rekha, Moushmi Chatterjee, Helen, Prema Narayan

SAMPOORNA SANT DARSHAN, 35mm, Colour
P: Jaymala; D: B.K. Adarsh;
M: Jitu Tapan
C: Jaymala, Ramesh Tiwari, Arpana Chowdhury, Helen

SWARG NARAK, 35mm, Colour
P: D. Rama Naidu; D: Dasari Narayana Rao; M: Rajesh Roshan
C: Sanjeev Kumar, Jeetendra, Vinod Mehra, Moushmi Chatterjee, Shabana Azmi, Kamini Kaushal, Helen, Madan Puri

1979

DUNIYA MERI JEB MEIN, 35mm, Colour
P: Bittu Anand and Naresh Malhotra; D: Tinnu Anand;
M: Rajesh Roshan
C: Shashi Kapoor, Rishi Kapoor, Neetu Singh, Ranjeet, Nadira, Agha, Paintal, Helen

GURU HO JA SHURU, 35mm, Colour
P: Nirmal Singh Chadda; D: Shiv Kumar; M: Kalyanji-Anandji
C: Ashok Kumar, Mahendra Sandhu, Prema Narayan, I.S. Johar, Ranjeet, Helen

JHOOTA KAHIN KA, 35mm, Colour
P: Ravi Malhotra; D: Ravi Tandon; M: R.D. Burman
C: Rishi Kapoor, Neetu Singh, Raakesh Roshan, Prem Chopra, Indrani Mukherjee, Helen

KANOON KA SHIKAR, 35mm, Colour

P: Shankar Kingai; D: Shankar Kingai; M: Meena Mangeshkar
C: Kabir Bedi, Neelam Mehra, Vikram Gokhle, Aruna Irani, Rehman, Helen

LAHU KE DO RANG, 35mm, Colour
P: N.N. Investment Corp.;
D: Mahesh Bhatt; M: Bappi Lahiri
C: Vinod Khanna, Shabana Azmi, Danny, Helen, Ranjeet, Prema Narayan

MAGROOR, 35mm, Colour
P: R.C. Kumar; D: Brij;
M: Laxmikant Pyarelal
C: Shatrughan Sinha, Vidya Sinha, Premnath, Helen, Shreeram Lagu, Nadira, Deven Verma

RAAKHI KI SAUGANDH, 35mm, Colour
P: B.S. Seth; D: Shibu Mitra;
M: Sonik Omi
C: Vinod Mehra, Sarika, Ranjeet, Madan Puri, Ajit, Amjad Khan, Helen, Jayshree T.

TEEN IKKE, 35mm, Colour
P: Prem Arora; D: Joginder;
M: Sonik Omi
C: Kiran Kumar, Romesh Sharma, Kunwar Ajit, Satish Kaul, Helen

THE GREAT GAMBLER, 35mm, Colour
P: C.V.K. Sastri; D: Shakti Samanta; M: R.D. Burman
C: Amitabh Bachchan, Zeenat Aman, Neetu Singh, Prem Chopra, Utpal Dutt, Helen, Madan Puri, Ranjeet

1980

ABDULLAH, 35mm, Colour
P: Sanjay Khan; D: Sanjay Khan;
M: R.D. Burman
C: Raj Kapoor, Sanjay Khan, Zeenat Aman, Danny, Sanjeev Kumar, Sp. App.: Farida Jalal, Helen, Om Prakash, Madan Puri

ANGAAR, 35mm, Colour
P: P.K. Rana; D: Ashok Roy;
M: Sonik Omi
C: Yogeeta Bali, Kiran Kumar, Jayshree T., Abhi Bhattacharya, Helen, Mukhri, Tarun Ghosh

BEREHAM, 35mm, Colour
P: K.D. Shorey; D: R. Jhalani;
M: Laxmikant Pyarelal
C: Sanjeev Kumar, Mala Sinha, Shatrughan Sinha, Reena Roy, I.S. Johar, Helen, Kader Khan

BOMBAY 405 MILES, 35mm, Colour
P: Brij; D: Brij; M: Kalyanji-Anandji
C: Vinod Khanna, Shatrughan Sinha, Zeenat Aman, Amjad Khan, Deven Verma, Pran, Helen

DOSTANA, 35mm, Colour
P: Yash Johar; D: Raj Khosla;
M: Laxmikant Pyarelal
C: Amitabh Bachchan, Shatrughan Sinha, Zeenat Aman, Prem Chopra, Amrish Puri, Helen, Pran

GARAM KHOON, 35mm, Colour
P: Tej Nath Zar; D: A. Salaam;
M: Shanker-Jaikishen
C: Vinod Khanna, Sulakshana Pandit, Bindu, Imtiaz, Ajit, Keshto Mukherji, Helen

HUM KADAM, 35mm, Colour
P: Tarachand Barjatya ; D: Anil Ganguly; M: Bappi Lahiri
C: Raakhee, Parikshit Sahni, A.K. Hangal, Helen

JAAYEN TO JAAYEN KAHAN, 35mm, Colour
P: G.P. Agarwal; D: Anil Kumar;
M: K. Babuji
C: Sachin, Sarika, Radha Saluja, Prema Narayan, Helen

KARWA CHOUTH, 35mm, Colour
P: Ramlal Hans; D: Ramlal Hans;
M: C. Arjun
C: Ashish Kumar, Kanan Kaushal, Bharat Bhushan, Meena T., Helen

SHAAN, 70mm, Colour
P: G.P. Sippy; D: Ramesh Sippy;
M: R.D. Burman
C: Sunil Dutt, Shashi Kapoor, Amitabh Bachchan, Shatrughan Sinha, Raakhee, Parveen Babi, Bindiya Goswami, Kulbhushan Kharbanda, Bindu, Helen

RAM BALRAM, 35mm, Colour
P: Tito; D: Vijay Anand;
M: Laxmikant Pyarelal
C: Amitabh Bachchan, Dharmendra, Zeenat Aman, Jeevan, Helen

1981

BHULA NA DENA, 35mm, Colour
P: Kumar Bhutani; D: Hersh Kohl;
M: Bappi Lahiri
C: Raakesh Roshan, Kajal Kiran, Shekar Kapur, Helen, Sujit Kumar, Jayshree T.

BULUNDI, 35mm, Colour
P: Mohan Rao; D: Esmayeel Shroff;
M: R.D. Burman
C: Raj Kumar, Asha Parkeh, Danny, Kim, Raj Kiran, Kulbhushan Kharbanda, Rakesh Bedi, Helen, Kader Khan

CHHUPA CHHUPPI, 35mm, Colour
P: Arun Jaitly; D: Arun Jaitly;
M: Hari Prasad Chaurasiya/Mishra
C: Deven Verman, Aruna Irani, Madan Puri, Paintal, Keshto Mukherji, Helen

JOSH, 35mm, Colour
P: Empire Films; D: Raj N. Sippy;
M: Bappi Lahiri
C: Amjad Khan, Vidya Sinha, Deven Verma, Raj Kiran, Sarika, Helen, Shakti Kapoor

PAANCH QAIDI, 35mm, Colour
P: Veekas & Veena Sharma;
D: Shibu Mitra; M: Bappi Lahiri
C: Amjad Khan, Mahendra Sandhu, Girish Karnad, Vijayendra, Sarika, Shakti Kapoor, Raza Murad; Guests: Zarina Wahab, Helen

RAAZ, 35mm, Colour
P: Virendra Kumar; D: Harmesh Malhotra; M: Ravindra Jain
C: Sulakshana Pandit, Raj Babbar, Shreeram Lagu, Kader Khan, Helen

SANNAATA, 35mm, Colour
P: Amarlal P. Chhabria; D: Tulsi, Shyam Ramsay; M: Rajesh Roshan
C: Sarika, Deepak Parasher, Shobhna, Vijay Arora, Vinod Mehra, Bindiya Goswami, Mehmood, Helen

SHAAKA, 35mm, Colour
P: Kailash Chopra; D: Sham Ralhan; M: Rajesh Roshan
C: Jeetendra, Simple Kapadia, Zaheera, Helen, Prem Chopra

1982

ALLAUDDIN AND WONDERFUL LAMP, 35mm, Colour
P: Ayyappan Productions; D: I.V. Sasi; M: Devirajan and Rangarao
C: Kamal Haasan, Jaya Bharathi, Rajnikant, Helen

AYYASH, 35mm, Colour
P: Shakti Samanta; D: Shakti Samanta; M: Ravindra Jain
C: Sanjeev Kumar, Rati Agnihotri, Arun Govil, Helen

CHORNI, 35mm, Colour
P: B.K. Sood; D: Jyoti Swaroop;
M: Shanker Jaikishan
C: Neetu Singh, Jeetendra, Jalal Agha, Helen

EENT KA JAWAAB PATTHAR, 35mm, Colour
P: Pachhi; D: Pacchi; M: Shanker-Jaikishen
C: Amjad Khan, Adil, Neeta Mehta, Premnath, Helen

HEERON KA CHOR, 35mm, Colour
P: S.K. Kapur; D: S.K. Kapur; M: Sonik Omi
C: Ashok Kumar, Mithun Chakraborty, Bindiya Goswami, Madan Puri, Helen

KACHCHE HEERE, 35mm, Colour
P: N.P. Singh; D: Narinder Bedi; M: R.D. Burman
C: Feroz Khan, Reena Roy, Danny, Sudhir, Shakti Kapoor, Helen, Aruna Irani

SAWAAL, 35mm, Colour
P: Yash Chopra; D: Ramesh Talwar; M: Khayyam
C: Waheeda Rehman, Shashi Kapoor, Sanjeev Kumar, Poonam Dhillon, Prem Chopra, Helen

TEESRI AANKH, 35mm, Colour
P: Shubir Mukerji; D: Subodh Mukerji; M: Laxmikant-Pyarelal
C: Dharmendra, Shatrughan Sinha, Zeenat Aman, Neetu Singh, Rakesh Roshan, Sarika, Helen, Mehmood, Amjad Khan

WAQT WAQT KI BAAT, 35mm, Colour
P: Matadin Kejriwal; D: Santosh Saroj; M: Rajesh Roshan
C: Rakesh Roshan, Rameshwari, Raj Kiran, Sarika, Vijayendra, Helen, Kader Khan

1983

HAADSA, 35mm, Colour
P: Akbar Khan ; D: Akbar Khan; M: Kalyanji-Anandji
C: Ashok Kumar, Akbar Khan, Ranjeeta, Smita Patil, Naseeruddin Shah, Helen

FILM HI FILM, 35mm, Colour
P: Shahab Ahmed; D: Hiren Nag; M: Bappi Lahiri
C: Bipin, Beena, Ramesh Deo, Pran, Farquan, Sonit, Helen

1984

PAKHANDEE, 35mm, Colour
P: Robert D'Souza; D: Samir Ganguli; M: Laxmikant Pyarelal
C: Shashi Kapoor, Sanjeev Kumar, Zeenat Aman, Asha Parekh, Ranjeet, Jagdeep, Helen

1986

BOND 303, 35mm, Colour
P: B.C. Devra; D: Ravi Tandon; M: R.D. Burman
C: Jeetendra, Parveen Babi, Prem Chopra, Helen

1989

PARCHHAEEN, 35mm, Colour
P: Narayan Tomar; D: Narayan Tomar; M: Ravindra Jain
C: Anil Dhawan, Bindu, Shyamlee, Helen, Jezebel, Oscar

1991

AKAYLA, 35mm Colour
P: M.R. Production; D: Ramesh Sippy; M: Laxmikant Pyarelal
C: Amitabh Bachchan, Amrita Singh, Jackie Shroff, Meenakshi Sheshadri, Aditya Pancholi, Shashi Kapoor, Keith Stevenson, Helen

1993

AANSOON BANE ANGAARE, 35mm, Colour
P: Paramount Pictures; D: Mehul Kumar; M: Laxmikant Pyarelal

C: Jeetendra, Madhuri Dixit, Prem Chopra, Helen, Anupam Kher, Nirupa Roy

1996

KHAMOSHI—THE MUSICAL, 35mm, Colour
P: Sibte Hasan Rizvi; D: Sanjay Leela Bhanali; M: Jatin-Lalit
C: Nana Patekar, Salman Khan, Manisha Koirala, Seema Biswas, Helen, Raghuveer Yadav

1998

SAAZISH—THE CONSPIRACY, 35mm, Colour
P: Shivkumar Damani; D: Sudhir R. Nair; M: Jatin-Lalit
C: Mithun Chakraborty, Pooja Batra, Helen, Kashmira Shah, Aruna Irani, Homi Wadia

1999

HUM DIL DE CHUKE SANAM, 35mm, Colour
P: Bhansali Production; D: Sanjay Leela Bhansali; M: Ismail Darbar
C: Salman Khan, Ajay Devgan, Aishwarya Rai, Vikram Gokhale, Zohra Sehgal, Helen

2000

MOHABBATEIN, 35mm, Colour
P: Yash Chopra; D: Aditya Chopra; M: Jatin Lalit
C: Amitabh Bachchan, Shah Rukh Khan, Uday Chopra, Jimmy Shergil, Kim Sharma, Preeti Jhangiani, Anupam Kher, Archana Puran Singh, Amrish Puri, Helen

2001

SHARARAT, 35 mm, Colour
P: Jayantilal Gada; D: Gurudev Bhalla; M: Sajid-Majid
C: Abhishek Bachchan, Hrishita Bhatt, Amrish Puri, Helen

2004

DIL NE JISE APNA KAHAA, 35mm, Colour
P: Mukesh Talreja and Sunil Machanda; D: Atul Agnihotri; M: Himmesh Reshammiya and A.R. Rehman
C: Salman Khan, Preity Zinta, Bhumika Chawla, Renuka Shahane, Rati Agnihotri, Helen

2007

MARIGOLD
D: Willard Carroll
C: Salman Khan, Ali Larter, Simone Singh, Nandana Sen, Helen

GUJARATI FILMS

LAKHO VANZRO (1963)
KAADU MAKRANI (1973)
VEER CHAMPRAJWALO (1975)
DAAKU RAANI GANGA (1976)
ANAND MANGAL (1979)

MARATHI FILMS

KEECHAK VADH (1959)
BAAT CHUKLELE NAVRE (1964)
DHAAKTI BEHEN (1970)
SHANTATA! KHOON ZALA AAHE (1975)

BHOJPURI FILMS

BIDESIYA (1963)
LAAGI NAAHIN CHHOOTE RAMA (1963)
JEKRA CHARANVE NEIN LAGLE PARANVA (1964)
BHOUJI (1965)
HAMAAR SANSAAR (1965)
SOLA SINGAAR KARE DULHANIYA (1965)
LOHA SINGH (1966)

MAGADHI FILMS

BHAIYA (1964)
MORE MAN MITHWA (1965)

RAJASTHANI FILMS

BABASA RI LADLI (1961)
DHANI LUGAI (1964)
DHOLA MARWAN (1964)